A GOOD SPY LEAVES NO TRACE

BIG OIL, CIA SECRETS, AND A SPY DAUGHTER'S RECKONING

ANNE E TAZEWELL

North Carolina

Published in the United States by WriteLife Publishing
(An imprint of Boutique of Quality Books Publishing Company, Inc.)
www.writelife.com

Printed in the United States of America
978-1-60808-263-6 (p)
978-1-60808-264-3 (e)

Library of Congress Control Number: 2021940135

Book cover and design by Robin Krauss, www.bookformatters.com
Cover design by Rebecca Lown, www.rebeccalowndesign.com
First editor: Caleb Guard
Second editor: Andrea Vande Vorde

PRAISE FOR
A GOOD SPY LEAVES NO TRACE
AND
ANNE E TAZEWELL

"Anne Tazewell has written an evocative memoir about her quest to unmask the life of her elusive father, a CIA officer who operated in the Middle East in the 1950s and 60s. It is an important spy story, charmingly told, and along the way readers will bump into a colorful cast of spooks, including Miles Copeland, Kim Philby and Kermit and Archie Roosevelt. A captivating story."

—Kai Bird is a Pulitzer Prize winning historian, Director of the Leon Levy Center for Biography and the author of *The Good Spy: The Life and Death of Robert Ames*, *Crossing Mandelbaum Gate*—and most recently *The Outlier: The Unfinished Presidency of Jimmy Carter.*

"*A Good Spy* tells a fascinating story of the author's journey to confront the facts around her mysterious CIA agent father—and at the same time shed light on her own shadow. A dedicated environmental, anti-war, anti-fossil fuels activist daughter of a military-industrial-complex, oil company mercenary soldier, she weaves a tale that is a microcosm for the dualities that confront our world today."

—John Perkins, New York Time Best Selling Author of *The New Confessions Of An Economic Hit Man.*

"*Mission Impossible* meets *Eat, Pray, Love*. This is a riveting, powerfully written espionage thriller with a deeply personal journey into the shadowlands of the human heart. Tazewell masterfully weaves together a search for her father's spy secrets with her own buried truths. It is a stunning, revelatory read."

—Will Harlan, author of the New York Times bestselling biography *Untamed: The Wildest Woman in America*

"In this captivating and moving memoir, a CIA daughter goes in search of the truth about her spy father, a brilliant but troubled man present at the creation of modern U.S.-Middle East relations."

— Hugh Wilford, author of *America's Great Game: The CIA's Secret Arabists* and *The Shaping of the Modern Middle East*

"A haunting story of a daughter searching for her lost father. An epic of international intrigue and shadowy Cold War geopolitics. The origin story for a champion of a new world of growth and alternative energy. *A Good Spy Leaves No Trace* is all of these books and more. Anne Tazewell turns this deeply personal story into a door that unlocks for us a little-known but important room in our shared history."

- David Taylor, author of *Cork Wars: Intrigue and Industry in World War II*

"Anne Tazewell's memoir is a genuine page-turner. I couldn't put it down. Herein lie the inside stories of how the world worked when her father was a CIA Station Chief in the oil rich Middle

East of the 1950s and'60s. Surrounded by close friends from World War II such as Miles Copeland, a schemer and a dreamer for the CIA, and CBS News reporter Frank Kearns, Ms. Tazewell exposes relationships both personal and geopolitical. She describes the heartbreaking chicanery within her family and by the U.S. government with its many friends who wanted to influence control of the oilfields. It's also a story of loss, of reconciliation and of love by a daughter for her father. Through her determined research she opens up the inner workings of people in her family, places both near and far, and events that quietly lay dormant in hopes of never being disturbed. As I read *A Good Spy Leaves No Trace* I kept wishing that I would have had access to what she has learned for my own uses. She's painfully honest in laying out the facts of her life and that of her unprincipled father. Because of that, she is a great storyteller.

This is a wonderful book for anyone who yearns to reconnect with their own past!"

—Gerald Davis, author of *Algerian Diary: Frank Kearns and the 'Impossible' Assignment for CBS News,* and producer, writer and director of the Emmy-winning documentary for PBS, "Frank Kearns: American Correspondent."

One of the joys of being a professor is learning the unique lives of your students. My former student, Anne Tazewell exceeds all of them, and her riveting story provides wisdom and inspiration for us all. Underlying her tumultuous world was a passion for nature and finding solutions to clean energy. A must read!

—Meg Lowman, Conservation Biologist and Arbornaut. Author of *The Arbornaut* (Farrar, Strauss & Giroux) 2021

"*A Good Spy* entwines a passionate quest to uncover her father's secret, real life Clancy-esque thriller life with an untold history of events in the Middle East that shaped the world we live in today. Anne Tazewell captures the intimate, the power, the personal pain and the sheer force of world events that make this true life saga one of the most critical foreign policy reads in decades. In other words—damn, it's great.

—Josh Tickell, Author and Film Director, including *Kiss The Ground - How the Food You Eat Can Reverse Climate Change, Heal Your Body & Ultimately Save Our World*

To the great spirit who connects us all: past, present, and future.

May we be at peace,
May our hearts remain open,
May we awaken into the light of our own true beings,
May we be healed,
May we be a source of healing for all beings.

—*Buddhist Metta Meditation of Loving Kindness adaptation*

TABLE OF CONTENTS

PREFACE

I wrote *A Good Spy Leaves No Trace* because I am interested in how the past influences the present. It is for those open to the mysterious forces—the things we cannot see but are here nonetheless—speaking to us, guiding us, encouraging us to find the light of our own true being. This is a story both personal and political. Given that all human experience is shaped by our personal vantage and social milieu, it is important to read between the lines of every thought and action to understand their origin and deeper meaning.

A Good Spy is a posthumous investigation of my father. I wanted to come to peace with this ghost of a man who deserted his young family in the Middle East. After decades of thinking my father's life had little bearing on mine, I was compelled to determine the forces that shaped his life to better understand my own. From this curiosity, I delved into the 1950s and '60s political history my father was involved in, especially his work with the CIA and its role in increasing our global reliance on oil. For more than twenty years I have worked professionally in the clean energy field to reduce our oil dependence and am acutely sensitive to the political and environmental costs this addiction extracts from our lives and that of the planet. Oil became a river of connection, though we stood on opposite banks of time and ideology around it.

Focusing on the past—one largely classified—of people long dead, comes with its limitations. I may have misinterpreted some people's intentions or actions. To the children of my father's

CIA colleagues, with whom I interacted over the course of this past decade, I hope I have not done the same to you. I am deeply indebted to them all for the gift of helping me better understand my own life.

In the end this has been my own journey of discovery and realization. My father was a writer who died a penniless alcoholic. He wanted to get his story out into the world but failed for reasons I will never know. Now what I have found about his story has become part of my story, and I am grateful to you, the reader, for this opportunity to share my story with you.

CHAPTER 1
2003—THE BEGINNING

The name catches my attention: Miles Copeland III, the music producer. I am listening to National Public Radio, stuck in bumper-to-bumper traffic on Interstate 40—the stretch in North Carolina that extends from Research Triangle Park to my exit in Chapel Hill. One consolation is that my Prius engine cuts off when I stop and will automatically turn back on when I push on the gas pedal. Since starting my job promoting alternative fuels—everything *but* gasoline and diesel—I have become hypersensitive to the invisible spew from my tailpipe. I turn up the radio knob to hear *All Things Considered*. Copeland is talking about his career. My ears perk up when he mentions that he and his brother Stewart, a drummer, named Stewart's band the Police in a loose reference to their father, who was in the CIA. Suddenly the annoyance of the long commute evaporates, and the radio story transports me back to my childhood in the 1950s.

A half century ago, Copeland's father, Miles Jr., worked together with my father first in Cairo, where I was born, then in Beirut. My mother did not much like Miles—she felt he was not trustworthy, but he and my father were close. It might even be fair to say that for a time they were best friends. I played with the Copeland kids, primarily Stewart who was closest to me in age. I don't remember much more about our interactions than their names. Suddenly, like a genie, Miles III's voice conjures up my curiosity—about the Copelands, my childhood, and most of all my father. He has always been a mystery to me.

In 1960, when I was six years old, my father abruptly left our family. I saw little of him after that. Now, staring out the windshield, I realize it has never occurred to me to search for him on the Web. My father had died in 1989, long before internet search engines were born.

Back home I drop my laptop bag on the Egyptian camel saddle seat, now serving as a piece of furniture, and flip on the lights in our wormwood paneled family room. I turn on our desktop computer, go to Google, and type my father's name, James M Eichelberger, along with "CIA," "Middle East" and "1950s" in the Web browser. A homemade-looking website pops up. It shows a series of names connected by assorted colored lines drawn to signify the strength of their relationships and the year.

The website is run by old "spooks," a term the spies use to describe themselves on the site they have created. In my father's case, it is particularly apt. He has always been a shadowy figure—a ghost from my childhood whose memory pops up unexpectedly from time to time.

In the search bar provided on the web page, I type in the years my father worked for the CIA and the regions where he was active: 1950s and 1960s in Egypt and Lebanon. The computer pauses a moment, then lines appear connecting my father to Kermit Roosevelt (Theodore's grandson), Miles Copeland, and Wilbur Crane Eveland, an agent I've never heard of before. Eveland, I discover, wrote *Ropes of Sand*[1], an autobiography. I order a used copy on Amazon. It's dawning on me: even though my father is gone, with the World Wide Web there may still be a way to uncover who he was and what he did.

My father abandoned us without warning, and like a thief, he snatched away my memories of life up to that time. My mother waited months for his return. When he didn't come back, she moved my baby brother, Jay, and me from Lebanon to Washington, DC. It was there, around the time of my seventh birthday, that my memories emerge: an image of my parents together and the question my mother asked me. He showed up at our brick home for an evening, and then vanished again. The rest of this part of childhood exists not in my mind but in the photographs my mother saved. During the time we lived overseas, she recorded my early years on the back of snapshots mailed to my grandparents in Ohio. There is one of me climbing our Beirut backyard gate with the Copeland brothers, and many of me with Jay and our parents the last Christmas we had together.

I imagine my life in Lebanon was quite different than it was in DC. I spoke French, Arabic, and English and went to first grade at a French school in Beirut. Although Rue Maamari was close to the American University of Beirut Medical Center, you could barely see our villa from the road given all the subtropical trees and bushes in our front yard. The backyard was where my parents held Easter egg hunts for the kids. In one color picture I'm in a petticoated party dress sitting on the edge of our sandbox, holding a soda bottle in the air with both arms stretched over my head like exclamation points. A towheaded boy sitting next to me is picking up one of the Easter eggs from his basket. The scotch taped caption on the back of the shiny Kodachrome has yellowed and started to peel. My mother wrote in blue ink on the onion skin paper, "This is certainly the best Coca-Cola I've ever had! But Stewie (Copeland) doesn't want one—he'd rather find another Easter egg because he thinks he's missing one!"

I find a photo of my father in the same group without a caption. Perhaps it's fallen off. My father's kneeling next to me, looking down at the camera hanging from his neck. I have a wicker basket for collecting eggs by my side. We are both in profile, our faces partially obscured. I wish I had a picture of me sitting in his lap for a story or walking our poodle, Go-Go. I am sure we must have done these familiar activities because—after all these decades—a deep abiding bond with that ghost of a father remains. This must be why I am now searching for the man I never really knew. It's an undertaking challenged by unanswered questions and knotted emotions that begins with only the bare bones of my knowledge of his life.

I know that my father also grew up without a father figure. His dad, my grandfather, died from syphilis when my dad was around nine years old. My father was an only child, raised by his mother in Pittsburgh. He convinced my grandmother to arrange for private French lessons while he was in high school, and the lessons paid off. During World War II he was a spy for the French Resistance. He was a Captain of Military Intelligence in the storied Office of Strategic Services, the OSS. After the war he went to graduate school in Chicago where he met my mother. There he also worked for J. Walter Thompson, the world's largest, best-known marketing and communications firm.

My mother and father married in 1947 at my grandparents' home in Bedford, Ohio—the two-story house I would visit every summer growing up. My mother designed her own wedding dress, a two-piece gray taffeta outfit with a long-sleeved top and mid-length full skirt. She had just graduated from the Art Institute in Chicago. My mom never met either of her in-laws; my father's mother died just three months before my parents wed.

Seven years later I was born in Cairo where my father worked under the guise of the US Embassy. "Eich"—my father's nickname—had been recruited to the newly formed Central Intelligence Agency, the CIA, at the suggestion of Miles Copeland. My brother was born five years after me in Beirut, where my father and Miles were oil consultants to government leaders and business executives. This is when our family began to come apart.

My father left us in 1960. He had a long-term relationship with another woman, Patsy Cooper, though they never married. Eich continued to be a consultant living overseas and jetting around the world until 1967 or so when he and Patsy settled in Laurel, Maryland, an hour's drive from where I lived with my mother and brother. After Patsy died, my father moved even closer than that, into subsidized housing for the elderly in DC.

I have letters from him: twelve to be exact, beginning in 1982 and spanning six years. There was another, but I believe I destroyed it because of how cruelly he wrote about my mother. In most of his letters he writes about his draft autobiography, how he is up to five hundred pages, how he will be sure to get me a copy. I never got one. In his last letter he suggests meeting me in London or Paris and informs how he and Miles Copeland have been talking about writing a book on covert political action. This is right after telling me he has cancer which has spread to his lungs but has been successfully treated, "with nothing to prevent me from living the good life that all sinful old men are entitled to."[2] He died three months later. What happened to this part of me who once had so much, then lost it all? I know he was a proud man, a brilliant man, a man with an ironic sense of humor, a lover of poetry and flights of fancy, but there is so much more I don't know.

After my father left us in Beirut there were long gaps between visits. My mother rarely spoke about him after he left, and I quickly learned to forget. Jay retains only one memory from my father: a vague recollection of Eich taking him to the movies once. In addition to the letters, I have gifts from him: a pearl necklace from Kuwait, an ivory necklace from the Congo. I know he loved me, but it was a strange, distant love that settled on my heart like a fog, obscuring my feelings.

My father once took me to New York City for spring break. I

was in sixth grade, and it had been five years since I had seen him. I remember feeling awkward on the cusp of becoming a teenager. He seemed kind but detached. I wasn't sure what to call him. "Daddy" didn't seem to fit. He took me shopping for a new spring dress and we went on a horse and buggy ride through Central Park before spending the rest of the week at his friend's house in Scarsdale. My father's timing was good. Had he waited until spring break the following year, he would have had a different daughter on his hands.

In seventh grade I shed half my name, from Ann Mary to Anne with an *e*. I discovered boys, snuck out at night, and had parties when Mom went out. In the summer after seventh grade I was hitchhiking to meet friends at the pool and the couple who picked me up asked if I smoked. "Sure," I said, thinking they were offering me a cigarette. It wasn't until I started giggling uncontrollably at the outdoor pool in Chevy Chase, that I realized I was stoned. After that introduction I tried many other drugs, from huffing glue to shooting heroin. It's no wonder Mom sent me to see a shrink. Although I resented having to see Dr. Grana, I was grateful Mom did not send me to the therapeutic boarding school he recommended.

Instead, Mom sent me to an all-girls Catholic boarding school. Two years later I convinced her to allow me to attend a co-ed school. My junior year was humming along until my friend stole two thousand Phenobarbitals from his doctor father and started passing them out like candy. My boyfriend overdosed and ended up in a mental institution. The school closed a week early for spring break and expelled me along with thirty other kids. Naturally Mom was not happy, but it allowed me to finish the year at the public high school near our house and participate in one of the defining experiences of my generation.

On April 24, 1971, I joined hundreds of thousands of veterans and others gathered on the great expanse of green between the Lincoln Memorial and the Capitol to express frustration with President Nixon, who was escalating the Vietnam War after vowing to end it. Some of the soldiers took their medals and lay them on the Capitol steps. I knew there was something deeply wrong with what our government was doing in Vietnam and felt proud to be a part of a movement that was promoting peace. After seeing President Kennedy assassinated, then his brother Robert and Martin Luther King being killed just a few years later, I was caught up in the massive wave of youth who understood our parents' generation to be corrupt. Unbeknownst to me at the time, perhaps my feelings were also a direct rejection of the world my father and his colleagues helped to create.

As I was leaving the demonstration to catch a bus back home, an old veteran appeared from the bushes edging the National Mall. The weather-faced man with a gray crop of hair motioned me with the crook of his finger to come closer. He looked straight into my eyes. "This is what war does," he said, as he popped his right eye out of the socket and into his palm. He laughed, like the cackle of a witch, at the way I recoiled in my bell-bottomed jeans from seeing the bare flesh where his eye had been. I doubt this man ever gave me another thought, yet the memory of his glass eye lingers and brings back into focus thoughts of my father. Eich was a veteran too, and he must have been close to this veteran's age, but he and I were totally estranged by this point.

The summer of eleventh grade, I discovered yoga and volunteered at the Golden Temple, a vegetarian restaurant near Dupont Circle started by devotees of Yogi Bhajan. I announced my decision to stop eating meat on Thanksgiving, while home from the boarding school in Connecticut I attended my senior year. The next May, Mom gave me eighty dollars and a backpack as a graduation present. So that fall, when others were starting college, I headed to Jamaica with my boyfriend.

I rarely thought about my father. It wasn't until I was married and began to have children, my first in 1979, that I saw him again. Even then, our visits were infrequent. Now I wonder, what did Eich do with Miles Copeland and his other CIA associates in the Middle East? Why did he leave his family? The six-year-old in me is still locked in the confusing room where my father should reside. *"How could he leave us like that?"* she yells at the walls and stomps around the room. The disillusioned, free spirit I later became is tempted to ignore her rather than reconcile his absence in my life. How will I handle discoveries about him that are such an anathema to my beliefs? Perhaps if I can fill in the details and move beyond the basic framework of what he did with his time on the planet, I can better understand what I'm doing with my own life.

The hardback copy of *Ropes of Sand*[3] arrives on my doorstep bubble-wrapped in a manila envelope. My environmental ethos has me carefully undo the wrapping to save the mailer for another use. The book smells musty when I open it, as if it has sat in someone's basement since 1980, the year it was published. The cream-colored pages and the raggedy edge of its spine reflect its age. I learned from the description on Amazon that the book by Wilbur Crane Eveland is a stinging indictment of US foreign policy and covert operations, his attempt to explain America's failure in the Middle East. With bemusement, I skim the Author's Note about Eveland's struggle with the CIA to get his story published. Why would the CIA inform him of an obligation to allow them a prepublication review, but then "decline to review the manuscript"? The focus of the book is Eveland's experience in the Middle East and begins in 1975 when Beirut's port was burning in front of him. I learn from the first paragraph that he thought the destruction of Lebanon was, "at least in part the result of our meddling."[4] Without patience to read the whole chronicle, I search the index and skip to the pages where he mentions my father.

The first reference is on page ninety-seven. I smile at the description of Eveland's first visit to the Copeland's villa in Mahdi on the leafy, affluent outskirts south of Cairo where he met several American couples, all part of the CIA station. Many of them brought their kids, who were running in and out of the house with an equal number of dogs. I love this description, not only because I can imagine myself playing with the other toddlers at the Copeland's house, but this could be a scene from any number of parties my husband and I had in Key West when our own children were young.

It was at the Copeland's villa that Eveland learned that my father's associate was under commercial cover as a business consultant with Booz Allen Hamilton while my dad had embassy status to protect him. I had known my father was some sort of diplomat. My mother explained as much when I asked her what the letters *DPL* meant after noticing them on DC license plates. She had also told me he worked for the CIA, so Eveland's introduction is not revealing anything I do not already know. Nonetheless, reading what someone else has written about my father is oddly thrilling. This book is providing me passage to another world, a time and place arousing my curiosity.

A few pages later I enter unfamiliar territory. A group of young revolutionaries in Egypt had recently installed themselves as leaders in a bloodless coup, and my father was advising them on newspaper articles and radio broadcasts. Eveland describes my father as the "idea man." The CIA brought Eich to Egypt as one of the leading American authorities on two forms of propaganda: "black" and "gray"—both of which they used to popularize the new Egyptian leader Gamal Abdel Nasser's government. Black propaganda is totally fabricated stories—fake news in modern parlance—while gray refers to stories with elements of truth. My father and Miles were setting up a state-of-the-art broadcasting network for Nasser known as the Voice of the Arabs. Later, Eveland describes a tense meeting he and my father had in London with their British spy counterparts at MI6 who wanted to murder Nasser.[5]

Why was our government sending people like my father to help leaders like Nasser while our friends, the Brits, wanted to kill him? I imagine the answers involved oil. Doesn't most everything in the Middle East have something to do with oil? My profession of the past few years promoting alternative fuels—everything but oil—has certainly opened my eyes to the political price we are paying for our addiction to petroleum. Suddenly, I feel a doorway into a vast, dark space, and a labyrinth of confusing corridors and shady secrets is opening. But with more pressing priorities in my life and deep trepidation with where my searching could lead, I back away from this entrance into my father's world. My work is finally bearing tangible results. Thanks to an air quality grant I wrote, the first gas station in North Carolina to offer biodiesel, a renewable fuel that makes your exhaust smell like French fries, has just opened at a BP station in Garner, a small town near Raleigh.

A "Biodiesel: No War Required" bumper sticker caught my eye—and the attention of the press at the ribbon cutting I organized at the station.[6] The horror of 9/11 two years ago is still with us, as are the media disclosures about President Bush's close relations with the Saudis. These coupled with the recent invasion

of Iraq make me apprehensive about delving further into my
father's life, given the possibility of discovering that his work was
secretly supporting activities directly conflicting with mine. I put
the book down and resolve to return another time. My work and
family are calling for my attention. The hunt for my father's ghost
will have to wait.

[1] Wilbur Crane Eveland, *Ropes of Sand* (New York: W.W. Norton & Company, 1980).

[2] James M Eichelberger, letter to author June 10, 1989.

[3] Eveland, *Ropes of Sand.*

[4] Ibid, 4.

[5] Ibid, 168.

[6] Patrick O'Neill. "Going for homegrown at the pump," (*Indy Weekly*, July 9, 2003).

CHAPTER 2

THE CASUALTIES OF CIRCUMSTANCE

I had always imagined there would be time to get to know my father while he was still alive. This is the natural order of things. Children are supposed to know their parents. But as I got older, the circumstances of my life created their own challenges like an obstacle course which rises over time and terrain. Consequently, I only saw my father seven times after he left Mom, my baby brother, and me in Beirut. Quickly, it seems, in the retrospective prism of time, my own family took residence in the space he once occupied. I see now that it was my having children that spurred me to make the effort to see my father the few occasions I did before his death.

After high school, I backpacked through the Caribbean, and South America. This experience introduced me to the natural world in a way previously unknown to me. I had been a big-city girl. In 1973, in an Ecuadorian highland field, I was struck by the magical vastness of the universe when my boyfriend and I watched Comet Kohoutek streak across the jewel-studded sky. So much is unknown, I marveled.

It was in Negril, Jamaica, the year before, where I first really tuned into the wondrous world around me. At our camp along the craggy limestone cliffs of the tiny beach town, I learned to treasure nature, from the lapping of the waves and the rhythm of the tides to the dancing crabs as they shuffled sideways across the pocked rocks. She is our mother and we her children. I learned about living close to the earth from the local men who would come to our cliff camp to sell honey. These two old Rastafarians, dressed in loincloths and simple muslin wraps, educated me on the basics of real food from nature. They clued me into the fact that bananas and oranges do not have to be all yellow or orange to be ripe. What I saw in the supermarkets back home had been gassed, dyed, and sometimes waxed to their picture-perfect color and sheen, they explained.

In 1976, after traveling together for four years, my boyfriend and I decided to open a vegetarian restaurant with another couple in Norfolk, VA. We named it Amrit—Sanskrit for "nectar of the Gods." Much to my chagrin, as soon as I had put down my share of the down payment, my boyfriend and I suddenly broke up. Shortly thereafter, at the Amrit, I met Richard Tazewell, my curly-haired musician husband-to-be, when he lent the restaurant a piano from his grandfather's house. Since we offered free food to musicians, Richard likes to quip that in meeting me he found his meal ticket.

I had hoped my father could be at our wedding to be held on the lawn of the Boush-Tazewell house. The Georgian-style home on the Elizabeth River once belonged to Richard's great-great-grandfather—a former congressman, senator, and governor—who allegedly lost it in a poker game. Of course, Amrit provided the food: hummus, tabbouleh, and nori rolls stuffed with a delicious concoction of tofu, tahini, and tamari, for the one hundred friends and family in attendance. Regrettably, my father was not among them.

When I asked Mom about inviting Eich to attend our self-styled wedding, she replied "No, darling, having your father there will make me and the friends I have invited uncomfortable. I'm sure you understand."

"Yes, certainly," I replied. Secretly, I had wished the happy occasion could bring down the wall between my parents. My father and Patsy had moved less than twenty-five miles from Mom, but I had not seen him since sixth grade. She and I rarely spoke about my father as I grew up in DC. Yet, as I imagine many girls do, deep in my dreams, I hoped he could be a part of this joyous event. I knew enough not to push my mother on this wish. My wedding was no time to pick at her pain.

Eight months later, Richard and I moved to Key West, Florida. I was five months pregnant and had grown weary of the twelve-hour workdays the restaurant demanded. The slower pace and the lush green landscape set on a sea of sparkling turquoise were calling me. In addition, I wanted a home birth. Our midwife friend Gazelle, as well as several musician friends, had already moved from Norfolk to the island city. Our daughter was born at our new home on Ashe Street—an old, wooden two-bedroom shotgun we shared with a housemate for $80 a month. "Nefertiti," Richard exclaimed when he saw her pointy head emerge from my body in one swell push. We named her Jamila, which in Arabic means the beautiful aspect of God. Was I subconsciously making a connection with my parents' world and my own birth in Egypt twenty-five years earlier? I think so.

It wasn't until Jamila's second summer in 1981 that I saw my father again, fourteen years since our last visit. It was important that he meet my husband, especially now that we had become parents ourselves. I had a visceral sense of the magnitude of commitment that came with bringing a child into the world and thought it only proper that they be introduced to the man responsible for bringing *me* into the world. Plus, it was convenient to our plans, as Richard had some gigs in Virginia and North Carolina. I can't recall the logistics leading up to this meeting, but I don't imagine I would have run them by my mom. I generally avoided speaking to her about my father, though at some point she must have given me Eich's contact information. After winding our way through a suburban Maryland neighborhood of strip malls, we knocked on the door of a drab one-story apartment.

My father greeted me warmly. I remembered his blue eyes. He was tall, a lot taller than Richard, but it was his girlfriend Patsy who left more of an impression. Family friends had related Patsy was a purported heiress and that she and Eich were going to "bust a family trust" to get her riches. On this day, Patsy was not the glamourous woman I had imagined. My father's gray-haired paramour greeted me in a housedress and bedroom slippers. She was friendly and seemed genuinely pleased to meet me. "I remember you as such a sweet young child in Beirut, not much older than your adorable daughter is now," she said.

The visit was brief and awkward. Too many years had passed and Eich had essentially become a stranger to me. All I can remember is my husband and father's handshake and the feel of his big hands on my back as we hugged goodbye.

The last time I saw my father was also fleeting. It was in 1988, and again Richard and I were on what had become an annual summer trek up the east coast. The mission this time was to introduce Eich to his grandson, Rio, born eight years after Jamila. My father was in a wheelchair outside Walter Reed Military Hospital when Richard, Jamila, Rio, and I drove up in our red Dodge Ram van, disembarking at the hospital entrance. I don't recall why he was in the veteran's hospital. Perhaps it was one of the times he went through alcohol rehab. What I remember is giving him a quick hug around the neck and holding my chubby, platinum-headed son front first so my father could get a good look at him. He was pleased to see us, and we promised to write each other more often. Perhaps now I recall the hug but little of the conversation because tactile memories are the most deeply rooted in my psyche. Troubling situations are something my mind wants to block out.

The next year Patsy's daughter, Delores, called me in Key West to tell me my father was dying. "Come to the hospital," she said. "He's slipping in and out of consciousness, but you can still say goodbye." I gave her my brother Jay's phone number in Maryland instead. "He's nearby," I said. "Perhaps he can go."

Although Jay had no relationship with Eich, I thought he and his wife, Maryrose, a doctor, would surely carry out this task, simply because he *was* Jay's father. While I felt some pangs of guilt, they weren't enough to change my plans. I was readying to travel to Ecuador with Richard, our two children, and five friends to help another friend set up a batik operation for her fledgling export clothing business. Our tribe of artist and musician friends were more important to me than my long-estranged father. Furthermore, adventure was calling. I had been to Ecuador four times before having children and now I looked forward to going back with them. I was drawn to the simpler life, one that was more in touch with the rhythms of nature.

While we were there, our merry group of friends attended a housewarming of an indigenous family in Otavalo. After sharing music and drink until twilight, we walked along an earthen path whose green banks shone with the waning light. I thought of Eich as we passed a poor, drunk Otavalan on the ground singing loudly and speaking Kichwa to himself. He was barefoot and incoherent. A couple of days earlier, my father had died. There would be no funeral, no obituary. His life was almost as anonymous to me as the drunk man we passed on the side of our trail, but I had little time to contemplate this, nor that I had forfeited my chance to reconcile with him.

Within a month of returning to our island home, Richard and

I found out I was pregnant. It was a total surprise. When my water broke early at twenty-nine weeks, Gazelle expected I would go into labor. Key West was no place to have a premature birth, so Gazelle and Richard drove me the three and a half hours up the Keys to Jackson Memorial Hospital in Miami.

I spent eight weeks on my back in the hospital waiting for our second son's lungs to mature. I chronicled the fifty-six-day hospital stay in a journal Jamila gave me on one of the family's bi-weekly visits. Mostly, I recorded my medical saga and the stories of the fifteen women with whom I shared a room at various times during my confinement. There was Yamalise, a young woman who came to the US as part of the 1980 Mariel boatlift that brought a hundred and twenty-five thousand refugees from Cuba to Key West. Yamalise was in one of the over fifteen hundred boats, full to the gills, crossing the rough seas to freedom when she saw a man from another boat fall overboard and be eaten by a shark. This image was seared in her memory. I remember this time quite vividly as well. Jamila had only recently been born when Key West experienced over twenty-two inches of rain in one day, so much rain that locals were rowing boats down Duval Street to see all the refugees come to shore.

Reading my hospital journal again after twenty years, I see how much fear claimed my time. Fear I would go into premature labor. Fear my baby could catch an infection since his sterile sac of amniotic fluid had a leak. Fear his lungs would not mature properly, or that I would die in childbirth.

Toward the end of my pregnancy, I collected the sterile fluid—which continued to periodically leak from my womb—in plastic jars for the hospital lab to analyze the maturity of our baby's lungs. I fretted each time the reading determined that his lungs were not mature enough to hold breath on their own. On June 16,

1990, eight days before my doctor induced labor, my musings had turned to my father:

> "I have prayed a lot today. I ask for strength and faith. I need help to cope with my fearful thoughts. Thoughts of my father popped into my mind. I thought when I first found out that I was pregnant that perhaps it was Eich's soul reincarnating since he died just a few weeks before I conceived. I thought of it again today because he died of lung cancer and perhaps that's why this babe is taking a little bit longer to mature his lungs. I struggle (like so many of us) to put some order and reason in my life but actually it comes down to a matter of surrender and faith in a power higher than our logic."

I understand now that my struggle for order and control must come from my family upheaval so early in my life. With the vantage of age, I can see how everything is connected in ways I could not fully realize in the moment. Two decades after Taylor's birth, I can see how much both of my sons take after their grandfather. Rio, and to a lesser extent Taylor, have the same abandon as Eich had with alcohol. Like their grandfather, both my sons are skilled at philosophical debates. Taylor especially takes after his grandfather, physically standing at almost six feet. He loves chess and is a voracious reader. He reads classic and historical works only Eich would pick up and read for pleasure. Taylor is serious like his grandfather and me, but he's more pensive than I am, and he's the most difficult of our three kids to pin down.

Now in 2010 all three kids are out of the house. Richard and I are still settled in Carrboro, NC. I work at NC State University promoting petroleum-reduction strategies, and Richard "plays music for rich people," as he likes to describe his dinner music gig at a fancy hotel. We are grateful that our offspring are happily on their own and share our love of adventure and the natural world. Jamila is married and living in LA, Rio has graduated from college and is working in Boone, NC, and Taylor is at UNC Asheville after taking a year off to backpack around the world.

I am finally free to pick up the research I started on Eich seven years ago. I also have time to get organized. When I am in the attic re-arranging the boxes of books Taylor put up there before going to college, I find *The Game of Nations*[7], a book written by my father's friend Miles Copeland. I recall the publisher had sent my mother a copy in 1969. This must be her copy. Tucked inside the cover, I find a small card from the publisher, Simon & Schuster, that reads "With the Compliments of the Author."

I open the book and look at the jacket copy. It describes Miles as "a man who helped organize the CIA, a former diplomat, businessman, Middle East expert, and sometime player in the Game of Nations."[8] I vaguely understand the purpose of the Game is to keep it going, as the alternative is war. It's a game of spies and diplomats that shows how various parts of government work or don't work together and uses what Copeland and my dad did in Egypt as a case study. I remember the book sat on our DC basement bookshelf. At fifteen, I was too busy fooling around with my boyfriends on our basement cot to give it much thought. Now I wish I had spoken to my father about the book. I would have asked, "Why didn't you get your own story out into the world before you died?"

After my mother died, I carted the book from DC to Florida to North Carolina, but I never opened it. The back cover claims, "The Game of Nations discloses the cynical, amoral maneuverings that characterize international power politics, revealing the secret actions that bear no relation at all to what politicians and statesmen tell the public."[9] This sounds both intriguing and disturbing. I flip to the index to find the pages that reference my father. There are many, but one jumps out because it is an entire essay written by my father that Copeland included at the end of the book. The essay is titled, "The Power Problems of a Revolutionary Government." The CIA translated it from English to Arabic and my father passed the document to Zakaria Mohieddin, an advisor to Egypt's new leader Gamal Abdel Nasser. The Egyptians then allegedly presented the report to the public (including the US State Department) as Mohieddin's insights, not my father's[10]. So, this is how our shadow government influences foreign policy. The CIA writes a document for another country's government to put forward as their own.

Reading it for the first time makes me feel sick. My father is endorsing an "end justifies the means" course of action for the fledgling regime to remain in power. Secret police, propaganda facilities, legislation, and military buildup are needed to support the repressive power necessary to keep the revolutionary government in control. His prescription for a militaristic Orwellian society is an anathema to me, so contradictory to my way of thinking. My dreams for government lay in the basis of mutual respect and the realization that we are all interconnected. We can't hurt someone else without hurting ourselves. I feel repulsed by what I am learning, but the subject still draws me to it like an itching scab. It feels good to pick at the old crusty shell, yet I don't want to draw blood. I need to be wary. I am uncomfortable knowing that this man is part of me. Clearly, he was morally compromised in advocating for the get-whatever-you-can-with-whatever-means-necessary line of thinking. Although I have trepidations, I can't stop reading.

I spend hours googling anything that might lead to more information about my father. This is followed by bicycle trips to the University of North Carolina's Davis library for books I

identify with references to him. I augment articles printed directly from the internet with books purchased on Amazon and hunt-
ed down in used bookstores like The Book Shop of Chapel Hill.

The Franklin Street institution has two cats, as large as small
dogs, who sleep in the sun by the front window. Inside, behind
the room with novels arranged by author, a step down the ancient
wood floor gives way to rows of bookcases on both sides with
labels like Philosophy and Religion. The owner has divided the
history and politics section into regions. There are several shelves
devoted to the Middle East. I am on the hunt for Saul Bellow's
travel biography, *To Jerusalem and Back*[11], because an internet
search claims that references to my dad can be found in it. I locate
the book, quickly purchase it, and pedal my bicycle home to
discover the Internet is correct.

In Bellow's 1976 book, he writes about taking a trip to the
Holy Land with his mathematician wife, who has a speaking engagement in Israel. In preparation, Bellow reads up on this part
of the world and is surprised to learn that American diplomacy in
the region relies heavily on management consultants and public
relations experts. He describes my father as "a State Department
political scientist who had been an account executive for J. Walter
Thompson, one of the world's largest advertising and public
relations firms."[12] The author says Eich was in Cairo to help
Nasser's new government by writing a series of papers identifying
problems and proposing solutions. He must have read the essay
by Eich included in the back of *The Game of Nations*[13] because
he writes that my father's recommendation of making the police
a partisan paramilitary arm of the revolutionary government
"is Leninism, neat without neither ice nor bitters." Bellow then
goes on to ask, "For an American, the most intriguing question
is this: Whence the passion for social theory among these high

functionaries of the advertising world? How did executive types ever learn about such things?"[14] I have the same question.

I knew my dad had worked for J. Walter Thompson in Chicago. Like Saul Bellow, he had also attended the University of Chicago. Perhaps he even took a class from the esteemed professor and author. Although I don't know what my father studied in graduate school, I know that Chicago is where my parents first met. When they married in 1947, she was twenty-two and he thirty. Was their courtship long or short, I wonder? Likely, it was short since my mom never met my grandmother, who had died just months before their wedding. How my parents met, I don't know either. Maybe it was over the *Iliad* book jacket my mother designed for the University of Chicago Press when Eich worked there. Or was it a chance encounter at a jazz club? My mother loved music. I can still hear the sultry sounds of Ella Fitzgerald singing "What is This Thing Called Love?" drifting up the stairs to my bedroom from our stereo late at night in DC. Or maybe they met at a poetry reading. My father loved the written word. All I do know is that after a few years of marriage, Miles Copeland recruited him away from J Walter Thompson to join the CIA.

Are our life paths just a game of chance, like a pinball game where a whack of the ball at the right time leads to a jackpot and the next whack could lead to a dead end? Is it possible my parents' relationship would not have disintegrated if my father had decided to stay in Chicago instead of following Copeland to the Middle East? What can I learn from my parents' lives? How can I square my father's unethical activities with who I am and who I want to be? This is what I hope to find out.

[7] Miles Copeland, *The Game of Nations* (New York: Simon and Schuster, 1969).

[8] Copeland, *The Game of Nations*, first U.S. printing book jacket flap.

[9] Ibid.

[10] Ibid, 87.

[11] Saul Bellow, *To Jerusalem and Back*, (New York: The Viking Press, 1976), 12.

[12] Ibid, 12.

[13] Copeland, *The Game of Nations*.

[14] Bellow, *To Jerusalem and Back*, 14.

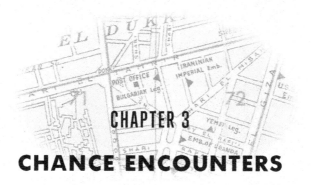

CHAPTER 3

CHANCE ENCOUNTERS

t's late fall 2010 in the Virginia mountains. I am sitting at the Formica-topped dining table in my friend Callie's cabin, staring out the plate glass door at her pastoral hillside view. The bare trees along the ridge are silhouetted against the brilliant blue sky. To protect this view, Annie Dillard purchased the forty-acre pasture which gives way to the wooded mountain top. Annie, the prize-winning author, has what she calls a cozy shack next to Callie's cabin. We are all part of a small community on a five-hundred-acre parcel of land in the middle of the national forest in southwest Virginia. Callie is in the bowl of land once cleared for farming, while Richard and I are up on the ridge. We are in the process of constructing our own cozy shack, a one-room cabin with a million-dollar view. I plan to meet the electrician about our wiring later, but my laptop is in front of me now, and I am researching my father again.

Both Callie and I had troubled relationships with our fathers. Callie's father committed suicide when she was twenty-one. Unlike my father, he left reams of material for her to sort through and parse some understanding, including a short story he wrote about fighting in World War II France. She thinks he never recovered from the Battle of the Bulge, a horror with a hundred and fifty thousand casualties. I know my father was writing an autobiography that included his war years, but after he died, the manuscript was not among his belongings.

"You know your father had a drinking problem," Patsy's

daughter Delores told me when I called asking for Eich's manuscript after his death. "He gave out a chapter here and there, and
I have no idea where his copies went." I am certain this is a result
of his alcoholism.

"Oh, what I would give to have his autobiography now," I lament to Callie.

"Do you think the CIA could have taken it?" she asks.

"I have no idea. I guess it's possible. I just know he promised
me a copy that I never got." It is difficult for me to imagine someone rustling through the mess of my father's rent subsidized
apartment looking for his manuscript, but certainly spies do these
kinds of things.

Callie goes to the next room to look through boxes of her dad's
things, and I turn back to my laptop to discover something new
on the internet: "Lost Victories, The CIA in the Middle East,"
an article by Said K. Aburish.[15] In the first paragraph, Aburish
mentions my father among other names that he says "mean
nothing to most people" but are, in fact, "a partial list of major
CIA agents who determined and carried out American designs
in the Arab world from the 1950s until now." My pulse quickens.
Immediately this journalist and historian—born in Palestine and
educated in the US—captivates me. He has authored thirteen
books, the most recent a biography of Gamal Abdel Nasser.[16]

"Callie," I yell, "Aburish's website says he wants to write the
definitive book on the Middle East's ruin by oil. That's perfect for
me." My profession is tuning me into how the Middle East and the
planet are being ruined by our global addiction to oil.

I had come to Callie's cabin directly from a retreat where I
led a discussion about forming a state-wide coalition to promote
petroleum-reduction strategies. The common focus of our work
is to get people, mainly managers of fleets of cars and trucks,
to use less gasoline and diesel in their legions of vehicles. The

attendees are affiliated with the US Department of Energy's Clean Cities program, a national endeavor to support this mission. My colleagues coordinate local coalitions in three parts of the state and my group at North Carolina State University wants us to link together by establishing a fourth coalition to coordinate state-wide efforts more effectively.

Before I was recruited to work at NC State, I had been the Clean Cities coordinator for the Triangle region where I live. I saw firsthand the advantages of being recognized by the federal government for our local efforts. It helps to have an organization that is bigger and carries more clout acknowledging your work. And since then, the importance of reducing our dependence on oil has only grown. Combining forces to better achieve our common goals were an obvious next step to me.

However, I came away from the meeting with a fistful of frustration from my colleagues' reluctance to seriously entertain my proposal. I am certain my associates feel that since I work for the state now, and they for local governments, I want to take them over. This is not true, and I am hurt by their lack of trust in our intention, especially given that my program supports local councils of government to conduct education and outreach on alternative transportation choices. With a federal air quality grant through the NC Department of Transportation, I'm paying two of the three Clean Cities in the state to work with us on educational initiatives. The third coalition in the Asheville area is not eligible for this funding because their air is "too clean." It is odd that a region must have dirty air to get support in cleaning it. What about *keeping* it clean?

While the mission of reducing our dependence on oil and improving air quality has its frustrations, it is providing a real sense of purpose to my life. It has ignited my passion for something bigger than myself and my immediate family. I am amazed sometimes that this once free-spirited nature lover who eschewed college to travel the world has now gotten herself wedded to the bureaucracy of air pollution and resource control. Nonetheless, even a workaholic like me sees the merit of stepping away from my work upon occasion. I am happy to have a break from the turf war and other petty frustrations to be with my friend in the mountains this weekend. Especially now that I have made this new discovery.

"You should try to get in touch with him," Callie says of Aburish.

On his website I find the email address for Aburish's London publisher and compose a note to the author with a request to kindly forward. Three days later, I receive a reply.

Aburish is in his childhood home of Bethany, Jordan recovering from an accident, he tells me. In February he will be in France and Italy, where he invites me to visit. What I read next is even more enticing: *it is a cia period that needs to be clarified and anything you do is likely to improve things. i have someone in mind for you to meet but let us wait until we do and discover our common grounds.*[17] Although I wonder about his lack of punctuation, I overlook it for the intriguing nature of what he is telling me. Who, I wonder, does he have in mind for me to meet?

The same day I receive Aburish's offer to meet in Europe, I fax a request to the DC Department of Health Statistics requesting my father's death certificate. I need this, as well as my birth certificate, to submit a Freedom of Information Act (FOIA) request to the CIA. I am requesting his personnel records—the dates and locations of his assignments, and his pay grade. Even this basic information can prove invaluable to my piecing together his past.

Within a week, the death certificate arrives in the mail. It lists his birth date: December 17, 1916; his death date: September 28, 1989; and other information, such as his occupation (writer) and the cause of his death (cirrhosis), that I can use to decipher his life. In the envelope with my FOIA request I enclose a copy of the folded certificate and hope for a speedy reply.

Six weeks later I receive a return letter from the CIA informing me that it is not likely they will be able to respond within the twenty working days FOIA requires, suggesting that a more "practical approach" is to allow them extra time to continue processing my request rather than exercising my right to appeal this delay. This seems reasonable. I am now preoccupied with finding a suitable way to communicate with Said Aburish. Although his invitation to visit in person is most generous, it doesn't make sense to drop everything and hop on a plane to Europe to visit a man I have never met before. I'm in the middle of a US Department of Energy grant to organize nationwide alternative fuel training workshops for fleet managers—those who care for dozens to hundreds of vehicles for businesses and local governments. Plus, I am having trouble with the person I hired to coordinate this effort. Maybe Aburish and I can establish a rapport through email and phone calls and plan an in-person visit for a later date.

Aburish provides me with his two phone numbers and I give him my three: personal cell, work BlackBerry, and our home phone. Bethany, Jordan is seven hours ahead of East Coast time. When I call the first number, it just rings and rings. There is no voicemail or answering machine. I keep trying, and on the couple of occasions Aburish answers, I can't hear him very well. The connection muffles his voice, like he is talking through the water of the undersea cable connecting us. The second number he's given me always has a busy signal or a *Lines are temporarily busy* message. I try scores of additional times with no success. Thankfully after all these attempts, Aburish emails and offers to call me.

Our plan is to speak the day after Christmas. It rarely snows in North Carolina's Piedmont, but this year a storm disrupts the power to our house along with the phone line. The four inches on the ground and white lacing on the trees are beautiful, but I am stressing about our plans to talk. Before my work phone runs out of juice, I email Aburish asking him to call my personal cell phone.

Apparently, he tried.

I receive Aburish's two voicemails much later. And when our electricity returns, I have an email from him that reads, *i think we better forget the whole thing.*[18] Instead of speaking, he asks me to provide him with a written synopsis of what I want. I feel crushed. "Said, please don't give up on having an actual conversation with me," I beg.

In preface to the list of written questions I hope he will answer, I confess the essence of what I am trying to understand: "What breaks a man?" I feel that Said holds the key to this answer because his own father, Abu Said—who had been *Time Magazine*'s bureau chief—had known Eich in Beirut, and it was in Beirut that Eich changed the course of his life by abandoning his family. And surely it is only a man who is broken who would do such a thing and then become an alcoholic. Aburish responds that he will answer my "difficult" queries in a week, and then he asks me a question:

> *did your papa work for INTERSER a company headed by former treasury secretary roberty* [sic] *anderson? knowing that would make some things easy.*[19]

I don't know the name Robert Anderson, but I understand this is a clue to something important since this is the only person Aburish has inquired about in relation to Eich. With phone conversation proving so challenging, I begin to reconsider his invitation to visit in France or Italy. If I want to earn his trust, perhaps I should try to meet him in person next month.

That's the bold and fearless part of me thinking. In truth,

however, I hate to fly. Ever since Mom nearly died after emergency cancer surgery and I had a turbulent trip from Key West to DC to visit her, I have avoided the pit in my stomach from climbing aboard a metal bird. But it's not just my flying phobia that's worrying me. The fits and starts of communicating with Aburish, punctuated by the seventy-five-year-old's apparent poor health, are troubling. I begin to realize I should have started this project decades ago when more people who could help were still alive.

On January 14, 2011 I check in with Said to ask about when he is traveling to Europe. He responds: *I GO TO EUROPE ON THE 19TH OF JANUARY BUT WILL BE IN TOUCH WITH YOU BEFORE.*[20] I wonder about the all caps of his message and hope that it indicates something big he will be getting in touch with me about.

Aburish does not get back to me, but I hesitate to bother him in Europe. The Arab Spring is sweeping across the Middle East, and it must be taking his attention. Just weeks after the student-led protests began in Cairo, Hosni Mubarak, Egypt's president of nearly thirty years, resigns and there is widespread euphoria. For decades Egyptians had bottled their fear of police brutality, press censorship, and political dissent crackdowns. January's *Foreign Policy* calls Mubarak's Egypt, "a textbook police state".[21] The Egyptian leader's actions were the same ones my father recommended in the essay he wrote over half a century ago, the essay that the CIA passed off as written by Gamal Abdel Nasser's second in command. Actions the US government has been tacitly supporting since.

This realization prickles me like stepping barefoot on cactus spines. It hurts to discover how my father's work is at the heart of what I am fighting against. I am rooting for the opposite of the old command and control strategies. I am rooting for the young people, the change agents, the ones who want to give voice to differing views, the people who believe that in respect, compassion, and diversity, we find strength.

—————

In March, I am in Los Angeles visiting my daughter and son-in-law on my way to an alternative fuel workshop we have organized in California's central valley. It's been over six weeks since my last communication with Aburish. Sitting on Jamila's living room couch, I fire off an email asking if he is still in Italy. I also add, "Please don't think I am being too forward, but you have grown in importance to me since our first exchange back in December. You are a window into a part of my father's life, one I wish I had taken the time to get to know better when he was still alive and am now deeply fascinated with. Even more so since the revolution in Egypt and the continuing changes . . ."

Later the same day, he replies: *Sadly, I am quite unwell.*[22] He did not go to Europe. Aburish is undergoing intensive medical treatment and is willing to work with me after whatever he is going through is over. At least this is what I read into the brief, typo-filled message. A few weeks pass, during which I decide to switch my tack. Instead of continuing personal conversations with Aburish, I tell him I want to interview him for the *Sun Magazine*. *The Sun* is a Chapel Hill, NC-based magazine that publishes long-form interviews with interesting, provocative people. Said qualifies on this count. Not only has he been a successful journalist and author, he has been an international business executive and even a Middle East arms dealer for a stint. I am lucky to know *The Sun's* founder and the managing editor who both have agreed to consider my pitch. They like the idea of exploring Said's work investigating the underbelly of Middle East politics, especially as it has to do with oil. And I am well-suited to write this as our country's oil addiction and all the problems it's spawned is now at the heart of my personal and professional interests. It's an understatement to say I am excited by the potential of this new idea of mine.

Aburish agrees to the interview, then changes his mind, then agrees again. As the magazine recommends, I prepare a list of twenty questions for him to consider. As we are arranging phone calls for the interview, I encounter the same difficulties we had months ago. The customer service representative I discuss my long-distance challenges with advises me to get Aburish's local numbers. He obliges. Still, the calls do not ring through. It's utterly maddening. My customer service representative also tries to call the number Aburish provided with no success. I try a different country code for Jordan before dialing the local seven-digit number Aburish had provided, and it connects, but no one answers. I email him to see if someone was home when I called. I want to determine if I *finally* have the correct combination of numbers.

His response is waiting the next morning: *Please let's terminate this contact, I will not answer you anymore, it's just too messy.*[23] The sting of rejection is sharp. It pushes me from the computer in our family room to our back porch. There is no way for me to respond. I had already urged him not to give up when we first started having difficulties speaking on the phone. My pride and pain won't let me go back and beg a second time.

I open the sliding glass door to sit at the wrought iron table my mother had made in Beirut. Thankfully, we have a very private back-yard. Five acres of our neighbors' woods hug two sides of our view. It is before the mosquitos will drive us from sitting on the deck but after I have refilled our pots with spring flowers.

Tears gush from my eyes, like a hidden spring of long-ago

emotion. Said is a living link to my father's world, the Middle East of my early years. I do not remember crying when I lost my father, but this ending feels like the same kind of loss.

When Eich left our family in Beirut, I must have thought he was just going away for one of his many business trips. How was I to know when he wrote my mother from Europe to say he was leaving us that he would not return until after we had left? A family friend, Elaine, told me that my mom hoped he would reconsider, or at least give her an opportunity to talk with him about this decision. I had finished first grade and my brother Jay was an infant, less than a year old, when we moved back to the States. We spent the summer with my grandparents as was customary before settling on Reno Road in Washington, DC. It was at this house, what became my home for the rest of my childhood, where I would next see my father. By then my feelings were locked inside my heart. I had experienced the ultimate rejection by a man who meant the world to me.

It's Memorial Day 2011, a little over a month since Aburish abruptly cut off our communication. Richard, Taylor, and I are visiting my brother Jay and his family at their home on the Severn River, outside Annapolis, MD. While my brother does not share my interest in exploring our father's life, my sister-in-law has a passion for ancestry and is curious about my investigation. After picking the sweet meat of Chesapeake Bay Blue crabs for our supper on their screened-in porch, I am showing Maryrose how I google Eich's name when I find something new—at least to my eyes. It is a post in a 2009 Association of Former Intelligence Officers newsletter. A man named Dan Egan is trying to reach "Former Chief of Station Cairo James Eichelberger." Egan is researching the Lavon Affair for a book about Israeli and Egyptian leadership, and his post says that he "met Mr. Eichelberger's son in a bar in Washington, DC back in 2005 but was unable to get in touch with him to schedule an interview with his father." This is impossible. I only have one brother and I just confirmed that he did not meet someone in a bar who was researching a book that would include our father. I immediately call the number Egan included with his now three-year-old post.

He answers on the first ring.

I tell him I just found his request in the AFIO newsletter. "I hope you can help me," I say. "I'm James Eichelberger's daughter, and I've recently started investigating my father's life." Egan explains how he was visiting DC from Chicago and, while in a Georgetown bar, he struck up a conversation with the bartender.

"I think his name was Brian," Egan tells me. At the time, Egan was considering a graduate degree in Political Science and was in the DC area to visit the National Archives. While celebrating some stock market successes with "copious amounts of Dom Pérignon," Egan explains that he told the bartender he was researching CIA activities in the 1950s Middle East. Brian mentioned my father's name. This is not what I was expecting. Egan is certain Brian asked if the name James Eichelberger meant anything to him. "James Eichelberger is my father," he clearly remembers the bartender saying. Furthermore, Brian said, "My father might be willing to let you interview him."[24]

Baffled by the story, the only explanation I can imagine is that the bartender was Patsy's son. But the other parts of the bartender's story don't add up. I don't believe Eich ever lived in South America—which is where the bartender said his family had moved after the Middle East. Yet, even in his drunkenness, why would Egan have made the story up, then posted it on the AFIO Association message board? Moreover, he seems genuinely interested in helping me with my quest. As we say goodbye, he tells me he's mailing me a couple of books I might find interesting.

My chance encounter with Dan Egan coincides with an NPR segment I hear about Gordon Thomas's book, *Her Majesty's Secret Service: The First 100 Years of British Intelligence inside MI5 and MI6*.[25] I google the author and learn he is a British investigative journalist, a cousin of the poet Dylan Thomas, and has published fifty-three books. How can anyone write fifty-three books? His niche is secret intelligence. At the library, I find a reference to my father on page four of his most recent hardcover:

> "Roosevelt had come to Egypt to develop secret channels, already started by the local CIA station chief, James Eichelberger, with the anti-British officer who had taken part in the coup. Eichelberger was a veteran Arabist, speaking the language and understanding the culture. He had money to spend and used it to buy American influence with the officers. His anti-colonialism gained him many friends."[26]

I didn't think my father had gone to Egypt before Kermit Roosevelt, or "Kim," as he was known to his friends. I thought it was the other way around. Theodore Roosevelt's grandson, my father's boss in the CIA, had been the first to cultivate relations with the young Egyptian army officers, including Nasser, who overthrew the British-installed King Farouk. Furthermore, I didn't think my father was a veteran Arabist. But what do I know? I am not an investigative journalist who specializes in secret intelligence, another reason I am anxious to get my father's personnel records from the CIA.

After six months, the Freedom of Information Act process with the CIA is feeling frustratingly slow, so I have enlisted the help of Congressman David Price. I discussed my situation over the phone with one of his aides, who seemed interested and sympathetic. Perhaps Congressman Price can help grease the wheels of our secret intelligence agency. I hope so.

In the meantime, I have just arrived in Cripple Creek for a long weekend of installing insulation to ready our eighteen-by-twelve-foot cabin for sheet rock. The electrician finished with the wiring, and we are now ready for walls. I'm looking forward to working with a friend to lay the soft rolls of insulation made from recycled soda bottles into our framing. It's a lovely summer day in the Appalachians, and I am taking in the view from our deck—the majesty of the oak trees and blooming rhododendron before me and the mountains beyond—when my cell phone rings. Perhaps it is the gentleman I spoke with from Congressman Price's office.

The woman on the other end is an intensive care nurse at Mission Hospital in Asheville. There has been a fire. Our son Rio is in critical condition. All I can clearly absorb is that he is on life support and I should come.

---

[15] Said K. Aburish, *Lost Victories, the CIA in the Middle East.* http://www.iiwds.com/said_aburish/a_lostvictories.htm.

[16] Said K. Aburish, *Nassar: The Last Arab: A Biography* (New York: Thomas Dunne Books, 2004).

[17] Said K. Aburish, email to author, 2010.

[18] Ibid.

[19] Ibid.

[20] Said K. Aburish, email to author, January 14, 2011.

[21] Elizabeth Dickinson, "Anatomy of a Dictatorship: Hosni Mubarak," Foreign Policy, February 4, 2011.

[22] Said K. Aburish, email to author, Spring 2011.

[23] Ibid.

[24] Dan Egan, phone call with author, May 2011.

[25] Gordon Thomas, *Her Majesty's Secret Service: The First 100 Years of British Intelligence inside MI5 and MI6,* (London: Thomas Dunne Books, 2009).

[26] Ibid, 4.

CHAPTER 4

INTO THE FIRE

A firefighter found our twenty-four-year-old son in a drainage ditch after he had jumped from the roof of a neglected 3,600-square-foot Victorian that burned to the ground. A friend of Rio's had offered him an extra bed for the night since he was coming to Asheville to attend a wedding. The old house had been a student rental for years. Eight people had been living there. All the others escaped unharmed, but our son is in a drug-induced coma on the fifth floor Intensive Care Unit at Mission Hospital. I am in a panic, working hard to stay calm.

A machine inflates Rio's lungs with oxygen, keeping him alive. In the X-ray the critical care doctor shows Richard and me, the collapsed one looks like a crumpled gossamer balloon. Although the impact of his jump partially collapsed his right one too, at least I can recognize it as a lung in the picture. With four broken vertebrae, Rio is lying on his back with his arms strapped to the hospital bed so he does not pull out the breathing tube in his throat. The rhythmic sound of the ventilator comforts me, while the beeps and alarms are disturbing, mainly because of their sounds and the peril facing my son. The biggest threat to Rio's life is in his lungs. There is no way to speed the healing and all kinds of risks—like pneumonia and other infections—to be concerned about.

Richard and I spend as much time in the ICU as the hospital allows, which is five half-hour visits a day. Richard strums his guitar and sings songs, mostly Bob Marley tunes like "Natural

Mystic" and "Redemption Song," two of Rio's favorites. Lying there, our boy, who so quickly has grown to be a man, is silent and immobile. There is nothing natural about this scene except our concern. From time to time, I massage his feet. The rest of the family—Taylor, Jamila, and her husband Jai Gopal—are in and out. Richard is calm, but I am a bundle of nerves wrapped in shock.

At night and in between visits to the ICU, I try to read Donald Neff's *Warrior of Suez: Eisenhower Takes America into the Middle East in 1956.*[27] Dan Egan—the man who thought he met my brother in a Georgetown bar—mailed me the two books he had promised, and Neff's book is the one I had at the cabin when the ICU nurse called about Rio.

Neff mentions my father on only one page. Like Eveland's *Ropes of Sand,*[28] he references Eich in relation to the meeting Eich and Eveland had in London with the British Secret Intelligence Service (SIS). The year is 1956 and the SIS has decided they must overthrow the governments of Egypt, Saudi Arabia, and Syria. The British are concerned Syria is about to become a Russian puppet, thus they reasoned: the "fates of Jordan and Syria depended on the prompt overthrow of the Syrian government." Saudi Arabia's King Saud and Egypt's Nasser would be next to fall under Soviet influence. Neff explains that my father and Eveland were "astonished" by Britain's new policy.

It is comforting to hear that my father was anti-colonialist and concerned about our ally's plans, but I am still trying to sort out who is who and why the British would feel the need to meddle so much in the Middle East's business. Neff's book is offering a clue. Britain is throwing all its weight behind Iraq "with its rich oil fields and pliant royal family."[29] Neff is a much better writer than Eveland. He was a foreign correspondent for *TIME*, United Press International, and the *LA Times* before becoming a freelance writer and author. A panel of judges nominated this, his first book, for the 1981 American Book Award. Still, it is difficult to absorb what I am reading with my son fighting for his life.

After seventeen days and a bout with pneumonia, the nurses finally take out Rio's breathing tube. Richard and I are there when our son's eyes open for the first time.

"Oh buddy, I am so happy to see you alive," I rejoice as silent tears slide down my cheeks.

"You won't believe where I've been," Rio begins, still under the dreamy effects of the Fentanyl and Propofol that have kept him sedated. "I was on a healing cruise, a sailboat, and my nurse made me her boyfriend," our supine son in a neck brace recounts to our rapt attention. "We were at a restaurant, and I was thinking I need to practice my table manners. Then—right before the breathing tube came out—I realized, no, I need to practice my breathing."

"Oh my god," I exclaim. "That's amazing!"

Rio winces, wracked by his broken body. "God, I am in so much pain," he moans.

Suddenly, our son is back and the drawbridge to his dream world has closed. The parallel universes of where he has been and where we are now strike me in their wake. To think while Richard was serenading him, and I was rubbing his feet, he was on a healing cruise!

Rio recalls jumping from the roof in a football-style tackle with the aim of grabbing hold of a pine tree in his sight. Instead, he smashed into the ground on his right shoulder. From there, he does not remember how he ended up in the drainage ditch, only that he could barely move and hot water from the firefighters was quickly filling the trough. He thought he could drown. At dawn a fireman found Rio, on a perimeter walk around the property, hours after they had come to put out the blaze. Now in his hospital bed, our son remembers asking his rescuer for a drink of water.

Finally, after nineteen days, the hospital releases Rio to

convalesce at our home in Carrboro until he is well enough to move back to his apartment in Boone. He has a titanium rod and six metal screws holding his shoulder together, a back brace, a four-footed metal cane, pain prescriptions, and a patch on his right eye. He had woken from the medically induced coma seeing double, and the hospital suggested we see a specialist back home since they do not have a neurological ophthalmologist. Rio manages the pain with his meds. It is seeing double that really agitates him.

The specialist we took him to said if the condition does not correct itself on its own, there is a surgery he could perform, but we will have to wait six months. As maddening as this news is for Rio, it is comforting to know that there is a cure; that in the doctor's line of work, this condition is common and the operation routine.

A few weeks later our friend Cindy is visiting and while I am at work she asks Rio if he wants to do some energy healing with her on his eyes. She is hesitant to ask, given his general irritation and chronic pain, but spirit encourages her to go ahead. "Okay," he agrees without much expectation. Rio removes his black eye patch. Then she asks him to close his eyes and visualize his own healing while she holds her hands inches over his head and focuses her intention on unifying both parts of his brain. A few minutes later, my son opens his eyes and exclaims, "Cindy, I only see one of you!"

Later that evening, I catch the glow of this magical manifestation of the universe. A twinkle has returned to Rio's eyes and their excitement in retelling the experience is palpable.

Then, a little over six weeks after Rio jumped from the burning roof in Asheville, he sheds his back brace. We are spending the 2011 Labor Day weekend at our cabin when he decides to remove the Velcro and plastic support system to swim in the pond. The family cheers from the shore. It feels like a miracle, like he is walking on water.

An email from Said Aburish is waiting when we get home. *Sorry for my messy dealings here,*[30] is all it says. The five words touch the tender spot left from his cutting off our communication over four months ago. It's tempting to write back. I'm torn. I want to rekindle our relationship but decide that all he really wants to do is apologize and I should accept the gift that this is. I don't reply. I hope he feels my appreciation, nonetheless.

In his place, another connection to my father materializes. Dan Egan provides me contact information for a man named Gerald Davis, who is making a documentary about my father's friend, Frank Kearns. Davis contacted Egan looking for information about Eich. By way of our introductory phone conversation, I learn that the filmmaker, who goes by the name Jerry, is a retired health care and marketing executive. His voice is warm and friendly as we talk over the landline connecting our family room to his home in Columbia, SC. I imagine he is about my age. Jerry helped coin the phrase, "I can't believe it's not butter!" for a popular margarine ad in the early 1980s. Now he's on a quest to document the life of one of his mentors. Frank Kearns, who had a lauded career as a foreign correspondent for CBS, was Jerry's journalism professor at West Virginia University. During WWII, my father and Kearns were flat mates with Miles Copeland in London, and the three friends and their wives socialized when they were all based in Cairo.

Seven years ago, Jerry met Kearns's widow at a press awards dinner where she offered him her late husband's personal papers —a full seven boxes—if he would take on the project of telling his story.

The filmmaker tells me he is in the final production stages of the documentary and would be most grateful for any visuals I can provide of my father or Frank during the war or when we lived in Cairo. "I don't have much—I didn't know my father very well growing up, but I'll see what I can find," I reply before asking him to tell me more about the film.

He is happy to oblige. "When Frank first came to Egypt, he was a freelance reporter, what's called a 'stringer,' for CBS."[31]

Kearns's stature grew, and he became CBS's African Bureau Chief, a man who embedded with troops and interviewed leaders in conflict-torn countries like Algeria and Egypt. According to Jerry, Frank faced death 114 times before he stopped counting. I tell him how impressed I am with Frank's bravery and the years of work he has devoted to making the film and writing a forthcoming book about his mentor.

"Really, I'm grappling with just one question in my film," Jerry responds. "Was Frank Kearns working for the CIA at the same time he was working for CBS? There is no direct evidence. His close relationships with Miles Copeland and your father are the only circumstantial indicators."[32]

"It's a mystery, then?" I say.

"Not according to CBS,"[33] Jerry tells me. During the 1975 Congressional Committee hearings on intelligence activities led by Senator Frank Church, he explains that the then-former president of CBS outed Kearns as also working for the CIA. It's a charge Kearns vehemently denied to his death eleven years later. *How sad*, I think, *that after so much success in his career, Frank's purported association with the CIA would haunt the rest of his life and tarnish his legacy.*

Jerry's story has me pause to consider the stakes for my father and his own relationship with the CIA. How difficult it must be for those in a profession looked upon by others with such contempt, as if the work were shameful, something to be vociferously denied under inquiry! What secrets did Eich carry to his grave? Perhaps it's not so far-fetched to think the CIA could have buried the book manuscript my father was working on—thereby keeping its potential revelations secret. Eich likely would have known if Kearns was on the CIA payroll. In one of his letters, my father told me he was writing about everyone he had known over his life, an intoxicating, addictive exercise in reflection that occupied his last years. I am panged by not having this manuscript now.

I rummage through the meager stores of memorabilia from my mother to find my dad's World War II government-issued identification card. Laminated with a brown-and-white border and a black-and-white photo, it has Eich's signature in blue ink, his name, and "Captain" typed on the front, along with the issue date, 28 May 1945. I take a photo of the ID and email it to Jerry. I also find Frank and Gwen Kearns's address in my mother's old red-leather address book and offer to take a photo of it for him.

Jerry likes the idea. He wants to flesh out Kearns's association with Miles Copeland and my dad as much as he can while still allowing viewers to draw their own conclusions about what Frank was doing there. "I love unanswered questions,"[34] he tells me. I don't share his enthusiasm on this point; the ambiguity of deceit disturbs me. I want to get to the truth of a matter, if there is such a thing. More than ever, I am realizing that, in large part, truth is in the hands of the storyteller. As someone who has spent most of her life living in the moment, I have a growing appreciation for those who mine the past for what it can tell us about the present. Although I harbor deep regrets from not having the manuscript Eich promised me, it is quite possible Eich could have become an unreliable narrator of his own story. He could well have lied about some things and embellished others. I must keep in mind, spies are sworn to secrecy. Deception becomes a valued skill, and honesty no longer their strong suit. Nonetheless, I wish I had his story in his own words so that I could be the judge.

Jerry and his film crew have recently traveled to southwest

France to interview my mother's old friend Lorraine Copeland, Miles Copeland's widow. Lorraine is ninety years old and lives in a château owned by her son, Miles III—the son I heard on the radio interview that sparked my quest in 2003. I'm delighted to hear she is still alive. Jerry reintroduces us via email, and I send a note right away.

In her response, Lorraine addresses me as Ann Mary, my childhood name, the name she knew me by. "Your mom was my best buddy for a long time and then we lost touch,"[35] she explains by way of asking me to fill her in on what happened to us after we left Beirut. I tell her about Mom's death in 1992 and how Jay has a successful financial advising company, that we are both married with five kids between us. Lorraine is concerned my mother thought she and Miles had taken Eich's side in my parents' split. I don't know how to respond. I have no recollection of our lives in Beirut, and Mom never spoke to me about their divorce or the circumstances leading to it. When I was with my mother, I felt like the subject was off limits, like it was cordoned off by the black-and-yellow tape blocking a crime scene. Especially after she was stricken with cancer.

About my dad's unexpected departure, Lorraine writes that they "were all devastated and scandalized at his action (and that of Patsy)."[36] I had previously heard from family friends that my parents' breakup happened when my dad had gone to Europe on a business trip. He wrote my mom telling her that their marriage was over, that he was not coming back to Beirut until she left. That my mother had to pack all our belongings and take my baby brother and me back to the States on her own, still makes me bristle with anger. How could my father leave his family like that? Why wasn't he brave enough to face her?

Since Lorraine had broached the subject of my parents' breakup and was one of my mother's closest friends at the time, I ask her if Eich and Patsy had gotten together before my dad went to Europe. I have no idea how he ended up with this woman—a mother of eight, no less.

"Yes," Lorraine tells me. "Eich and Patsy had already 'found' each other before he left," she and Miles figured. Further, Patsy's husband, Charles Cooper, who also worked for the CIA, was a third partner in Miles and Eich's Beirut consulting group. This is startling information.[37]

The three couples—the Copelands, Eichelbergers, and Coopers—would go to Lorraine's and Miles's Beirut beach hut where they picnicked and slept on the sand "under the stars with the sound of lapping waves."[38] I love the poetic nature of her language at the same time as I am disturbed by what is being disclosed. The six of them did a lot of hanging out together. It was simply so much easier for them to relax in each other's company since they didn't have to watch what they said. Lorraine adds to this disclosure, as a note of explanation, "CIA personnel have to get used to 'living a lie' in public."[39] It must be a difficult way to live, to be one thing but pretend to be another. I really appreciate her candor. My mother never spoke to me about what it was like to be a spy's wife. And I never thought to ask her. Maybe because of the deeply disturbing things my mother's friend is telling me now.

Lorraine remembers that, one evening, Patsy decided to sleep inside the hut, although it had no furniture. At the time, Lorraine and Miles did not think anything of it when my dad went to the shack to get a drink and did not come back out. But, they surmised, this must have been when it started.[40]

I imagine my mom left alone to sleep on the beach that night. They would have unfurled a cotton spread from which to watch the sea of stars and listen to the lapping of the Mediterranean on the sandy shore. My brother Jay was less than a year old, and I was six, undoubtedly left at home with our nanny. Wouldn't she have gone looking for him if he had wandered off and not come back to where they were on the beach? Or did he slip away after she fell asleep, after they made love? Or instead, did my parents have a fight that night, my mother voicing her anger at my father for his emotional aloofness? This could have prompted Eich to get another drink and fall into Patsy's arms.

My mother could be the life of a party, but she certainly was not what you would call "easy-going"; she had a temper. She was high-strung and moody. I recall in one of my father's letters him telling me that he came home once to find my mother chasing one of our servants around with a lit cigarette. Was this misplaced anger? Was my mother worried about the danger my dad was in with his work, or was it something else altogether? I wonder, did she figure out my father's indiscretion with Patsy after he left for Europe on the business trip—after she received his letter informing her that he was not coming back to Beirut until she left? Although she would not have known the exact nature of what my father was doing, I have the sense that my mom was not comfortable with the missions Eich and Miles were involved in for the CIA. Perhaps Patsy was more accepting of it all. This might explain why my father left my mom in favor of his lover. But does this explain why he would leave his children?

Lorraine's email continued: "The idea of Eich being attracted to Patsy was ludicrous and never crossed our minds—they were so different. Eich was intellectual, introspective, taciturn, while Patsy (with no figure after eight children!) was outgoing, garrulous, Catholic."[41] I read her email with equal parts fascination and disgust. Not only was my father duplicitous in his professional life by working undercover for the CIA, he was duplicitous in his personal life by having an affair with his partner's wife. It was a double deception.

Patsy's husband Charles had joined Miles and Eich's consulting group in Beirut due to his valuable connections with Saudi princes. He was an economic advisor on the payroll of the royal family. The three partners had been building a business advising oil interests, airlines, and the hospitality and film industry—governments and businesses wanting to take advantage of the Middle East's growing riches. Lorraine assures me Charles was a delightful person but when what she calls the "big bust-up" happened, Charles managed to embark on what Lorraine describes as his "Saudi career," and they did not see him after that. When my father left, she told me their consulting clients "skedaddled," leaving her and Miles with no income. Miles was left scrounging for work in Beirut and the US while my father went to Europe.[42] What was my father thinking starting an affair with his partner's wife? That he could get away with it, like his other clandestine operations?

It's a lot to digest. I promised myself that I would not let my search into my dad's life interfere with mine, but I feel like a volcano—an underground chamber that could explode if I don't step away from the edge. It's a relief to turn my attention toward my son instead. Rio is anxious to get back to his life in Boone, his new apartment and job with the clean energy nonprofit he was working for before the fire. He assures Richard and me that he can handle being on his own, but I worry about the high doses of medication he's still on to manage his pain. Rio had trouble on and off with drinking through high school and college. Though that had stopped well before the fire in July, his medical circumstances add to my concern that he could relapse. "Let him go," Richard advises. "He's ready."

I still think of the dreadful scene daily, although it has been a couple of months since the fire. Before Rio jumped, the flames were practically licking his heels from their spread out the windows below. The asphalt shingles were melting where he was standing, and he thought the roof was about to cave. With only moments to spare, our son leapt. It was an action that saved his life.

One afternoon, Richard and I were on our way to the hospital for our visit to the ICU when a traffic jam brought us to a stop. A siren's shrill warning and the smoke rising next to the hospital began my panic that Rio could get caught in another fire. I jumped out of our car to ask the cop directing traffic about the standstill. It was a fire in the medical offices next to Mission Hospital, he told me. Just days after fighting the fire that Rio survived, a fire fighter, Captain Jeff Bowen, lost his life in the medical office blaze.

I had pieced together that the Fire Chief was also at Rio's fire because he was one of the twenty men listed in the fire department report. Bowen left behind a wife and three teenage stepchildren. I had clipped an article from Asheville's *Citizen-Times* with the address to send contributions to the children's college fund, and it's been on the pile of papers crowding my desk at home, hounding me to act. As I am getting around to sending a condolence note and check to his widow, I keep in mind that the woman I am writing to lost her husband. With my son alive and well enough to allow me the psychic space to turn to other pursuits, the discomfort of chasing my father's ghost pales next to her family's suffering.

Oddly, though, realizing this woman's profound loss prompts me to face my fears in searching the rubble of my father's life. In one of her emails, Lorraine Copeland asks about the eight Cooper children. The only Cooper I had ever been in touch with is Delores, who is two years my junior and the second youngest of Patsy's children. It was Delores who called me when my father was dying. And then when I received Eich's death certificate as part of my quest to get his CIA personnel files, I discovered, with a jab of jealousy, that she is listed as "friend" where next of kin belongs. She is the person who cared for my father at the end of his life while I selfishly tended to my own family and our travel plans to Ecuador.

It is a Carolina blue sky day in September, and I am sitting on our living room couch typing Delores's name into a PeopleSmart. com search window. A match comes up. I recognize the address but not her current last name. She is still living in DC. After paying the five dollars to get her phone number, I dial the 202 area code, feeling anticipation mount in my stomach like barometric pressure. It has been over twenty years since we spoke. I don't know what to expect.

After decades, it seems she is expecting me. "I've been hoping someday you or Jay would get in touch with me," she says. "I am so happy you called. I have been saving a large envelope since your dad died, full of things about your grandmother. You won't believe what an amazing woman your grandmother was!"[43]

My surprise and appreciation tumble out together. I shower her with thanks and explain that I truly know little about my grandmother since she died before my parents married. "Do you have the manuscript Eich had been working on before he died?" I ask. This is the main reason for my call.

"No, I don't think so, unless it's in the attic of our Connecticut house. We just don't have room in our DC apartment to store much," she replies. Her husband Robert has a family home in Connecticut. I think he may have inherited it, although I don't ask. They, or perhaps the relatives they inherited the house from, have crammed the attic full of stuff. She may have put some last remaining things of Eich's up there after cleaning his apartment. She does not remember, and I do not press for details. "Most of what was in your father's apartment was worthless,"[44] she tells me.

"I hope it's there," I reply, stymied as to why Eich would not have kept a copy of the manuscript at his apartment in the Roosevelt. He'd told me he had a copy for me.

Three days after my call with Delores, I receive a thank you note from Stacy Bowen, the fire captain's widow. She tells me her husband was the fireman who found Rio. So, *he* was the person who saved Rio from the drainage ditch as he lay in fear of drowning. Tears spring to my eyes when I get to the end of Stacey Bowen's note: *I am glad he was the one to save your son!*

To think, our son survived the fire, and five days later her husband died in another inferno adjacent to where Rio was fighting for his life. Now two months after this misfortune, Rio is back in Boone picking up where he left things while I wait in anticipation for Delores's package to learn about my grandmother. I wonder about fate and luck and how this widow can carry on with so much grace while I totter on a seesaw of gratitude and doubt. I appreciate my blessings. I make a practice of this. At the same time, I am continually expecting the next shoe to drop, like my distrust could run away with my good fortune at any moment.

---

27 Donald Neff, *Warriors of Suez: Eisenhower Takes America into the Middle East in 1956* (Brattleboro: Amana Books 1988).

28 Eveland, *Ropes of Sand,* 168-7; Neff, *Warrior of Suez,* 216.

29 Neff, *Warriors of Suez ,* 216.

30 Said K. Aburish, email to author, September, 2011.

31 Jerry Davis, phone conversation with author September 6, 2011.

32 Ibid.

33 Jerry Davis, email to author September 5, 2011.

34 Ibid.

35 Lorraine Copeland, email to author, September 8, 2011.

36 Ibid.

37 Lorraine Copeland, email to author, September 11, 2011.

38 Ibid.

39 Ibid.

40 Ibid.

41 Ibid.

42 Ibid.

43 Delores Cooper, phone call with author, September 2011.

44 Ibid.

CHAPTER 5

BEIRUT TINDERBOX

Delores's package is full of memorabilia my father must have carted around the world after my grandmother's death. There are several newspaper clippings, including a yellowed 1931 *Pittsburgh Gazette* interview, "Can Girls Succeed In Business?" about how my grandmother had been a housewife until her husband died and then became a grocery store executive. With no way to support her only child, widowhood pushed my grandmother into the workforce. She credits her husband for inadvertently preparing her for a career in marketing. He had been in advertising, and after work she would pepper him with her curiosity, intensely interested in the workings of his world. Mary Eich—as others affectionately referred to her—started as a stenographer at McCann & Co, where she worked her way to Vice President of Marketing, attending night school to gain more business acumen.

I find a newspaper photo of my grandmother at a dinner with executives and department heads—the only woman around a rectangular table with twenty-seven men. They were celebrating the opening of their downtown Pittsburgh grocery emporium on East Liberty Street. The seven-story building, taking up an entire city block, was the largest food store of its kind in the US. The grocery began on the street as an egg and butter stall and grew to employ five hundred people in three Pittsburgh stores. Most remarkable is that the president handed ownership of the company to his employees and made no more salary than a salesclerk. I knew nothing about my grandmother before reading these newspaper clippings, and now she is coming to life before my eyes.

The envelope full of mementos about my grandmother has scant trace of my father's father. There is just one photograph of my father with his parents. It is a three-by-four-inch black-and-white snapshot in a gold-colored metal frame. It is the only photo of the three of them, the only one I have seen of the man who must be my grandfather, and the only picture I have of my father as a child.

They are standing close to each other in the tall grass of their overgrown backyard. All are smiling, especially Eich and his father. My grandfather's hand cups his son's shoulder like warm comfort. My father's head tilts toward his father's heart. His eyes are squinting from the sun, his mouth upturned in a grin that only the profound security of family can convey for a nine-year-old.

I feel like Mary Eich is sprinkling me with stardust, her quiet brilliance and the newspaper quotes illuminating my world eighty years after hers. When asked how to get ahead in the world she responds, "Get a definite picture in your mind of what you want to do, then leave no stone unturned until you have accomplished your goal." I feel she is speaking directly to me, encouraging my quest to understand my father, her only child. Next to this guide star, Eich's father, my grandfather, feels like a sea of dark space, a mysterious black hole.

Based on the few things Mom had told me of Eich's childhood, at the end of my grandfather's life, syphilis overtook him to the extent that he did not recognize his own son. This must have happened shortly after the photo was taken of my father with his parents. Could this be the seed of my father's alcoholism later in life? After Jimmy Eichelberger visited his father, Homer, at the Pennsylvania sanitorium and his father asked, "What is your name, son?" my father could have masked his heart and lived in his head. He could have been afraid to trust again. He could have been afraid, much like me, of ever having to feel the kind of pain that comes from losing a parent at such a tender age. What might the loss of a father to such a hideous disease do to the Depression-era boy who was raised by a single mom? What might it have done to the man with a desire to make a success of his life? A man who wanted to tell his story but, in the end, did not.

I file these troubling questions away for another time by reminding myself to focus on the steps I am taking, rather than the immense chasm of my not knowing. I write Delores a thank-you note and make plans for Richard and me to meet with her and her husband the next time we are in DC. In the meantime, I continue to piece together information gleaned from Miles Copeland's memoir, memorabilia my mother saved, scholarly articles, and the news media. It's all information that feeds into my father's life.

Books and photos are spread across the four-foot circular copper tray Mom bought in Lebanon. She told me the Bedouin desert dwellers carried these types of trays on their camels to use as their dining tables when they set up camp. On it is an inscription in Arabic that reads, *This is my path.* Now, as our living room coffee table, it is serving as my pathway to uncover my family's life in this seaside city. Beirut was in its heyday in July 1957 when my parents moved to the Lebanese capital after Cairo and a short stint in DC. Tourism was taking off. You could sun on the beach, ski in the mountains, shop for the latest in French fashion, and savor a drink at a world-class hotel along the Corniche—Beirut's three-mile promenade along the Mediterranean—all in one day. Lebanon was thriving because of Middle East oil. The largest pipeline in the world, the Trans-Arabian Pipeline (TAPline) had recently opened, bringing crude oil from Saudi Arabia over a thousand miles to its terminus at Lebanon's port city of Sidon.

My father and Copeland started their consulting business to take advantage of Beirut's commercial opportunities. In addition to oil, new airlines were adding flights to the Middle East, US construction companies were looking to gain from the flush of financial growth, and a fledgling film industry was taking hold in the cosmopolitan capital. Beirut held the potential to make them rich.

"Perhaps their new business was also a front for CIA work?" I wonder aloud to Richard from our living room couch.

"Of course it was," he responds. "They were out to make money, and taking advantage of their CIA connections would make it easy."

I agree with him. After all, Miles says as much in *The Game Player*[45] when he writes about how the CIA was paying them to throw lavish parties in Beirut to keep an eye on Kim Philby. Philby was the British double agent who defected to Russia from Beirut a couple of years after my parents broke up. At the time, his cover was writing for *The Economist* magazine while working for MI6, Britain's equivalent of the CIA. The cocktail parties and catered dinners my dad and Copeland hosted were a perfect platform for the press, political and profit-driven communities to mingle.

My growing fascination with my father's life and times is ignoring just how contrary his pursuits were to mine. I reject the definition of success as the accumulation of wealth, and I am extremely concerned about our continued reliance on oil. In addition to all the military intervention this substance has been responsible for, we are racing toward a fossil-fuel-induced climate catastrophe—a warming planet precipitating sea level rise, droughts, mass migration, and famine—upturning civilizations that have been thriving for centuries. The 2011 pro-democracy movement in Syria, now morphed into a civil war, is one example. It was fueled by famine resulting from a historical three-year drought. The fertile crescent is drying out due in large part to fossil fuels use.

The negative effects of oil dependence are the reason why I am so passionate—my husband would say obsessed—about my work promoting alternative fuels. Transportation in the US is the number one source of climate-change-inducing carbon dioxide emissions. Each gallon of gasoline and diesel burned in our vehicles puts more than nineteen and twenty-two pounds of CO_2 respectively into the atmosphere. This invisible gas is now blanketing the earth, trapping in the heat from the sun and creating what is now widely understood as the greenhouse gas effect. It is no wonder why this is such a difficult problem to tackle.

I, like everyone else, love the freedom of jumping in my car anytime day or night to go where I want to go and do what I want to do. It's not the eagle that symbolizes America's freedom. It's the car. And it's easy to look the other way when it comes to considering what that fuel is doing to the environment. The greenhouse gas effect was discovered well over a hundred years ago but ignored in favor of the convenience and comfort that cheap fossil fuels can bring. I am fascinated (in a disturbed kind of way) in realizing that this orgy of oil has been going on my whole life, fueled by Madison Avenue marketing, supported by the CIA, and facilitated by men like my father.

"Someone should make a movie about this time period in Beirut," I comment to Richard, who is now at the piano in our living room. "It could be a combo of Mad Men, James Bond, and Erin Brockovich. Julia Roberts can play me."

"Yes, indeed. And I can do the soundtrack," he says, fingering the horn part of the 007 theme song for *Goldfinger* on his keyboard.

The consulting group Copeland and Eichelberger opened swanky offices right next to TAPline's office on Hamra Street, the intellectual center of the capitol given its proximity to the

American University of Beirut. Their first client was Pittsburgh-based Gulf Oil, who had a half stake in the Kuwait Oil Company. At the time, two-thirds of Gulf's earnings came from operations in Kuwait. Gulf was making more on investment in Kuwait than the US by a factor of eighteen. Copeland and Eichelberger's assignment was to keep an eye on all the Middle East activities that could affect that investment. Previously, Gulf did not have its own regional representatives but rather relied on intelligence from British Petroleum, which also had a stake in Kuwaiti oil. Miles describes their job as reporting on "the fluctuating anxieties of the Kuwaiti royal family due to unsettling political developments in Iraq and Egypt."[46] There was plenty to report on, and in the late 1950s, Beirut was the place to be.

In early 1958, the country's Christian president Camille Chamoun was walking a tightrope between his past and present—a balancing act made more difficult by the Pan Arab movement resulting in the recent union of Lebanon's neighbors Syria and Egypt. Lebanon's charter requires equal political representation of Muslims and Christians, although by convention the president is always a Christian. During Lebanon's struggle to gain freedom from France ten years earlier, the colonialists imprisoned Chamoun for his nationalist beliefs. By the time my father arrived, some viewed President Chamoun as compromising the country's new autonomy by accepting support from Washington. Eich, I imagine, was one of the men encouraging the president to lean on US backing. Lebanese tension came to a head in May 1958 when a riot was sparked after unknown assailants murdered a prominent Arab journalist in Beirut.[47]

The tinder box really caught fire with the brutal murder of Iraq's King Faisal II a couple of months later—some five hundred miles away from Beirut. In Baghdad, Iraqi military men under the leadership of Abdel-Karim Qāsim, an Army brigadier and nationalist, corralled the twenty-three-year-old British-installed king and four members of the royal family into the palace courtyard. Although the young king did not resist the coup d'état, the men ordered him—along with his mother, brother, sister-in-law, aunt, and several servants—to turn toward the wall, after which the military men summarily shot them. The next day, a mob killed the prime minister as he was fleeing the country disguised as an old woman. What became known as the 14 July Revolution sent ripples through the region. The US feared Lebanon could be next to slip from Western control.[48]

President Eisenhower authorized US military troops to support Chamoun's government the following day. He dispatched fourteen thousand soldiers to the bikini-covered beaches just outside Beirut. I remember my mother saying she could hear the explosions from our balcony. It was the first use of the Eisenhower Doctrine—the bulwark against Communist aggression—and the first US invasion in the Middle East. There would be many others, dressed in ideological garb but underneath having to do with the power that comes with access to oil.[49]

Three days after the Iraqi royal family massacre my mother and I were boarding a French luxury liner. The SS Liberté set sail to New York from France. The only way I know this is that the ship's program lists Mrs. Alice Eichelberger and Miss Ann Mary Eichelberger as passengers. I found the eight-page pamphlet, with a watercolor cover of nautical flags, in the plastic container under our futon couch among the jumble of memorabilia I have brought down from our attic. The timing was perfect for my mom and me to take the luxury liner to the States for a summer visit with my grandparents. Given all the fast-moving developments, my father would have appreciated not having the distraction of his family nearby.

The very next year, the US was working on deposing Qasim,

the military leader responsible for the massacre of the Iraqi royal family. A young Saddam Hussein was hired to carry out the dirty work. I've found a United Press International article that claims my father knew Hussein. Informed by former US intelligence officials, the article states, "During this time Saddam was making frequent visits to the American Embassy where CIA specialists such as Miles Copeland and CIA station chief Jim Eichelberger were in residence and knew Saddam."[50] Reportedly, Hussein botched a 1959 CIA-supported assassination attempt on Qasim when he lost his nerve and fired his gun prematurely, killing the Prime Minister's driver and only wounding Qasim. Hussein then fled to Syria before landing in Beirut where the CIA installed him in an apartment and provided the twenty-two-year-old with training. It's possible my path crossed Saddam Hussein's.

I know it's a sick pastime to imagine an association with one of the most brutal tyrants in recent history, but I begin to consider that this is one way to exorcise the ghost of my father. I want to vilify my father because of the work he did and how he treated his family. At the same time, I want to find a way to forgive him for the damages he caused, the exorcism now a swing dance of emotion.

The rendezvous between Hussein and Eich would have taken place at the St. George's Hotel. Said Aburish devoted a whole book to the iconic Beirut landmark. In the 1950s and 60s, the indoor bar and terrace restaurant overlooking St. George's Bay was the premier place for spies, journalists, oil men, movie stars, and politicians to congregate. I imagine even roughnecks like Hussein could have come through its doors. Aburish's father—the decades-long *TIME* magazine bureau chief—set up an informal shop at the St. George's bar to keep track of comings and goings. Kim Philby proposed to one of his wives, who at the time was married to a *New York Times* reporter, at the St. George's bar. And when Philby disappeared and defected to Russia, questions quickly filled the watering hole with speculation.[51]

A place where nothing is as it seems is fitting for my flight of fancy. I am eating a cookie while my dad is having a drink on the restaurant terrace overlooking the pool and sea. I adore going out with my dad for sesame tahini cookies. My blonde, pixie-cut hair has a side ponytail and ribbon, and I'm wearing my tan school pinafore that has Ann Mary embroidered in blue cursive over my heart. We are conversing in French about how I like the new school I'm attending when Saddam Hussein walks by, bends to my father's ear for a moment, and whispers a secret. After they are finished speaking, my father and I hold hands for a walk along the Corniche.

I keep this kind of active imagining to myself when Richard and I first meet Delores and her husband Robert for dinner in Washington, DC. I'm sure she has far more stories than I do about growing up in the Middle East—actual real memories. Delores already told me over the phone that as an eleven-year-old, all she knew how to say in English was "Coca-Cola." This would have been 1967, when Eich arranged to have her and Patsy evacuated from Beirut to the States at the start of the Six Day War. "I didn't even have time to say goodbye to my friends at school," she said matter-of-factly.

We meet at Mama Ayesha's, the Lebanese eatery on Calvert Street in the Adams Morgan neighborhood of DC, a mainstay for Middle Eastern food since opening in 1960. They are already at a table near the entrance. Delores is slim with short, dark, gray-speckled hair and warm, inviting eyes. She looks elegant yet understated in her choice of jewelry, white blouse, and skirt. I don't recall meeting Delores in person before, although she says we did decades ago, when Eich was alive. I learn she is a retired accountant. Robert, more heavy-set than his wife with bushy brows, works for the federal government as a statistician. My nerves calm with a mango martini while the others have wine. We order some hummus and baba ghanouj as appetizers and remark on how we love Mediterranean food.

Both Delores and Robert are friendly and engaging conversationalists. Immediately, I am impressed with how much Middle East history they both know. At the same time, I sense their guardedness. While I want to ask what effect my father's relationship with her mother had on her, I try to be careful with my questions—probing but not too personal.

Over dinner Delores shares a couple of her early memories. She and her family lived outside Beirut on an old estate, a pastoral setting with fruit trees and farmland. Next to their home, a large above-ground cistern stored water used to irrigate the fruit trees. Delores was five or so when her nanny allowed her to stay up one night to watch one of her parents' parties.

From her recounting, I see the scene unfold in a crowded, smoky room. I picture the woman in front of me as a young child peering around a corner, hidden by a half wall. There is loud, boisterous talk and then splashing. In front of her eyes, her parents and their friends are jumping fully clothed in tuxedos and ball gowns from the second-floor window into their cistern pool. As she is describing these details, I file the images of inebriated spies, business leaders, politicians and officials jumping into the makeshift pool as a movie scene.

We are only getting brief snippets of her childhood. In the early sixties, the Saudi royal family held Delores's dad against his will in the desert kingdom for four years. I don't mention that Lorraine Copeland has recently explained to me that Delores's father embarked on a Saudi career that coincided with my parents' split-up and my dad getting together with her mom.

"I don't think much of the Copelands, especially Miles," Delores remarks in an offhanded way.

"My mom did not much like him either," I reply, keeping to myself how grateful I am for the books Miles wrote, even if he was known as a liar.

Delores does not know why the Saudi Royals detained her father, only that they sporadically permitted him to come home to Beirut.

On one of these occasions, she was eating breakfast when the maid informed her of her father's pending arrival. "Pappy's coming!" Delores exclaimed prancing around the kitchen in her nightie. At this point, my father—in his bathrobe with the Cooper's percolator coffee pot jiggling in his hands—scurried toward the back door while her dad was coming in the front. We laugh at the humor in her imagery, the conflicted chortle of strangers who share a troubling past. It is far easier to look at the surface of the scene and be engaged by the dark comedy of circumstance than examine the confusing role my father played in both our lives.

My father lived with Patsy and her children off and on for years. While Eich was in and out of the country conducting CIA business, and Robert Cooper's Saudi Arabian problems had him periodically indisposed, I surmise the two men shared a residence and a wife in Beirut. It was around this time that Patsy had her eighth child, a son. He is two years younger than Delores, who is two years younger than me. Moreover, being Catholic, her parents never divorced. I do not dare ask if this person could be my half-brother. Delores is decidedly not as interested as I am in exploring her past, or at least not plumbing its depths with me. I ask about meeting some of her other siblings and get a tepid response. She is gracious and charming and does agree to look for Eich's papers in the attic of their Connecticut house the next time she is there.

I understand not wanting to explore a troubling past. My father's death as some penniless alcoholic haunts me, as does the blame he cast on my mother for the disintegration of their marriage. Maybe because I am a product of this marriage, I feel equally responsible for its unraveling and doomed to a similar fate.

Shortly after Jamila was born, I wrote my father asking why he left my mom. I thought I had destroyed his response for its vitriol—pages on how he never loved my mother, that he had to leave our family to save himself. At the time, Richard and I were struggling with our own marital problems, including an affair, and had decided to patch things up. His thoughtless treatment of my mother, in my memory, had me throw the letter away. Why in the world did he need to tell me his cruel thoughts about a woman who did her best to raise me?

But one day, as I am looking for something else altogether, I find the seven-page typed missive in our attic. I'm grateful now I kept it. Along with the lacerating he gives my mom, it is the most thorough account of his career I have. In the letter, Eich recounts his bitter disappointment with an oil deal gone awry and references INTERSER, the consulting group he and Copeland started in New York City, after my parents split. The business deal involved Former Eisenhower Treasury Secretary Robert Anderson.[52]

My father's relationship with Robert Anderson was the only thing Said Aburish had questioned me about over our five months of correspondence.[53] I feel like I am on to something, something having to do with money and politics and the price we pay for our reliance on oil. Some of the very things that get me out of bed every morning.

45 Miles Copeland. *The Game Player Confession of the CIA's Original Operatives,* (London: Aurum Press, 1989), 212.

46 Ibid, 211.

47 K. S., "The Lebanese Crisis in Perspective." The World Today 14, no. 9 (1958): 369-80, accessed June 6, 2021, http://www.jstor.org/stable/40393919.

48 Bruce Riedel, "1958: When America first went to war in the Middle East," July 2, 2018, accessed June 6, 2021, https://www.brookings.edu/blog/order-from-chaos/ 2018/07/02/1958-when-america-first-went-to-war-in-the-middle-east/.

49 Shibley Telhami, "The Persian Gulf: Understanding the American Oil Strategy," March 1, 2002, Brookings Article, accessed June 6, 2021, https://www.brookings.edu/ articles/the-persian-gulf-understanding-the-american-oil-strategy/.

50 Richard Sale, "Exclusive: Saddam Was Key in Early CIA," UPI, (April 11, 2003), https://www.upi.com/Defense-News/2003/04/10/Exclusive-Saddam-key-in-early-CIA-plot/65571050017461/.

51 Said K. Aburish, *The St. George Hotel Bar,* (London: Bloomsbury Publishing Ltd, 1989), 75-85.

52 James M Eichelberger, letter to author, December 14, 1982.

53 Said K. Aburish, email to author, December 28, 2010.

CHAPTER 6

THE GHOSTS BETWEEN THE LINES

How did the oil age begin? What drove it? Just how much did underhanded politics play in its making? How was my father involved and to what lasting effect? He is certainly guilty by association. In his memoir, Miles Copeland boasts of his hand in the overthrow of Syria's government in 1949[54], actions that led to the rise of the Baathist party, the Assad regime, the current Syrian civil war and the deaths of millions.

Eich's boss in the CIA, Kim Roosevelt, led US efforts in Iran to overthrow the democratically elected leader Mohammad Mosaddegh after he nationalized the Iranian oil industry. The CIA meddling then reinstalled the last Shah of Iran.[55] This move ushered in lucrative US oil deals until the 1979 revolution when Khomeini's Islamic Republic severed relations, a situation that continues to haunt America's relations with the world's fourth largest oil producer.

This is well-trod ground for spy world historians, but for someone working to undo the oil age, it's disturbing to place my father amidst its founding fathers and ponder the three degrees of separation between what was driving my father's world and what is driving mine. At what price comes this skullduggery? I am connecting to my father through oil, which, given my work, makes Eich and his colleagues easy to loathe.

In one of my emails, I ask Lorraine Copeland about good references to learn about my father's world—the host of relations Eich and Miles were navigating in the 1950s and 60s Middle East.

She responds with one suggestion, a book by Anthony Cave Brown, *Treason in the Blood*.[56] When the used copy arrives from Amazon, yet again, before so much as opening the front cover, I flip straight to the index and run my finger down the *E*s to see if it references my father. It does not. I size up the 677-page tome about my father's colleague Kim Philby, a British spy-turned-traitor, and his father St. John, as not relevant enough to my research about Eich to warrant immediate attention. I already have a rough sketch of Kim Philby's infamy. The younger Philby defected to Russia as a double agent in 1963, shortly after we moved to DC.

Before shelving the hardcover, I give it another look. It reveals a lot about the dawn of the oil age and the deviousness that drove it. I also notice it references Lorraine. Miles Copeland is listed in many of the books I'm reading, but I have never seen her quoted before. I turn to page 488. The heartbreak in Lorraine's words strike me like a fire poker. "It was painful to think that during the years we all loved Kim and had him constantly in our homes, he was all the while laughing at us."[57]

Lorraine and Miles trusted the younger Philby. They were close, made closer by the British heritage Lorraine and Kim shared. Further, Lorraine had served Britain's Special Operations Executive, a clandestine World War II government organization. She was an SOE agent when she met her future American husband. The SOE was the precursor to the MI6, the intelligence agency Kim worked in. On a parallel track during WWII, Eich and Miles worked for the Office of Strategic Services (OSS) and the Counter Intelligence Corp (CIC), the precursors to the CIA. Miles, my father, and many other CIA counter intelligence agents collaborated with Kim and his colleagues in Britain's MI6.[58]

As it turns out, their charming friend and colleague had been eating at their table and coming to their cocktail parties at the same time he was feeding information to the Russians. Lorraine's feeling of betrayal certainly matched that of my father and many others. What does this line of work do to people who deceive for a living, when the very colleagues holding their confidence deceive them? I suspect it causes them to hide more and trust less. Under no circumstance should you share what nourishes you. The consequence could be death, like food poisoning, unexpected and final.

I imagine that one could never fully recover from this breach of confidence. All Philby's colleagues, my father included, would have had to review, in their mind's eye at least, every conversation they had with the traitor for damaging disclosures. Stakes are high in the spy world. It is not an exaggeration to consider the many lives lost because of their collegiality. I doubt the group of Beirut friends would have even told each other of their unintentional breaches at the time of Philby's defection. The wound of deceit was theirs alone to tend. But no doubt it haunted them. Good spies do not talk. They keep their secrets to themselves. They carry them to their grave.

In this regard, my father was a good spy.

From *Treason in the Blood*, I learn the apple doesn't fall far from the tree in the Philby family. St. John, like his son, was prone to deceit. It appears the elder Philby was instrumental in facilitating US access to Saudi oil. St. John Philby's influence on Ibn Saud, the desert ruler who founded the Kingdom of Saudi Arabia, was what opened the tent flap for American business. His sway over the king to sell Saudi oil rights to the Americans handed the US a prize that should have gone to his homeland. Little did anyone know at the time how big it would be. Saudi Arabia is now the world's second largest oil producer, the US its largest consumer.[59] With assets of over $10 trillion, the Arabian American Oil Company (ARAMCO), now officially named the Saudi Arabian Oil Company, is also the world's wealthiest business.[60]

Sadly, the brilliant explorer and Middle East expert died unsatisfied. After heavily drinking with his son over two days in September 1960, the elder Philby collapsed at a party in Beirut. His last words were reportedly, "God, I'm bored."[61] Are we destined to repeat the foibles of our fathers to the peril of our hearts and history? I hope not. I am trying mightily to counter the ways of my father with my family and work. For me, Kim and St. John Philby's stories illustrate how chance, circumstance, and intention play a tune to which our personal and political actions dance into the future.

Both father and son felt strongly that their English homeland was hypocritical, saying one thing and doing another, to the detriment of principles they held dear.[62] I often feel the same about my government. In the US we espouse an abiding belief in democracy and personal freedoms within the rule of law while supporting repressive regimes around the world who do the opposite. I don't believe my personal convictions would allow me to use deceit to correct the injustices perpetrated by my government. I prefer my grievances are known through peaceful protest, like the one we just attended in DC against the Iraq War. The same cannot be said for my dad, his colleagues, as well as St. John and Kim Philby.

Father and son both used deception to enact their ideas for a better world, a better life. In the end they were too proud to admit a disappointing outcome. Each went to their graves defending his duplicity, despite the collateral damage it may have caused their family and country.[63] In this they remind me of my father. In his letters and in our few meetings, Eich never expressed any remorse for the deceit or double-crossing with which he was involved.

St. John's story is fascinating to me because it traces just how quickly things changed with the discovery of oil and how deceit underpins America's special relations with Saudi Arabia, a vast desert known as *terra incognita* on maps of the day. In October 1917, St. John became the first British imperial agent to its desert ruler Ibn Saud. There, St. John's belief in Arab self-determination took a gut punch with the turn of events after the first World War. In 1918, in accordance with covert plans, our allies France and Britain installed as kings the sons of Saud's enemy, Hussein the Sharif of Mecca. King Faisal (the grandfather of King Faisal II, the young Iraqi ruler executed in 1958 when I was living in Beirut) became the ruler of newly formed Iraq. King Abdullah became the leader of newly formed Transjordan, carved from British-mandated Palestine as a home for the Arabs after the Jews were regranted their own homeland. The duplicity of British leaders, professing support for Arab autonomy while conspiring to make the Middle East their own, soured St. John on his homeland.[64]

After Saud's fifteen-year struggle to unite the Arabian Peninsula's Bedouin tribes and establish the Kingdom of Saudi Arabia in 1932, St. John Philby drew closer to the Saudis. He converted to Islam, and King Saud provided him a seat on his private council along with several homes and a Muslim wife. When Philby wed his second wife, his son Kim was in British boarding school while Eich was in high school in Pittsburgh, PA. While Philby was establishing a new family in Saudi Arabia (a wife and soon-to-be son), he didn't divorce, nor did he totally abandon his family in England. On both sides of the globe, in his own perverse manner, St. John sought a way to support his family in England—at least financially—while helping the House of Saud.[65] This is more than I can say for my father, who separated from us completely.

To my knowledge, the only aid we received from Eich was a down payment on our house in DC. He never gave my mother any child support. He never helped pay for the boarding schools I attended as a rebellious teenager. The taste of sour grapes lingers in my mouth as I make this realization. How could my father just disappear from our lives and not try to help us financially or see my brother and me with some frequency? I can't imagine this happening if Richard and I were to split up. We are both equally devoted to our children. And when we were briefly estranged, we shared expenses and took turns staying with three-year-old Jamila.

In reading about St. John's facilitation of the Saudi-American alliance, it is disturbing to consider how our deep-seated interest in oil has caused the US—a country that professes democratic ideals—to look the other way in its dealings with one of the world's most autocratic countries. Under the present male guardianship system in Saudi Arabia, women have few rights. For normal activities that I take for granted, such as getting a job, traveling internationally, or getting married, Saudi women need to have permission from their father, husband, or another male relative. I am afraid desire and deceit are the double faces that continue to act out the power play of our relations with disregard for human rights and peril to our planet's future.

St. John's and Saud's ticket to financial self-sufficiency turned out to be oil, a top priority for Allied governments and business interests after WWI. A global race was on and the oil business was booming. In 1932, while Eich attended high school in Pittsburgh, Gulf Oil completed the construction of its headquarters downtown, an iconic Art Deco skyscraper that was the city's tallest structure until 1970. At the time, Saudi Arabia remained impenetrable to resource exploration, its oil wealth yet unknown. The desert kingdom had purposefully isolated itself from Western cultural influences. The Ikhwan, Saud's fearless warriors, as well as the religious council the Ulema, were wary of outsiders. St. John Philby counseled the king to view the Americans differently. A main point of Philby's pitch was that the Americans were not colonialists like the British. If the Americans discovered oil, they would provide the kingdom much-needed revenue with no interest in influencing Saudi politics.[66]

Philby's lobbying was successful. Saud gave consent to US oil exploration, a significant milestone in the dawn of the oil age. To realize US dominance in the field of resource control, much changed quickly. In some places, my father and his CIA colleagues most certainly played a part in the new venture. I know the US government prefers its shadow side, its clandestine operations, to grease the wheels for business. Another book, another story illustrates the doublespeak of this secret world in ways that I am unable.

Crossing Mandelbaum's Gate[67] is Kai Bird's memoir about growing up in the Middle East. His father worked for the State Department in some of the same countries our family was stationed. Perhaps his father knew Eich. I emailed the author asking as much. Though the Pulitzer Prize winner was kind enough to respond *and* ask his parents—which means a lot—the answer was no. Bird's book describes the same duplicity I have discovered in my father's world and more broadly in US and Saudi relations regarding its oil. It underscores the importance of my reading between the lines of everything, to examine who wants what out of any given situation, and why governments and businesses are so secretive in their transactions.

In his book, Bird recounts a story about Colonel William Eddy, an academic and oil consultant whose name I just discovered in my mother's red address book. In 1960 the US government countered pro-democracy strategies in Saudi Arabia. There was speculation that Saudi Arabia was heading toward establishing a constitutional monarchy. Crown Prince Faisal, next in line for the throne, had already abolished slavery and censorship of the press. Foreign-educated princes, led by Prince Talal (Faisal's half-brother), were pushing for a more representative national assembly than the absolute rule established with the monarchy. There appeared to be strong popular support for Talal, especially among a growing middle class in the kingdom. The US talked outwardly about supporting democracy, yet was quick to quash it if it impeded business.[68]

Despite Faisal's progressive steps, Talal concluded that the Crown Prince was less interested in democratization than his brother, King Saud. Given the shifting sands of Saudi leadership, Talal looked to the United States to be a power broker in the region to help his interests.

In June 1960, Talal met with the US government to request support for the democracy movement. The American *chargé d'affaires* in Jeddah responded that the "United States could not involve itself with the internal politics of the Kingdom." Prince Talal questioned the bureaucrat's response. "If that was the case, then why was Colonel Bill Eddy constantly meeting with the king?"

"Why should that matter?" the American responded. Col. Eddy was not representing the US government; he was representing ARAMCO's interest. No, Prince Talal countered, he "believed Eddy was now working for [CIA Chief] Allen Dulles."[69] The CIA continues to keep Eddy's reports classified. The Colonel was "undoubtedly urging King Saud to reject Price Talal's demands,"[70] Bird explains. Eich, I imagine, was like Eddy in that he played multiple roles in any given situation and justified the duplicity to satisfy the mission at hand. How I wish I could have had a heart-to-heart with my father toward the end of his life. If only he hadn't succumbed to the ravages of alcoholism, I may have heard an honest retrospective on what the CIA was doing in Saudi Arabia. Instead I continue to piece together a shroud of disparate clues with which to sketch a portrait of a man and his times. Maybe it will lead to some postmortem reconciliation.

In our email correspondence, Lorraine Copeland describes a "junket" to Saudi Arabia with her husband Miles, my father, and Archie Roosevelt (who'd followed his cousin Kim into the CIA).[71]

After an interminable tour of the oil installations, Eich was heard to murmur that he had not yet seen any evidence of actual oil. Consternation [sic], a small Arab boy was fetched who turned a tap and a tiny drop of the black gold appeared.

Why they were touring the oil operation I don't know. I'm certain it wasn't to assess the engineering. Perhaps it was to cultivate relations with informants as seeds for some future fruit. What this tidbit supports is Eich's sharp sense of humor. I see my father casting light on the odd situation of being in a place awash in oil but never seeing a drop of it. I wonder if he'd appreciate the irony of my discovery that his work in oil underpins all that I am working against to reduce our dependence on fossil fuels?

When your father is a secret agent, when he is a ghost, when he is someone you didn't really know, you need to look at the smallest of details to paint a picture of the man. A sense of adventure provides the bold colors of his background. There is no doubt that Lorraine, Miles, Archie Roosevelt, and Eich shared a sense of adventure in the places which they traveled. Still, it's the shadows of deceit and greed that continue to unsettle me.

54 Copeland, *The Game Player Confession of the CIA's Originial Operatives*, 92.

55 Ibid, 187.

56 Anthony Cave Brown, *Treason in the Blood H. St John Philby, Kim Philby, and the Spy Case of the Century* (New York: Houghton Mifflin, 1994).

57 Ibid, 488.

58 Copeland, *The Game Player*, 211-212.

59 US Energy Information Agency 2019, "Frequently Asked Questions," accessed September 1, 2020, https://www.eia.gov/tools/faqs/faq.php?id=709&t=6 .

60 Christopher Helman, "Big Oil, Bigger Oil,"*Financial Times*. February 4, 2010, https://www.ft.com/content/c5b32636-116f-11df-9195-00144feab49a, July 2010; "The World's Biggest Oil Companies," *Forbes*, cited December 14, 2014, *Forbes*, https://www.forbes.com/pictures/mef45gkei/1-saudi-aramco-12-5-million-barrels-per-day-2/?sh=649c95193303.

61 Ben Macintyre, *A Spy Among Friends: Kim Philby And The Great Betayal* (New York: Broadway Books, 2014), 232.

62 Brown, *Treason in the Blood*, 3; Macintyre, *A Spy Among Friends*.

63 Ibid.

64 Brown, *Treason in the Blood*, 101-102.

65 Ibid, 119-121.

66 Ibid, 148-157.

67 Kai Bird, *Crossing Mandelbaum Gate: Coming of Age Between The Arabs and Israelis, 1956-1978* (New York: Scribner, 2010).

68 Ibid, 122-127.

69 Ibid, 122-123.

70 Ibid, 72-73.

71 Lorraine Copeland, email to author, January 27, 2012.

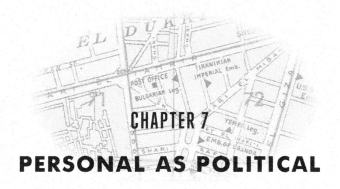

CHAPTER 7

PERSONAL AS POLITICAL

F or men like my father—the second generation navigating the sea of Middle East oil—the prevailing winds began to change in 1960. It had been little more than twenty years since the formation of Saudi Arabia's Arabian American Oil Company (ARAMCO), a creation that became the single largest US foreign investment. When the Arabs sought more from the pool of profits under their sand, Western oil companies were not appropriately attentive to this sea change. Until this point, the oil companies had the upper hand with their technical knowhow and expertise. It was understood that without foreign industry help, the Arab oil would still be in the ground and the desert rulers' poor. Eich and his cohorts were maneuvering the political winds as best they could to benefit those captaining the ship—the foreign oil companies—and themselves.

As I am considering my father's role in the Middle East oil industry, my attention shifts between my laptop and the view from our cabin deck. It is early spring 2012 and morning clouds are slowly lifting from the valley so the mountaintops look like islands floating in a sea. There is the faintest hint of green dressing the trees. The view is a constant distraction and wonder. When it is quiet and still with just a whisper of breeze, like it is now, having so much nature around me is a balm to my soul. Always her rhythms inform my life and work; I want, in whatever ways I can, to protect her. It's this view, the five ridge tops before me, that recharges my batteries to continue the fight against the vise grip that oil has on our lives. My soul feels at home here in the world that Annie Dillard laid at our feet in *Pilgrim at Tinker Creek*: "Our life is a faint tracing on the surface of mystery, like the idle curved tunnels of leaf miners on the face of a leaf. We must somehow take a wider view, look at the whole landscape, really see it, and describe what's going on here."[72] This is what I am doing now. With the grace of time, I am allowed to sit in this remote corner of southwest Virginia with the World Wide Web at my fingertips and what looks like heaven in my sight to consider my father's very different goals relative to oil.

I am trying Google's book searching feature for the first time. In scrolling pages of bolded references to James Eichelberger—many not the man I am hunting—I spot an intriguing book: *Queen of the Oil Club: The Intrepid Wanda Jablonski and The Power of Information* by Anna Rubino.[73] The title alone has allure. In my father's letter (the one I thought I had destroyed), he mentions a stint working for Jablonski. Eich wrote, "I had come back at your mother's request from London to accompany her, you, and Jay to Bedford, after I made the down payment on the house on Reno Road. At that time, I had been in New York where I started a newsletter called *Petroleum Intelligence Weekly* with Wanda Jablonski, who had been the editor of McGraw Hill's Petroleum Week."[74] Now, to my good fortune, I've discovered a biography devoted to this woman. I order a used copy of Rubino's book in anticipation of treasure.

Of the people in my father's world, Jablonski is one I am coming to admire. As the daughter of a Polish petroleum engineer, the "queen of the oil club" was a petite, fashionable woman who forged her way into a man's world. Jablonski understood the industry and had traveled widely when she was young, developing a deep sensitivity to other cultures. Her *savoir faire* helped hone her skills in the mid-1950s Middle East to establish a worldwide reputation. In a rapidly changing world, Jablonski was a change agent. The formation of the Organization of Petroleum Exporting Countries was a watershed event in the history of global oil, and she became known as OPEC's midwife. To discover a woman providing voice to the Arabs in an exclusively man's world is exciting. To have an inkling of the connection between her life and my father's is more so.

Jablonski was close with Saudi Arabia's first oil minister Abdullah Tariki. She appreciated Tariki's soft side—his fondness for animals and flowers—but also how he "combined bluntness with great personal charm." They liked socializing and talking business. At that time, the Saudis were struggling and angry with a 10 percent price cut the major oil companies had imposed on country producers due to a global glut of crude oil.[75] She introduced Tariki to Venezuela's oil minister, Perez Alfonzo, who was just as angry about the price cuts as well as the US's newly established import quotas. Robert Anderson, Eisenhower's Treasury Secretary, and soon to be one of Eich's ill-fated business partners, was behind these new limits.

At the time, the pace of oil discovery and development in the Middle East far outstripped that in the US. During this surge, global market share of US oil decreased from 64 percent to 22 percent.[76] Stateside oil companies were pushing for regulation to help them maintain market share and higher prices. The large multinational oil companies who benefited from foreign oil were happy, but the independent producers who helped birth the US industry were not. Enacted by the Eisenhower Administration in 1959, a new quota system limited how much oil each company could import into the US from less expensive foreign sources. The foreign quotas benefited both the international and domestic oil companies by limiting supply, forcing US prices up.

Foreign oil-producing countries like Saudi Arabia were

distressed by the sales cut. In retaliation against the new US policy, the Saudis kept producing, increasing the global supply. The oil glut continued into the next year as another 7 percent price cut was announced for Middle East crude.[77] OPEC was founded to counter the power of the international oil companies. Saudi Arabia, Venezuela, Iraq, Iran, and Kuwait announced its formation in September 1960. The following month at the second Arab Petroleum Congress in Beirut, Jablonski reported Tariki gave a "riveting" speech in which he provided a detailed plan to restrain output to drive up prices.

Curious if my father attended, I find the registration list for this seminal meeting at the bottom of a pile of photos in the storage container under our futon couch. The cover has a large red *2* for "Second" curled around "Arab Petroleum Congress" in bold font. Printed in the E section of the twenty-five-page directory is James Eichelberger, with "Copeland and Eichelberger Consultants" and "Resident" in the row with his name. Others who are not residents have their hotel listed in the right margin along with the company they represented.

October 1960 was nearing the end of our time together as a family. My brother Jay had been born the previous July. I was in first grade learning how to read and write in French while speaking Arabic with my neighborhood friend Renda. A favorite snapshot from this time is from Christmas of that year, our last together as a family of four. I'm sitting on our fireplace mantle in a velvet holiday dress flanked by my parents. Jay, in Mom's arms, is reaching for the tiny ornamental tree I am holding. In the same cache of memorabilia, I find my mom's American University of Beirut registration card for the fall 1960-61 semester. Nearby I find a letter dated February 21, 1961 from AUB thanking both my parents for their book donation to the Education Library. This is how I know when she was packing to leave the Middle East.

I learn from Rubino's book that in August 1961 Jablonski was setting up her own oil journal in New York City. After my parent's separation, Eich was one of the first employees she recruited to *Petroleum Intelligence Weekly (PIW)*—a publication that almost immediately became known as the bible of the international oil world. Anna Rubino recounts, "Her first good prospect was not a journalist but a former CIA operative—one of Kim Roosevelt's "cowboys" Jim Eichelberger. He would help her gather intelligence, and she and others would write it up."[78]

Eich did not last long working for her. Although he helped by searching for staff, leasing office space, and lining up a printer, my father was not a good fit and quit after just four weeks. I'm pleased to read in Rubino's book that his departure was not like that of other staff she mentions. Jablonski fired one man, who was hired about the same time as my father, because of his "drinking problem."[79]

In his letter to me, Eich mentions his short stint working for Jablonski as part of the diatribe against my mother. "Typically she had trouble understanding and thought I had my priorities mixed up," he wrote.[80] I imagine there were many times in the Middle East when he was called away from family life to conduct his secret work, activities that likely rattled my mother either consciously or unconsciously. Typical of that time, men worked out in the world and women in large part tended to housekeeping and child rearing. My mother would not have had much room to question or complain about what went on outside the home.

In Eich's letter, he is referring specifically to the forty-eight hours in which he and Jablonski were frantic to get the first issue of *Petroleum Intelligence Weekly* to the printers. Mom had asked him to accompany our poodle, Go-Go, from New York to DC after the dog's transcontinental flight from Beirut. Eich describes the chore as bringing Go-Go to us by air and "having him clipped and laundered before doing so."[81] It bothers me that my father is referring to our dog as an inanimate object but then realize this is what I should expect from a man coldhearted enough to announce the end of his marriage to his wife via a letter from Europe.

I do not remember him leaving us in Beirut. I do not remember the months my mother waited for his return. I do not remember visiting my grandparents in Ohio during the summer of 1961 while my mother looked for a house in Washington, DC. My first real memory of my father is from an evening late that summer in our new home. I could hear the cicadas in our backyard from my bedroom. I was lying in bed in my new room playing my favorite pillow game. I would pretend my pillow was an airplane and balance the fluffy rectangle with my extended feet while lying on my back—flying my pillow until it fell from the sky onto my single bed.

"Darling," my mother called to my bedroom. "Can you come downstairs for a moment?"

As I descended the stairs in my nightie, my bare feet brushed the soft carpet before I settled on the down pillow of one of our wingback chairs. I looked up, and there was my father. It was the first time I had seen him since he left us a year earlier. Now I was about to start second grade in a new school in a new city. Yet something in the room kept me from running toward him for a hug. I kept my mouth buttoned and arms sidelined.

After mustering a hello, I focused on the furniture. My parents sat opposite each other on our gold-patterned love seats, smoke from their cigarettes circling like halos. The rectangular living room was not large, but my parents seemed distant from each other. It felt odd to see them together. The brass screen stood guard in front of our fireplace; its peacock-like feathers fanned out in plumed symmetry as it had at our home in Beirut the last time we were together. The mummy head my mother had bought in Cairo stared at me from its glass case above our new stereo speaker. The Egyptian princess died a young girl, Mom had told me. My eyes preferred seeing these familiar objects and the bright green of the slipcovers my mother had chosen for my favorite perch rather than looking in my father's blue eyes and revealing my confusion.

Gray-haired Go-Go was sitting next to my mom on the love seat when she posed the question.

"Who would you rather live with, your father or me?" she asked between puffs of her Salem.

I froze. She was not crying, but the sadness in her face made me feel like someone had died. My father was quiet.

"I dunno," I mumbled, looking down at the ruffled lace on my nightie, then my tanned feet, before she excused me to go back to bed.

How was I to know which one I would rather live with? I most certainly would have wanted our life back to how it was in Beirut. Daddy would come and go, but Mommy was always there if I needed her. This was the natural order of things, the comfort of childhood, the rhythm of having two parents in my life.

My mother and I never spoke of this instance again, but her question has haunted me ever since. What if I had said yes, I want to live with my dad? Was this even a real possibility? Could they have taken turns with me? Or was putting such a terrible question to her firstborn my mother's way of bridging her sadness with the challenges she faced as a single parent?

Eich had broken her heart, crushed it with his leaving—I knew this by osmosis. As a woman artist who suddenly faced becoming the family breadwinner, my mother was haunted by her own demons. She may have felt the pain was hers to bear alone, not something to share with her children. Consequently, she rarely spoke about him. Given her lead, I chose to follow suit. Until, that is, this search for my father decades after my parents' deaths.

Freshly separated from his wife, could part of the reason Eich left *Petroleum Intelligence Weekly* be that he saw too much of my mother's demanding nature in his new boss? Perhaps. Both Wanda Jablonski and my mother set exacting standards and were challenging taskmasters. But there is more to why he left *PIW* and why he left his family than what he admitted to me.

In his letter, my father confided his need to leave my mother to save himself. When Eich wrote to her from Europe saying he was not coming back, he had seen a psychiatrist who determined the immediate source of his problems were his "wife troubles." He also admitted that there were "other, deeper things going back to childhood."

Why he left *PIW* is easier for me to figure out. It was to make money, hopefully lots of money. A dear friend of my mother, Elaine Atkins, said as much in response to a letter I had written inquiring about Eich. "As for why your dad dropped out of the CIA, it was quite simply money—I think he was rather unsophisticated in the ways of 'big money' and imagined it was easier to come by than it proved to be. He was certainly lured away by Miles Copeland."[82] I know that Elaine does not mean that he left the CIA completely, only that he had dropped his government cover job with the Embassy (like he had in Cairo) and perhaps went to CIA contract work when he and Miles started their consulting business.

Eich's letter says that INTERSER—the New York-based consulting group he and Copeland started about the same time Jablonski was launching *PIW*—had "mercifully" sent him to Kuwait where they "almost made a few million bucks."[83] The "mercifully" part directly follows his account of taking our dog, Go-Go, from New York to DC. It's clear he was grateful to get away from my mother. I struggle to not take this part personally, to not let his abandonment anger me, to focus instead on the events of his life at the time. Emotionally, it's far easier for me to try to investigate his life and the political events shaping it, than to gaze into the abyss of his absence.

However, now that I recognize the pain from my father's disappearance and the wider political world I have chosen for my profession, I see the relevance of casting the personal as political, of considering how our private lives can reflect a wider political whole. Although it is unclear where the "personal as political" phrase originated, it appears in C. Wright Mills's 1959 book *The Sociological Imagination*[84]—which discusses the intersection of public issues and personal problems. The phrase was popularized by the women's movement in the 1960s and '70s when political barriers restricted the personal choices for women.

With the increasing urgency of climate change, the personal as political takes on new meaning. The public issue is the political denial of fossil fuel endangerment to the air we breathe, the water we drink, and the earth we tread upon. The personal problem, it can be argued, is the denial that our fossil-fuel-driven lifestyle, and the pursuit of wealth and political upheaval that underlies it, has not brought happiness. Comfort, yes, and immense wealth for some, yes, but happiness in the form of contentment, no.

As a culture we seem to be steamrolling over consideration for the planet in favor of consumption. It's showing in our personal lives. Antidepressant use is on the rise, along with the convenient use of petroleum-based, single-use plastic products. We are distracted by our electronic devices and harried by busy lifestyles, continually reminded that we need to push harder and do more, or risk being left behind the parade of what passes as success. Like many, I struggle with how to maintain a work-life balance. There is always something I need to do or accomplish that gets in the way of my contentment. This imbalance has become more acute over the past two decades of my career, and I now see it is directly tied to my childhood and a broader political story.

The personal pain inflicted by my father's absence parallels a wider political abandonment of the interest in our planet's well-being. Moreover, my reluctance to look at the pain my father caused in my life and the effect it had on my ability to trust, my ability to value my self-worth, is reflected in a broader reluctance to reconcile the ramifications of the injustices to the earth and those less fortunate who struggle to eke out a living from it. An innate desire for control of our lives, and by extension our environment through overzealous resource exploitation and wealth accumulation, has created economic inequities and countless other injustices. With all this in mind, I see my father's abandonment of his family and interest in capitalizing on his political connections as a perfect example of the personal as political run amok.

---

72 Annie Dillard, *Pilgrim at Tinker Creek,* (New York: Harper & Row, 1985), 11.

73 Anna Rubino, *Queen of the Oil Club the Intrepid Wanda Jablonski and the Power of Information* (Boston: Beacon Press, 2008), 137.

74 James M Eichelberger, letter to author, December 14, 1982.

75 Daniel Yergin, *The Prize: The Epic Quest for Oil, Money & Power* (New York: Free Press, 2009), 482.

76 Ibid, 481-482.

77 Rubino, *Queen of the Oil Club,* 194.

78 Ibid, 222.

79 Ibid, 227.

80 James M Eichelberger, letter to the author, December 14, 1982.

81 Ibid.

82 Elaine Atkins, letter to author.

83 James M Eichelberger, letter to author, December 14, 1982.

84 C. Wright Mills, *The Sociological Imagination* (Oxford: Oxford University Press, 1959).

CHAPTER 8

SHIFTING SANDS

NTERSER, the New York-based consulting group my father was involved in, had all the necessary ingredients for success, including posh offices at 1 Rockefeller Plaza. In the heart of Midtown Manhattan—the largest central business district in the world—I imagine the address as a gold-plated calling card. The location alone should help anyone get rich quick. But the men involved with INTERSER were not just anyone. In addition to Miles Copeland, the group was composed of "James Eichelberger, a former CIA operative in Cairo, superspy Kim Roosevelt, Robert Anderson, former Eisenhower Secretary of the Treasury and CIA troubleshooter, and one businessman, Jack McCrane."[85] INTERSER, Aburish explains in one of his books, "specialized in helping large American corporations with their Middle East business" and was a "CIA front organization, though the business-man in the group may not have known this."[86]

Lorraine Copeland also mentioned INTERSER in one of our email exchanges, but she conflated the New York venture with the Beirut-based Copeland and Eichelberger consulting group, a perfectly understandable mash-up for someone ninety-one. I know from my own experience how the passage of time affects memory, like a desert sandstorm that leaves only one or two key reference points to recollect your way. According to Lorraine, INTERSER fell apart when my father unexpectedly left my mother. With Eich suddenly out of the picture, she remembers the oasis of their Beirut consulting business drying up and Miles reduced to selling encyclopedias for a time.

Eich and Copeland needed money. Aburish further corroborates this point, indicating Miles was trying to borrow money from friends in New York City for his daughter's school tuition at the time INTERSER was getting started. Like Icarus flying toward the sun, out of the ashes of Eich's marriage and the dissolution of the Eichelberger and Copeland consulting group in Beirut, they were going for the gold from New York, pinning their hope on an oil deal in Kuwait. They needed Eich to go to the Arab state to explain the deal.[87] What exactly the deal was, I don't know, but it hinged on the star of the INTERSER team, Robert Anderson.

The man who served as US Treasury Secretary from 1957 until January 1961 was also Eisenhower's personal choice to succeed him as President. According to Anderson's personal papers, instead of running for president, he decided to "become an international investment specialist."[88] Distrustful eyes like mine translate this to mean that Anderson declined Eisenhower's request in favor of a more immediate path to greater wealth. He wanted to cash in on his political connections. For the trouble, public service simply did not pay enough to suit his tastes—thus aligning Anderson's priorities right along with those of Copeland and Eich, and the INTERSER group.

The first time my father and Anderson likely crossed paths was in 1956 in Cairo when I was two years old. President Eisenhower sent Anderson to Egypt to convince President Nasser to make peace with Israel; an effort that did not pan out. His second trip to the Middle East did not meet with any more success. Eisenhower sent Anderson to Saudi Arabia upon Exxon's suggestion.[89] His mission was to convince King Saud to get Nasser to back down from nationalizing Suez Canal operations. If Saud did not cooperate, Anderson explained, the US had better options than buying their petroleum. Nuclear energy was a new alternative to oil, obviating the need for Saudi petroleum and the Suez Canal to get it to Western markets. The mission failed. King Saud already knew that nuclear energy was not a realistic alternative to oil. I chuckle reading this story. At work we are continually promoting the perfect alternatives—biofuels, natural gas, propane, electricity—but oil is still king. Fifty-two years later, petroleum still provides 93 percent of the fuel to power our transportation needs.[90]

As Treasury Secretary, Anderson had made an impressive set of connections which now aided the new consulting group. He was also intimate with the oil industry. After law school, Anderson started his career in the Texas legislature, then presided over the Texas Mid-Continent Oil and Gas Association, the state's primary oil lobbying group.[91] Anderson's entree onto the national stage came by way of a chance meeting on a train with Dwight Eisenhower, then a young army officer. A friendship was born over a bridge game from Texas to DC.

I love the serendipity of coincidental meetings that set the course of history, both personal and political. The first rhyme I recall writing and the only one I have locked in my mind pays homage to the subject: "Every meeting has a reason. Every voice can sing a verse. If we could only hear the song, heaven could be on earth." I tapped into this stream of cosmic consciousness at the all-girls Catholic boarding school I attended in ninth grade. Everything does happen for a reason. It's for us to find the still, quiet voice within to mine the nugget of its beauty.

I don't know that Anderson or Eisenhower ever reflected on any deeper reason for their meeting. It appears that the friendship wrought from the chance meeting brought oil money to Eisenhower's presidential campaign and led to Anderson's first appointments to federal posts as the Secretary of the Navy and Secretary of Defense. Such a career path makes sense for an oil man. The US military is the largest single user of oil in the world, and the defense industry has profited mightily from our oil dependence. Later as Treasury Secretary, Anderson led the team that devised an import quota system that unintentionally led to the formation of OPEC and the subsequent rise in clout for the Arab oil producers.

In 1961 there was no better person to facilitate US import opportunities with the Kuwaiti government than Eisenhower's former Treasury Secretary. He would have known all the work-arounds in the import quota system he devised. In the plan for the Kuwaiti oil deal, INTERSER was to represent Anderson with Eich as his emissary. It was an apt pairing since Eich had written the history of the Kuwaiti oil industry for Gulf Oil—with whom Copeland and Eichelberger had a contract—when we lived in Beirut.[92]

Oil had transformed Kuwait since its discovery in the 1930s. At that time, Kuwait City had a population of seventy thousand living in mud-walled houses clustered around the port. Before oil, trade, pearl diving, and ship building drove the economy. Archeologists found the world's oldest reed boat north of the city. Held together by bitumen, the seven-thousand-year-old vestige from the cradle of civilization evidences the importance of oil, even in ancient history.[93]

I am staring at my own sea-going relic, one I inherited from my mother. An antique Kuwait chest sits landlocked on our floor across from the desktop computer where I am sitting in our family room. Seafarers decorated the heavy wood trunk with brass nails and cut metal sheets that can shine like the sun when polished. The chest came to my mother in Beirut as a surprise gift. Did the massive treasure arrive before my father left us in Beirut or after? Was the trunk a thank you gift for the history of Kuwaiti oil my father had written? All I know about this family heirloom is what my mother told me, that an Arab friend shipped it to her as airline baggage.

Kuwait Air had begun flights out of the capital just a few years earlier and the friend knew my mother admired fine craftsmanship from this part of the world. Previously, the trunk—which Richard and I can barely lift an inch off our floor—would have traveled from Kuwait to Beirut eight hundred miles overland through Iraq and Syria. Or it could have come by boat—south through the Persian Gulf into the Arabian Sea, then north into the Red Sea, and through the Suez Canal to the Mediterranean. That a friend had the unexpected gift flown from Kuwait to Beirut gives testimony to Arab generosity and to how quickly the cradle of civilization changed after the birth of the oil industry.

In 1961 when my father went to Kuwait on assignment for INTERSER it had a population of little over three hundred thousand, quadruple what it was when oil was discovered less than twenty-five years earlier.[94] Dwarfed by its three neighbors—Iran, Iraq, and Saudi Arabia—Kuwait is about the size of New Jersey. Yet in the early 1960s this small country was the world's largest oil exporter, resulting in the world's highest per capita income. Wealth multiplied exponentially along with rapid change. A year earlier, Kuwait had joined OPEC as a founding member to help coordinate petroleum policies. Their aim was to counter the power of multinational oil companies and the noose US oil import quotas had put around their necks. The government and Kuwaiti business interests also organized the Kuwait National Petroleum Company (KNPC) and wrested some power away from international companies British Petroleum (BP) and Gulf Oil, who had each had a half share of Kuwait's oil.[95]

Here at home as a promoter for cleaner burning alternative fuels, I am extremely sensitive to the might of the multinational oil companies. In North Carolina we only have a few dozen stations selling a 20 percent blend of biodiesel with petroleum. Far fewer stations are selling E85, a biofuel blend of 85 percent ethanol with gasoline that could be used by millions of flex fuel vehicle drivers, most of whom don't realize they could be using this alternative fuel. There are far fewer natural gas, propane, and electric vehicle charging stations. With a gasoline station on almost every corner and lawmakers in their pockets, Big Oil is still having its way.

This is not to say that the alternative fuel industry hasn't received any concessions from lawmakers. Despite the number of oil lobbyists and the obscene amount of money they spend on Capitol Hill, there are now federal tax credits for alternative fuels and vehicles as well as usage requirements for biofuels. I play a small role in this system and appreciate the opportunity to go to DC every year to educate lawmakers and their aides about what proposed bills will provide the best opportunities for the alternative fuels industry to get ahead. It's not unlike what the independent producers did by pushing the Eisenhower Administration to develop import quotas for the multinationals when Anderson was Treasury Secretary.

In the early 1960s the Neutral Zone between Saudi Arabia and Kuwait, a kind of no man's land that neither country controlled in 1932, was thrust into play. To expand oil opportunities, Kuwait's Neutral Zone concession went to a company of independent oil producers Aminoil, short for American Independent Oil.[96] Perhaps Anderson, and INTERSER by extension, represented Aminoil. The rapidly changing field presented plenty of prospects for profit. My father, Robert Anderson, and the other principles at INTERSER intended to be part of this get-rich group.

It did not happen, at least not for my father. The Kuwaiti Emir Abdullah Hussain presented Eich a $100,000 check for INTERSER's efforts and asked him to deliver it to Robert Anderson, the payee on the check. As Eich stated in what I call *the* letter, he never saw a "red cent of the money after that."[97] From what I can tell, the failed Kuwaiti deal spelled the end of INTERSER.

The global game of resource control is making a few rich at the cost of everyone else. It is an enticing game, fraught with unintended consequences and what economists call "externalities," effects of an action that are not counted in the financial equation. The high stakes have been the downfall of many and are arguably leading to our planet's destruction. For me, it's a cautionary tale.

Eich told me he had to leave my mother "or be destroyed in front of your very eyes—since I had not the money for psychoanalysis." He admitted, "money is miserably at the bottom of so much else." My father explained he did not have the bus fare from Laurel, Maryland to Washington to come visit my brother and me—to take us to the movies or visit the zoo. It did not work out so well for Robert Anderson either. I read in his *New York Times* obituary, "his career became clouded in later years by a brief prison term for income tax evasion and operating an illegal offshore bank." Anderson died in August 1989, a month before my father, and had "been hospitalized for alcoholism ten times since 1981."[98] From what I recollect being told decades ago, Eich had been in the VA hospital for alcoholism treatment three times, although he never mentioned this in his letters to me.

My calculating mind is always trying to make connections. I wonder now if the pursuit of wealth and drinking can be two sides of the same coin. Power usually comes from money. Pleasure comes from drinking. Both are intoxicating, addicting, and in excess can wreak havoc. With alcoholism, there is a worldwide refuge in Alcoholics Anonymous for those recognizing a problem in themselves and wanting to overcome it. There is no such support group for recovering "wealthaholics." We barely acknowledge the problems of extreme wealth, nor recognize the environmental and social exploitation that comes at the cost of its pursuit.

Individuals, businesses, and nations have little recourse in considering the "externalities" of their excess, such as air pollution. In the case of Middle East oil, the list of industry externalities is long, beginning with manipulation of nascent nations by people like my father, as evidenced by the CIA's early grooming of Saddam Hussein to carry out an assassination attempt on Iraqi leadership in 1959. For men like my father and Anderson the misguided mission for money by means of oil-tainted foreign policy led to no good. This combined with alcoholism was ruinous. It was a calamity made especially acute when the excessive alcohol and wealth-seeking was powered by deceit and double-crossing.

Nonetheless, something is spurring me on. There must be more to the story than just treachery. There must be more than the scorn I feel for my father and his ilk—for their get-rich-quick ambitions and embrace of the underworld. There must be other people to help me make my way out of this dark passage.

85 Said K. Aburish, *A Brutal Friendship: The West and The Arab Elite*, (St. Martins Press, 1998), 327.

86 Ibid.

87 James M Eichelberger, letter to author, December 14, 1982.

88 "Robert B. Anderson: Papers 1933-89," Dwight D. Eisenhower Library Abilene, Kansas, July 2004, 2.

89 Wilbur Crane Eveland, *Ropes of Sand, America's Failure in the Middle East* (New York: W.W. Norton & Company, 1980), 209-213.

90 "Annual Energy Review 2011," US Energy Information Agency, September 2012, 57, https://www.eia.gov/totalenergy/data/annual/pdf/aer.pdf.

91 Robert Sherrill, *The Accidental President* (New York: Grossman Publishers, March 1968), 122.

92 Miles Copeland, *The Game Player*, 209.

93 Richard Weeks, "Secrets of world's oldest boat are discovered in Kuwait sands," *The Telegraph*, April 2001, accessed January 19, 2015, http://www.telegraph.co.uk/news/worldnews/middleeast/kuwait/1314980Secrets-of-worlds-oldest-boat-are-discovered-in-Kuwait-sands.html.

94 "Population of Kuwait," Muzaffar.com, http://muzaffar.com/Kuwait/population.htm; "Kuwait Population," PopulationOf.net, accessed April 6, 2021, http://www.populationof.net/kuwait/.

95 Rubino, *Queen of the Oil Club*, 214.

96 Yergin, The Prize 419-20; Office of the Historian FOREIGN RELATIONS OF THE UNITED STATES, 1950, THE NEAR EAST, SOUTH ASIA, AND AFRICA, VOLUME V March 1950, accessed June 26, 2021, https://history.state.gov/historicaldocuments/frus1950v05/d13.

97 James M Eichelberger, letter to author.

98 Eric Pace, "ROBERT B. ANDERSON, EX-TREASURY CHIEF, DIES AT 79." *The New York*, August 16, 1989, accessed October 27, 2018, http://www.nytimes.comn/1989/08/16/obituaries/robert-b-anderson-ex-treasury-chief-dies-at-79.html.

CHAPTER 9

EGYPT: THE UNSETTLED TIME
OF MY BEGINNING

There is little hope for new understanding of my father's fallacious actions through Said Aburish. He died early this morning—August 29, 2012—in Bethany, Jordan. I am reading the email announcement from his nephew at my work desk in Raleigh. My office is in a one-story standalone brick building at the gateway to the University's new thousand-acre Centennial Campus. Two windows offer a view of the crepe myrtle crowns alongside our module. Before looking back at the email, I notice their magenta tops, the fleeting late summer blooms a fitting juxtaposition to the finality of this news.

With the seven-hour time difference, family and friends must be gathering now for what his nephew describes as the "last pray" at Al Ozair mosque. Then they will bury the Palestinian author at the cemetery in Bethany—Said Aburish's home village where Jesus raised Lazarus from the dead. In *Bethany's Children: A Palestinian Family*,[99] Aburish describes how his grandfather had bought the land with the cave said to be Lazarus's tomb. He became rich by charging admission to the growing number of seekers who traveled the road from Jericho to Jerusalem.

"May Allah bless his soul." The nephew's note ends as my silent wishes pass through layers of regret. Why didn't I drop everything and fly to Bethany to visit the old man when he first extended the invitation two years ago? The reasons have not changed: I was afraid; I hate flying. I thought we could cultivate a long-distance relationship. Another reason though, is that I let my job consume much of my life. At the time of his invitation I could not imagine stepping away from my work.

Now in 2012 we are negotiating a new agreement with the North Carolina Department of Transportation (DOT) for a $6.2M grant to reduce emissions from cars, trucks, even train locomotives. We just wrapped up a $2.6M award from DOT, so this is another big step for my team. The money to improve air quality, most of which we will continue to distribute to local governments and businesses for the use of alternative fuels, puffs up my pride. Our projects are priming the pump to reduce oil dominance across the state's urban crescent from Charlotte to Raleigh. I also see my work in context of what my father was doing in the Middle East and what Said Aburish exposes in the books he wrote. I find that having people pay attention to you because you control the spending of money or have something to say is intoxicating.

To my surprise, I find Aburish's obituary from the *New York Times* reprinted in our local paper. Reading the Sunday newspaper has become a ritual for Richard and me now that the kids are out on their own. We are sitting on our living room couch savoring our favorite morning beverages—mine English tea, his Cuban espresso. I like the feel of the paper in my hands, the crinkling as I turn the pages a tangible link to the wider world, even though so much of the news is disturbing. On page 6B, next to an article titled, "Sept. 11 volunteer day draws big response," my eyes land on *Journalist Aburish afflicted Arab rulers*.

I read aloud from the obit, "Mr. Aburish's writing was notably blunt. He accused Arab leaders of being stooges of Western powers and indifferent to the well-being of their citizens."

"Yeah," agrees my husband, "They want our weapons and we want their oil in a devil's bargain that screws the poor people." Richard can be blunt too.

"I don't think Aburish was including Nasser in this summation of Arab leaders," I respond. Since Aburish's death I have begun rereading his 2004 book, *Nasser The Last Arab*,[100] written twenty-four years after the Egyptian ruler died unexpectedly of a heart attack. Aburish recounts hearing the news while driving a rental car half a world away in California. The author was sobbing uncontrollably when a state trooper stopped to inquire why he had haphazardly pulled the car to the side of the road.

"Officer, there has been a death in my family. I've just heard it on the radio."[101] Aburish was speaking metaphorically. The author, who had seen his family scattered around the globe in the Arab diaspora, had his own blood invested in Nasser's vision for Arab nationalism. The Palestine-born US citizen, a man of the world, was not alone with his devastation.

"Did you know," I ask Richard, "over five million people, some say up to seven million, crowded Cairo for Nasser's funeral in 1980?"

The first two years of my life, 1954-56, spent in Egypt, were critical times for Gamal Abdel Nasser to consolidate his control as a voice of the people. Under these circumstances, my father was ostensibly an advisor to the new president. His cover for the CIA was to serve as a State Department Economic Attaché.[102] In 1952, Nasser and a band of young Egyptian military men over-threw King Farouk in a bloodless coup. The leave-taking of the British-installed ruler, a playboy king on his yacht with 204 pieces of luggage, is an apt image for the end of colonial control in Egypt. Since 1882 the Brits had run the Nile kingdom, and before them, the Ottoman Turks. As a Gandhi follower, Nasser knew it was important that the takeover be nonviolent. As a committed pacifist myself, this point is key to my esteem for the Egyptian leader.

It was a time of hope. In July 1954, after seventy-two years as an occupier, Great Britain made an agreement with Egypt to evacuate the Suez Canal zone. They agreed to exit within twenty months. Concurrently, the US was working on an intelligence-information sharing agreement with Egypt as well as an Israeli and Arab agreement to share the Jordan River. Countering these hopeful signs, Israel had moved its government offices to Jerusalem, at the time a disputed territory. The same month, there was a series of bombings at movie theaters and libraries frequented by Americans in both Cairo and the seaside city of Alexandria.

I can only imagine my mother's concern. If unknown enemies were randomly bombing places I frequented, I would not have taken it very well, especially while pregnant. However, my mother never mentioned this terror as part of her experience with me in utero and later I did not know enough to ask her. To an outsider, Egypt was looking downright hostile to Western interests. According to Aburish, this is exactly what the perpetrators wanted.

What became known as the Lavon Affair uncovered an Israeli spy ring using Jewish Egyptians to conduct the terrorist activities, rather than anti-Western Arabs as most people presumed. With the secret plot uncovered, Nasser reacted quickly, hanging two of the Israeli spies and imprisoning the others. This betrayal by Israel sowed the seeds of mistrust between the two countries more deeply, and Nasser's interest in obtaining weapons and building Egypt's military strengthened.[103]

My life began in this unsettled world. I do not know exactly when my parents moved to Egypt, but after seven years of marriage, the fertile Nile delta was to be my birthplace. My mother would reminisce how on August 26, 1954 I was one of only two babies born at the Anglo-American hospital. "The nice British Dr. King helped you into the world," she would say. Even in the mid-1950s the hospital was a throwback to another era. The hands of Egyptian labor built the Anglo with arched doorways and fireplaces at the turn of the twentieth century to serve British and American nationals.[104]

After the customary post-birth week in the hospital it took just a few minutes to drive to 19 El Gabalaya Street, my first home. My parents' fifth floor apartment overlooked the narrow part of the river separating Zamalek—the island where we lived—from Dokki, the Giza pyramid side of Cairo. The two-by-four-kilometer island in the middle of Egypt's capital, with its tree-lined streets, was a fashionable place to reside. It had once been part of the estate of Khedive Ismail, the Ottoman Empire-appointed governor during the 1860s and 70s. Ismail the Magnificent, as he was also known, oversaw the construction of the Egyptian portion of the Suez Canal.

Lorraine remembers dinners at my parents' apartment in Zamalek and picnics along the Nile in the traditional wooden boats common to the waterway. "At night a group of us and other friends would hire a Felucca and install ourselves with picnic food—and, of course, cooled martini glasses and other necessities—and sail up the river for a few hours of tranquility. Besides the early Step Pyramid at Saqqara we had a 'secret' spot, a destroyed pyramid where we could often find artifacts in the sand." Memory is a dreamy friend of romance—a link to the past that has become more precious as I age. Charmed by her recollection, I remember myself at the same stage of life.

We, too, lived on a small island. Richard and I enjoyed suppers with friends along the turquoise necklace of the Florida Keys and sailing with Jamila in our Sunfish off the old Sands Beach in Key West. Like the Copelands and my parents, we did not have family nearby. As our children were born, our friends became family.

This is where the similarities end. I know these were not

peaceful times for my parents, especially for my father. Just two months after I was born, Nasser survived an attempt on his life. As he was giving a speech in Alexandria celebrating the Suez Canal evacuation agreement with Britain, a member of the Muslim Brotherhood fired at close range. A bulletproof vest loaned by the CIA saved him.[105]

I wonder if my father had anything to do with making the arrangements for the vest. Would the Embassy assign this type of technical detail to someone else, rather than the Economic Attaché? This type of question keeps popping up as I read about this period of Egyptian history. What did my father do day-to-day in his dual roles with the State Department and the CIA? Aburish references my father once in his 311-page biography: "He [Nasser] was tolerant of human weakness and never spoke of the shortcomings of others. There were patterns to his behavior, for example having American friends (Roosevelt, Lakeland, and James Eichelberger of the CIA among others) with whom he thought he could discourse."[106] I have discovered my father and Nasser had several things in common. Both were voracious readers, loved to play chess, smoked incessantly, and had lost a parent at an early age—Nasser his mother and Eich his father. Moreover, both men had reasons to like each other. The US was trying to establish a foothold of influence in the region and Nasser was looking for friends to secure his base. Nasser was drawn to the democratic vision and free spirit of the Americans much more than to the Russians, who were also courting him, as the Middle East emerged from the post-World War II era in an advantaged position.

Both the US and Britain recognized the strategic and economic importance of Arab oil. With no wells at home, Middle East oil was Europe's life blood while US interests were more economic. US oil companies were profiting from Middle East oil because it was less expensive to produce than the crude back home. In 1953, US companies extracted 70 percent of Middle East oil, and much of that oil was shipped through the Suez Canal to reach European markets. In Miles Copeland's book, *The Game of Nations,* he recounts just how that game was played. A key strategy in playing, Miles explains, is spreading money around in exchange for influence. Not that different from what I am trying to do by providing grants to vehicle fleet managers to use alternative fuels.

In November 1954, less than a month after the assassination attempt just two months after I was born, the US announced $40M in aid to Egypt. In addition, Egypt was "allowed to purchase $20M worth of military equipment at reasonable prices and easy credit terms." Copeland explains the aid and favorable terms for the military purchases go hand in hand because the aid money frees the state budget to buy American weapons.[107] The US hoped the deal would convince Nasser to sign on to the Baghdad Pact—a US-led defense alliance with Turkey, Pakistan, and Iraq to contain the Soviets. This same agreement resulted in fourteen thousand Marines landing on Beirut beaches in 1958 when we were living in Lebanon. According to Copeland, he and my father were responsible for explaining the pact to Nasser, who was none too happy. The agreement stood in the Egyptian leader's way of creating a unified block of Arab nations—one not controlled by either the US or Russia.

In addition to the $40M announced in economic aid, Miles Copeland hand-delivered $3M in cash from President Eisenhower's discretionary fund. I imagine my father readying the transfer with Copeland. The afternoon sun beat down on the two men as they stepped into the cooler air of the Cairo safe house. The living room, furnished with an Art Deco bar in the corner, has a couple of couches and a coffee table. A ceiling fan is whirring overhead. The two friends are relishing a drink of scotch on the rocks as they move bundles of bills from a diplomatic pouch into a couple of leather suitcases to give to the Egyptian leader, or more likely one of his aides. The gift reportedly offended Nasser—it looked like a bribe—but he accepted the cash nevertheless to build the Cairo Tower.[108]

The Cairo Tower is the tallest structure in Egypt and a monument to the times. Nasser began construction in 1954 and completed it six years later. The 614-foot phallus rises from the banks of the Nile close to the Gezira Sporting Club. With a commanding view and revolving restaurant at the top, the Tower is now the second most-visited Cairo tourist attraction after the pyramids. The granite-latticed structure also transmitted the Voice of the Arabs, Nasser's radio mouthpiece to the people. After continual US funding delays for the larger aid package, extending into months after Copeland made the delivery, DC back channels heard Nasser referring to the cash gift and resulting communications tower as "Roosevelt's erection." The Roosevelt to which he referred is Kermit "Kim" Roosevelt, Theodore's grandson, Eich's boss, head of the CIA's Near East division. No doubt frustrations were mounting with the "Game."

Nasser aimed to be a strong voice for non-aligned nations, what he called positive neutralism. He did not want to be a pawn of either Russia or the US. Increasingly, he also wanted to prevent other Arab countries from seeing Egypt as too friendly with the US. When my babyhood had just passed the six-month mark, the Israelis raided an Army post in Gaza to avenge Egypt's execution of the Israeli spies, killing fifty-seven. Nasser did not retaliate, although the small strip of land along the Mediterranean Sea was part of Egypt and the UN Security Council condemned the attack. Even so, there were signs Nasser would not sit idly by after such aggression. Three months after the Gaza killings, Nasser met with the US Ambassador to Egypt, Henry Byroade, to let him know Egypt was considering purchasing weapons from Russia.

According to Miles Copeland, Ambassador Byroade was a tremendously likeable guy, the type of person who never met someone he did not like. Nasser had made it clear all along— through the Embassy and CIA—he would have preferred doing business with the Americans. Nonetheless, the Ambassador was not able to speed up the promised Washington aid to Nasser's satisfaction. Consequently, prospects deteriorated for the Ambassador in Cairo.

One month after my first birthday, in September 1955, Nasser announced Egypt's agreement to purchase weapons from the Russians. My father was one of the first to hear the news before the public announcement. An Egyptian informer paid by the CIA told him it was a done deal. After the tip, at three in the morning, Eich called Egyptian journalist and Nasser confidant Mohamed Heikal. Agitated, my father begged Heikal not to let Nasser fall into a communist trap. Tell him to "keep his pants on," Heikal quotes Eich as saying.[109] Later the journalist and author writes, "Egypt has been the graveyard of so many diplomats' careers." Heikal was referring to Henry Byroade, not my father. The cascading events took their toll on the American ambassador, with some fallout I presume for my father as well.

With news of the arms deal heating up in DC, US Secretary of State Foster Dulles sent Kim Roosevelt and Miles Copeland to Cairo. Copeland had just returned to the US after the end of his Egyptian assignment with Booz, Allen, and Hamilton— presumably, a CIA cover. Dulles wanted his Middle East experts to dissuade Nasser from the weapons deal with the Soviet Union. Roosevelt and Copeland met with my father before they met with Nasser, but the premier was immovable.

That evening the Egyptian ambassador to the US, Ahmed Hussein, was hosting a dinner party and had invited my father, Nasser, and many others. He had recently returned to Cairo for vacation. Upon hearing about the Czech arms deal (so called because the Soviet weapons would go through Czechoslovakia), he too tried to dissuade Nasser. Hussein reminded the Egyptian premier about the CIA's recent hand in overthrowing the left-leaning government in Guatemala. "To hell with Guatemala," Nasser said.[110] He needed the weapons for self-defense and was tired of waiting on the US aid package. The wrath of the Dulles brothers—Secretary of State Foster and his brother Allen who headed the CIA—would not change his mind.

I imagine my father going to the Egyptian Ambassador's dinner directly from the Embassy. Given the harried day, he would not have had time to change his suit. He meets my mother at the ambassador's home. My mother is wearing the Damask silk dress she had recently designed and had sewn by her favorite tailor in Zamalek. It is the perfect late summer dress—sleeveless and knee length, cinched at her twenty-four-inch waist with a full skirt and petticoat. Her brown bobbed hair and light complexion complement the rich teal green, blue, and purple plaid of the silk. After an initial drink together, my mother takes leave of her husband to speak with the other Embassy wives.

My father shares a bottle of brandy with Hussein. Although he is exhausted from the previous late-night efforts to dissuade Nasser about the arms deal through his confidant Heikel, Eich starts to relax. As soon as Roosevelt and Copeland walk into the party with Nasser's deputy, Zakaria Mohieddin, he remembers. My father's pulse quickens with the realization of his political faux pas. Damn it! He forgot to tell Ambassador Byroade that Dulles dispatched his colleagues to Cairo—that they had met with Nasser to try to dissuade him from the Russian arms deal. How could he have forgotten to inform the US Ambassador about the Washington visitors? With Roosevelt and Copeland's unexpected appearance one hour into the party, Eich knows his oversight will further aggravate the Ambassador's state of mind, given what Byroade had heard earlier that day.

Byroade had learned one of Nasser's men nearly beat to death a US labor attaché in Suez. The Ambassador is drinking scotch to settle his nerves. It is not clear who arrived first but Nasser, who did not drink, had just taken the first sip of his orange juice when Byroade launched into a tirade about the "Egyptian police state" and how the Egyptian government was "behaving like a bunch of juvenile delinquents."[111] The room goes silent. Byroade demands to know why the Egyptian police beat his labor attaché. Nasser, who knows all the details of the situation, replies that the man had been acting like a spy. Byroade denies the accusation, explaining the man had only gone to Suez to study the oil industry. He then adds bitterly, "I am sorry; I thought we were in a civilized country."[112] Nasser snubs out his cigarette and strides out of the party, offended. His ministers follow. This statement ends the Ambassador's career.

Reading firsthand accounts by Mohamed Heikel and Miles Copeland are like finding jewels. The way they reflect my father is a glimpse into his world, albeit a troubling one. I reread *Power Problems of a Revolutionary Government,* the fifteen-page treatise attributed to Eich that Copeland published as an appendix in *The Game of Nations.* My father states that "a revolutionary government must do *whatever is necessary* to actualize more power—repressive and constructive—than is allowed to remain potential." This includes a "politicalized" police force that becomes "to whatever extent is necessary a partisan paramilitary arm of the revolutionary government." After the first phase of repression, "constructive action becomes the basis of power."[113] A key component of constructive action is building a power base—a massive group of supporters—which in Nasser's case I see as the poor landless masses. They were the ones cheated by colonial business interests and the oil which made the Middle East so desirable. Reading this essay my father penned over sixty-five years ago is tough going for me. I am sympathetic to the goals and aspirations spurring Nasser's revolution. Promulgating social justice in the face of the inequity of colonialism is important—critical if we are to create a more just world. However, the methods recommended by my father, widely adopted, and currently practiced, make me shudder with fear for our future.

It is a strange twist that the downfall of Ambassador Byroade was accusing Nasser of uncivilized governance because the Egyptian government beat a suspected spy for gathering oil industry intelligence. Nasser's enforcement accorded with my father's advice. Knowing the Ambassador did not know my father wrote the *Power Problems of a Revolutionary Government* adds to the irony. In another layer of the cloak and dagger, the CIA passed the essay to the State Department as the work of Nasser's Lieutenant Zakaria Mohieddin—the escort of Copeland and Roosevelt to the party that evening. In yet another example of foreign meddling's negative reverberation, Eich's work led to the oil consultant's beating by the Egyptian police.

I have come to understand the oil industry employs many of the same tactics recommended by my father. They muscle their way into whatever part of the world they wish to plunder, react with swift violence to any dissent, and with the help of expensive PR firms they greenwash their footprints to the rest of the world, all the while being one of its largest polluters. I appreciate Nasser's voice for the people, although not his tactics, and am horrified by my father's role in recommending such actions. Did my father ever feel trapped between his undercover role and the world stage unfolding before his eyes? Did he believe in what Nasser was doing in Egypt or side with the political forces in DC turning against the revolutionary? At what point did my father disassociate himself, as Copeland claims, from the *Power Problems of a Revolutionary Government* essay? I still have so many questions. One thing is certain: it is a dirty, double-crossing business in which Eich invested his life. Not only that, the inherent deceit in the work makes it difficult to decipher the truth today.

I had hopes that by getting to know Said Aburish, I could shed more light on my father's role in the Middle East than I am able to glean from books. Our communication ended almost a couple of years ago. Aburish's death has put a final lock on the door. Another opportunity has passed. I am praying for others to appear. I want to reconcile the troubling affairs of my father's life. The past is speaking to me; I struggle with what it's trying to say.

99 Said K. Aburish, *Children of Bethany: The Story of a Palestinian Family,* (New York: Bloomsbury Publishing, 1988).

100 Said K. Aburish, *Nasser: The Last Arab* (New York: Thomas Dunne Books, 2004).

101 Ibid, 310-311.

102 Miles Copeland, *The Game Player,* 161.

103 Aburish, Nasser, *The Last Arab,* 67-74.

104 Samir Raafat, THE ANGLO-AMERICAN HOSPITAL APPROACHES ITS CEN-TENNIAL, *Cairo Times,* May 28, 1998, http://www.egy.com/zamalek/96-01-13.php.

105 Robert C. Doty, New York Times October 26, 1954, "Nasser Escapes Attempt on Life" accessed June 8, 2021, https://www.nytimes.com/1954/10/27/archives/nasser-escapes-attempt-on-life-assassin-who-fires-8-shots-is-held.html.

106 Said K. Aburish, *Nasser: The Last Arab,* 125.

107 Miles Copeland, *The Game of Nations: The Amorablity of Power Politics* (New York: Simon and Schulter, 1969) 154.

108 Bruce Riedel, Beirut 1958: America's origin story in the Middle East, October 29, 2019, accessed June 8, 2021, https://www.brookings.edu/blog/order-from-chaos/2019/10/29/beirut-1958-americas-origin-story-in-the-middle-east/ .

109 Mohamed Heikal, *The Cairo Documents: The Inside Story of Nasser and His Relationship with World Leaders, Rebels, and Statesmen* (Garden City: NJ. Double Day & Company, 1973), 50.

110 Ibid, 51.

111 Copeland, *The Game of Nations,* 162.

112 Heikal., *The Cairo Documents,* 53.

113 Copeland, *The Game of Nations,* 300.

CHAPTER 10

COMMON GROUND

t is not long before the past invites me to look further. One Saturday morning, before heading to the farmer's market and the thrift store, I check my email at our desktop computer in the family room. Waiting for me is a surprise inquiry from a professor who found my post about Eich on the OSS listserv. He is writing a book about some of my dad's colleagues and wants to talk with me. I tell Richard the good news.

"That's great," he replies. "Hopefully, you'll have better luck with him than you had with Aburish."

"This guy's in California, not halfway around the world in Jordan," I say, more to convince myself than my husband that this man's inquiry will lead to anything useful.

Dr. Hugh Wilford teaches in Long Beach, CA, and the book he's about to finish is about Kim Roosevelt's efforts to build relations with Arab leaders, chiefly Gamal Abdel Nasser. Kim's cousin, Archie Roosevelt, features prominently, as does Miles Copeland. "I am very keen to include more about your father, as it is clear from other sources that he played an important role in the events I am describing," he writes. *Yes, join the club.* If only I had the autobiography Eich was working on, I think to myself for the hundredth time. "I have little to offer your research given my parents' divorce," I forewarn the professor. It doesn't matter. Wilford still wants to speak with me, and we have set up a phone date for this coming Friday evening.

I answer my cell at our dining room table, two smooth rectangles of polished marble set atop wrought iron legs my mother had designed and made in Egypt. I am sitting on one of the eight matching chairs she had also made, the one closest to the picture window overlooking the small fish pond Richard constructed when we first moved to our Carrboro home. My back is to our galley kitchen. It is my favorite seat at the table. While I did not appreciate my mother's minimalist modern style when growing up in DC, now I find the clean lines soothing.

"It's Hugh Wilford. Is this still a good time to talk?" Immediately, his voice charms me. Not only does he have a British accent, he is polite, and our phone connection is clear. Our conversation unfolds like a map. He is the seasoned explorer. I am the novice looking for the promised land. I ask Hugh about the document he attached to his request to speak with me. It's a signed memo that my dad wrote.

"I found the memo while on a research trip to the National Archives," Hugh says. "It was in a box of State Department files on 1956 Middle East policy. It really surprised me to see his name typed at the end of it. I've never found a CIA memo before while searching through a State Department box. They are usually classified." The professor apologizes for the clumsy copy he sent. "I photographed the pages horizontally rather than vertically, and then the low resolution makes them more of a strain to read."

I'm just glad he found the pages and found me. This memo sheds light on what happened with US-Egyptian relations after the 1955 Czech arms deal. Besides my small handful of letters, this is the only document I have directly attributable to my father. This after my father told me he ghostwrote several books for the CIA. I ask Hugh what he thinks about my father's comments.

"I found the memo very interesting. Your father is recommending the US take a more moderate approach to managing Nasser."

"That's good, because the British were not," I say, hoping to sound like I know what I am talking about, at the same time not offending the Englishman regarding his country's 1956 position in Egypt. Thankfully, our sentiments seem *simpatico*.

The three pages Hugh sent me have TOP SECRET stamped in red at the top and bottom. My father wrote the memo for the Middle East Policy Planning Group. It's titled, "Cairo Station Views Pertinent to OMEGA Planning." OMEGA was the Eisenhower Administration's secret endeavor to subdue the non-aligned movement—countries that wanted to assert their independence from an increasingly polarized world, with Russia on one side and the US on the other. Eich is advising against direct attacks on "full independence, self-determination," and "Arab nationalism," because they will backfire and strengthen Nasser's hand. He goes on to write that "Western propaganda in the area based upon the traditional 'Soviet menace' theme is unlikely to be greatly effective under current conditions."[114]

Eich realized the Soviets were not the threat others were making them out to be. Yet he does recommend the following "propaganda lines" to meet US objectives: "Create suspicion throughout the area as to the ultimate extent of Nasser's ambition. Does he wish to establish dictatorship over the whole area? Gain control over Arab oil resources?"[115]

I wonder, did my father no longer trust Nasser's intentions, or was he writing to placate headquarters' dislike of Nasser's increasing anti-Western rhetoric? Either way, I am happy with the memo's conclusion: "We wish most strongly to emphasize that any course of action which involves the US Government in direct combat with Arab Nationalism as such is almost certain to lead to the defeat of Western interests in the area."[116] Finally, my father and I agree on something. There was a brief period after WWII when the Arab world looked at US interests in the region with appreciation. But with dubious motives and misguided actions, Arab trust in our intentions would fade fast.

I feel I am starting a conversation with my father through this long-ago document. *See, Anne, I believed in the Arab cause and trusted Nasser, but the higher ups in DC did not want to listen to what I was saying from the field,* the ghost of my father is telling me. Yet I am having trouble responding with any generosity to his situation, given the deep-seated anger I still feel from how he left me. Rather, I want to focus on the professor on the phone, the angel who gave me this document.

I would like to give him something in return. Hugh's manuscript has already gone to the publisher, but they may consider some photos of Eich from when we were in Egypt. I will look in the cache I inherited from my mother. After forty-five minutes, Hugh and I agree to speak again the following night.

In the OMEGA memo, Eich writes: "British policy favors the use of force, overt and/or covert, to reestablish British influence in the area."[117] I am lining up this statement with the passages in Wilbur Crane Eveland's *Ropes of Sand* that so confused me when I first read them nine years ago—passages about how Eich's counterparts in Britain wanted to murder Nasser, while the CIA sent Eich to Cairo a couple years earlier to help him. Finally, I understand enough of the world stage and can read between the lines of what others have written to form a plausible interpretation of the events. And in the case of Britain's interest in murdering Nasser, my father's opposition to this crazy idea is right where I would want him to be.

In March 1956, a month before my father wrote the OMEGA memo, he was sent to London where he shared a suite with Eveland at the Connaught Hotel. My father and Eveland knew each other but were not close. I imagine the nineteenth-century hotel was memorable for my father. During World War II, Eich lived with Miles Copeland and Frank Kearns in a flat off Grosvenor

Square, just two blocks north of the Connaught. While Eich came from Cairo that morning, Eveland had flown overnight from DC, preparing for the meetings by reading the London papers.

In rereading Eveland's memoir, the situation he and my father faced in Britain comes to life for me with the conversations he quoted. "The press was lashing out at the 'communist-serving Nasser' and calling King Saud degrading names,"[118] Eveland remarked as Eich hung his suits in the closet. He wanted to know what to expect at their first meeting later that morning. When Eich informed him that they were meeting with the Secret Intelligence Service—Britain's MI6—Eveland jokingly inquired if the SIS would ask that they join them in doing away with Nasser. My father replied in all seriousness, "If our British cousins had their way, that would be just the plan."[119] Eich pulled an unfiltered player from a pack on the table, then realizing his colleague's concern about the rising tensions said, "Don't worry, our instructions are to stall any decisions until Allen Dulles and Kim Roosevelt get here next week. We're just here for exploratory talks." Eveland didn't know the CIA director and his Near East chief were coming, nor the purpose of his own trip when he received the cable to meet Jim Eichelberger in London. He was depending on Eich for navigation.

For March the weather was fair, and the pair walked to the Bond Street station where they took the underground to St. James Park in the city center. Exiting the station, Eich pointed out their destination: The Broadway Buildings were officially known as the Government Communications Bureau but also served as the headquarters of the SIS. British double agent Kim Philby worked here. I imagine this was where my father first met the charming British spy with a stammer. During the war, Eich and the newly formed OSS looked to MI6 for their intelligence gathering experience. While the Brits had uncovered two of Kim's colleagues spying for the Russians in the early 1950s, Kim's double life was still a secret in 1956. If my father had been reminiscing about his first meeting with his friend and colleague Kim, it would have evaporated as soon as he and Eveland exited the elevator on the top floor and the soles of my father's shoes were clicking across the marble.

Eich and Eveland were trying to get a read on MI6 Deputy Director George Kennedy Young. Brief introductions aside, the Englishman launched right in.

"There's been a change with regards to UK policy in the Middle East, the details of which we've already communicated to your leadership. Therefore, chaps," the burly man paused for a breath, "the purpose of our meetings the next couple of days is to develop a joint intelligence appreciation justifying our new strategy."

Eich was not about to commit to this. "We're just here on a fact-finding mission," he replied.[120]

"Egypt, Saudi Arabia, and Syria are threatening our survival," Young retorted with rapid fire, his voice mounting. "Nasser is an out-and-out Soviet instrument and Syria is about to become a Soviet satellite. We can't sit here idly. Nasser will use Soviet bombers to eradicate Israel, and the fates of our allies in Jordon and Lebanon depend on our swift action in Syria. And since Saudi Arabia is financing Arab moves with its petrol, King Saud needs to go too."

Young sounded borderline unhinged to the two Americans. With each successive meeting, he became more hostile.

Eveland baited Young to reveal MI6's first plan of action. The deputy director explained the UK would take care of Syria by having Turkey create some border incidents. Then, with the British controlled Iraqi leadership stirring up the desert tribes and Lebanon's *Partie Populaire Syrienne* infiltrating the borders, the resulting mass confusion would justify the use of Iraqi troops to "stabilize" the situation.

Though Britain planned to go after Syria first, they had a special vengeance for Nasser. The Egyptian leader had unseated the British after more than seventy years of rule. At their final meeting, the SIS Deputy Director asked Eveland and Eich to summarize their impressions of British plans. He was sizing up the Americans, and Eveland had hoped to sound more diplomatic than what came out. "You are counting on a lot from the Iraqis that could come to pass, but unseating Nasser sounds like wishful thinking."

Young was not the least bit fazed. "Gentlemen, you forgot one thing in this equation—the snipcocks," he replied.[121]

Eveland had never heard the term before. When a perplexed expression crossed his face, Eich leaned over and whispered into his colleague's ear, "the Israelis." Britain would get Israel to do its dirty work. George Young flashed a devilish smile. Handing Eveland a summary of their talks, he suggested the two men use it to prepare a cable to CIA director Allen Dulles. Young told them he would come by the Connaught to review their draft.

At the hotel the next day, Young requested several additions to their report, to which they agreed. "Britain is now prepared to fight its last battle . . . no matter what the cost, we will win." And finally, "we have to face the possibility that Nasser might close the canal and would like to know how the US would react to that."[122] After Young left and Eveland sent the cable to Dulles, he and Eich reflected on the series of meetings over a bottle of Dewar's White Label. They needed to debrief.

"There is absolutely no evidence that Nasser is a tool of the Russians," Eich said. "I hope the talk we just heard from Young is more bluster than substance. It will only make Nasser more popular if our cousins go on the offensive in the Middle East."

Eveland was not so sure. He understood Eich to be "part of the Kim Roosevelt clique that had taken such pride in 'inventing a pro-Western Nasser.'"[123]

The men parted ways—my father to DC for follow-up meetings with CIA headquarters while Eveland stayed on for Kim Roosevelt's arrival. There is no doubt that with the mounting tensions, Eich was under pressure—lots of pressure—on the powder keg leading up to the Suez Crisis four months later. My understanding of the global situation, and my father's role in it, at last engenders my empathy for him.

———————

As he had promised, Hugh Wilford emails me Lucky Roosevelt's contact information. Lucky is the widow of Archie Roosevelt, Kim's cousin and Eich's colleague. Selwa "Lucky" Roosevelt is known in her own right. Born to Lebanese parents in Kingsport, Tennessee, she graduated with honors from Vassar College, became a journalist, and then went on to become Ronald Reagan's Chief of Protocol for seven years. I remember my mom's friend Elaine Atkins talking about Lucky. Their DC address is in Mom's address book, but it's different from the one Hugh gave me. I imagine she moved after Archie's death in 1990. I write the now eighty-three-year-old a handwritten note in hopes she has some memories of Archie and my father from their time together in the CIA. I then search through my haphazard piles of photos from my parents' time in the Middle East to find one that Hugh may want to use in his forthcoming book.

I scan five snapshots to compile into one file for Hugh to consider. One is a black-and-white close-up of Eich sitting in our living room next to the marble table my brother Jay now has in his house. On it is an iron peacock with silver-and-gold-threaded inlay that now stands on the bookshelf in our guest room. The close-up is my favorite photo of Eich. He's is in a white Oxford shirt with sleeves rolled halfway to his elbow so the leather band of his watch is visible. His dark tie is tight to his neck. I look at his eyes. He is wearing horn-rimmed glasses and not looking at the camera but somewhere into the distance. Young and handsome, he is in the prime of his life. This black-and-white shot allows me to peek into his soul to wonder what he was thinking. The second one is Eich seated on a round leather pouf holding a book in front of a wall of books that would be in his study. Hugh emails back right away and asks that I send these two photos as separate files to give to his editor.

When we speak again, I ask him if he would be willing to share the Freedom of Information Act letter he wrote to the CIA requesting Miles, Kim, and Archie's personnel files. Hugh tells me he would have asked for Eich's as well had he thought of it, but alas he did not.

"I really didn't receive much of anything useful from the FOIA request. Most of the pages the CIA sent were redacted," he says.

"At least you got something. All I received was a letter saying they could 'neither confirm nor deny' a relationship with him," I gripe. It is maddening to hear that Hugh only had to send a written request that included their names, birth dates, and their newspaper obituaries, while I had to prove Eich was my father *and* send his death certificate. "It doesn't seem fair," I say, recalling the excitement of finally seeing the taped envelope from the Central Intelligence Agency Information & Privacy Coordinator in my mailbox.

"You should try again," Hugh counsels me. Once I get over feeling frustrated with the length of time it took them to respond *and* the result, I may consider it. As it was, it took over a year and a half for the CIA to tell me that they couldn't tell me anything. His encouragement helps, though. I am not going to give up trying to find out what I can about my father with or without the CIA's help. There is no sense in aborting my quest after coming this far.

---

114 US Department of State, Omega, James M Eichelberger, Omega Folder Vol. 4, Record Group 59, Lot 61D417, Box 55 College Park, MD: National Archives and Records Administration, Retrieved 2013.

115 Ibid, 2.

116 Ibid, 3.

117 Ibid.

118 Wilbur Crane Eveland, *Ropes of Sand: America's Failure in the Middle East* (London: WW Norton & Company, 1980), 168.

119 Ibid.

120 Ibid, 169.

121 Ibid, 171.

122 Ibid.

123 Ibid.

CHAPTER 11

A GOOD SPY LEAVES NO TRACE

"Thank you so much for calling me, Mrs. Roosevelt," I half yell into my phone, hoping the appreciation in my voice carries over the thump, thump, thump of the bus's massive wheels rolling over gravel. I am straining to hear Lucky Roosevelt as my ride to work moves onto the shoulder of I-40 to bypass the bumper-to-bumper traffic between Chapel Hill and Raleigh. A new policy allows transit buses to move ahead of the mostly single occupancy vehicles by driving on the shoulder, but it is difficult to hear Archie Roosevelt's widow over the bumpy din.

"Since you included your phone number, I thought it would be better to call rather than respond to your note. Tell me again, who was your father?" she asks.

"James Eichelberger—he was a colleague of Archie's when you lived in the Middle East."

"James Eichelberger? I am afraid I don't remember him. There were so many people and it was so long ago."

"I understand. Do you remember Elaine Atkins?" I reply, hoping to jog her memory.

"Yes. Yes, I do. We went to Vassar together."

"Elaine and my mother, Alice Eichelberger, were close friends, and Elaine's husband, Teddy, also worked for the CIA with Archie and my father." Still no luck.

"I'm sorry, I'm old now and Archie had so many CIA colleagues, I just don't have any recollection of your father."

"That's okay. We are going to see Elaine in Florida this December on our way to a family holiday. I will be sure to give her your regards," I say, wanting to make a connection before the conversation ends.

"Yes, please do," she replies.

It was kind of Lucky to call, but her forgetfulness brings into focus, once again, why I should have started this project twenty or thirty years ago. Even ten would have helped. I know better than to indulge in this line of thinking. The ocean of regret will drown me if I don't get out of its undertow. It does no good to feel like a victim of time. Yet each reminder of its deadening passage makes my heart wince.

Walking helps. It is mid-October and the leaves are dropping with the breeze as I make my way from the bus stop past the foliage next to NC State's Horticulture Building. The cerulean blue sky and puffy white clouds complement the gold and red fall harbingers. It is stunning, but I do not much like what it will bring: winter. The days shorten, and the abundance of summer's foliage is left to wither in the chilled air. Another year will soon pass. I consider the rest of Eich's year in 1956—after his meetings in London with Eveland and the OMEGA memo Hugh gave me— as I walk up the long hill to my office.

The meeting with MI6 Deputy Director George Young in London so alarmed Eich that he leaked much of it to Cairo. In *Suez Through Egyptian Eyes*, Mohamed Heikal recounts, "The message Eichelberger sent was that the British were now desperate and were determined to 'do a Mossadeq' with Nasser."[124] Young had talked openly about assassinating Nasser instead of using "a polite euphemism like *liquidating*," my father said. "This was perhaps the last useful contact Egypt was to have with the American undercover organizations," the Egyptian journalist wrote. The Mosaddegh reference goes back to the CIA operation that Kim Roosevelt proudly led three years earlier to overthrow the democratically elected leader of Iran after he nationalized his country's oil.[125] The tide was rapidly changing in Washington, and I imagine my father felt the rip currents wracking through the Middle East more than most. He did not want the British to overthrow the Egyptian leadership to better suit their fossil fuel interests, although the US had recently done the same in Iran.

My sympathy grows as I realize the stress Eich must have felt from circumstances outside of his control. I don't think I would hold up under that kind of pressure. This is more reason to immerse myself in the history of my father's times. It helps me reconcile our broken relationship and my hard feelings for him. Understanding does not excuse my dad's poor behavior toward his family and more broadly the nefarious work of the CIA in overthrowing governments, but it helps in developing my compassion.

Just a couple of weeks after the OMEGA memo, Nasser formally recognized Communist China as a country. He did this in part to get around the potential for a United Nations general arms embargo, since China was not part of the international organization. In the Cold War build up and the rise of non-aligned nations, this did not make the US happy. Secretary of State Foster Dulles responded by authorizing a French supply of fighter planes to the Israelis under a tripartite agreement intended to maintain a balance of arms in the Middle East.[126] I now realize they used these planes to bomb Egypt in retaliation for Nasser's nationalization of the Suez Canal later that year.

Earlier, Nasser had gone to the World Bank for help to build the Aswan Dam. His mission was to end the Nile's annual flooding and bring electricity across Egypt. The massive project would not come without environmental consequences but, Nasser reasoned, the needed hydroelectric energy would alleviate poverty. The

$1B project was too expensive for the World Bank to finance on its own so Britain and the US were to help. When both countries reneged, the deal fell through. On July 19, 1956, two months after the OMEGA memo, the US withdrew its offer to help finance the Aswan Dam.[127]

Nasser publicly responded eight days later, on July 26 in Alexandria. Was my father at the president's speech? Could my mom and I have accompanied him to the seaside resort? Although she was not much of a swimmer, I know Mom loved the beach. She also loved the ancient city and the seaside air. I have a black-and-white photo of me on a white sand beach holding a bucket. Perhaps it was taken there. Nasser was staying in Alexandria with his wife and five children at the time. The Egyptian premier was both a teetotaler and a devout family man, who went home to lunch every day with his family[128]—traits I admire in a father so opposite mine.

The President made his way to Mansheya Square in the old city center, standing in an open barricade of vehicles. He waved to the crowd of a hundred thousand people gathered to hear his response to their loss of financing for the dam. It was the same site as the failed assassination attempt during which the CIA provided a bulletproof vest the year before. Nasser in his suit took the podium at nine p.m., the heat still stifling. "We will not be manipulated," the leader said. The crowd erupted in cheers. "Today we are going to get rid of what happened in the past."[129]

The Egyptian leader had disclosed his plans to few. He had put in charge Mohammed Younis, the Egyptian responsible for all oil-related relationships. When the president said a specific code word in his speech, Younis had instructed a handful of engineers and administrators to take over operations at the four Suez Canal facilities. Nasser said the code word Ferdinand De Lesseps—the name of the Canal's French developer—thirteen times to make sure the planning team got the signal over the national broadcast. "Some of your fellow citizens have just taken over the Canal," he announced to erupting cheers in the Square.[130]

It was a bold move that shocked some in Nasser's cabinet; informed only earlier that evening. "More than one minister mentioned Mossadeq; he had nationalized his country's oil industry and this had proved a failure."[131] The Egyptian president knew the world would measure his success by how seamlessly the flow of petroleum tankers continued to bring Mideast oil to markets. Egypt had sovereign right to the Canal, but a company of primarily British and French investors managed it. The president assured compensation to the shareholders and the free flow of oil. He would use toll revenue to build the high dam.

Britain and France did not believe the Egyptians capable of running the Canal. By 1955, petroleum accounted for half of the canal's traffic, and, in turn, two-thirds of Europe's oil passed through it.[132] That number would only grow as the international oil industry continued investing in the Middle East. Not only was their pride as former colonists and commanders of foreign lands threatened, but their economy was at risk. My father accompanied Secretary of State John Foster Dulles to the first London conference on Suez one month after Nasser's surprise takeover—hastily organized for the maritime nations using the waterway. At the second conference, Secretary Dulles proposed my father's idea of forming a Suez Canal Users Association, a collaboration of government and industry that would manage the pipelines and canal like the US did railroads.[133]

Eich writes that during the Suez meetings, he was also representing the CIA in London on "a clandestine plan for the Middle East with the British government."[134] My father flew trans-Atlantic seven times in 1956 while Britain, France, and Israel secretly coordinated plans for a military invasion and reoccupation of the canal zone.[135] Was he trying to be a voice of reason to the Brits' bellicosity? He must have known about the pending invasion and, I imagine, advised against it.

President Eisenhower opposed the allies' plan that began on October 29 with the Israeli takeover of the Sinai Peninsula. Eventually, he forced Israel, Britain, and France to withdraw from their invasion of the Suez Canal, but not before the US allies had already convened approximately a hundred thousand Israelis, forty-five thousand Britons, and thirty-four thousand Frenchmen; two hundred British and thirty French warships, seventy merchant vessels, hundreds of landing craft; and twelve thousand British and nine thousand French vehicles to the area.[136] Historians estimated that thousands died in the invasion, the majority Egyptian. It would not be the last time such hubris prevailed.

Unfortunately, in subsequent decades of Middle East engagement, it would be the US that led a "coalition of the willing" to fight a "global war on terror" that tallies in the trillions of dollars.[137] The Suez crisis was the first time a US president stood up to aggression from its close friends. And I might add, it was the last. In fact, since the Suez Crisis, the US has been the lead aggressor in the Middle East.

A wave of satisfaction washes over me, for I sense that my father steered the president to the right side of history in this instance. Eich told me his cables, "from Egypt concerning the Middle East were being read by the president himself." If Eisenhower didn't see a message in the morning, he would ask his advisor Bill Bundy for "what Eich says."[138] For the first time, I feel a daughter's pride in her father's work. It is immensely fulfilling to know that the US stood up to our allies in defense of Egypt and my father had something to do with the president's position.

By the time the British Royal Air Force bombed Cairo West

Airport two days after the Israeli incursion, our family of three must have already moved from the Egyptian capitol back to Washington. I'm certain my mother would have told me, had she been living in a war zone. Elaine Atkins agrees. She remembers my parents in Cairo. This is where they met, when her husband, Teddy, was a junior case officer, and she recollects that we left sometime before the Suez invasion. After their early years in Egypt, Elaine became my mother's lifelong friend. She and Teddy settled with their kids near us in DC where my mother looked to Teddy as a potential father figure for me when I was a troubled teen.

We—Richard, Rio, and I—are with the spry eighty-three-year-old widow in Sawgrass, the Florida retirement community near St Augustine where she and Teddy moved decades ago. She takes us to her beach club to have a view of the ocean for our short visit. It's windy—too windy—and cold for a dip in the sea. We are on our way to Key West by way of Sarasota for a Christmas week reunion with Jamila, our son-in-law Jai Gopal, and Taylor. Since Taylor will be flying into Sarasota from Austin tomorrow, we are on a tight schedule. The visit is too brief to hope for any useful information for my hunt.

Elaine is interested in what she calls "the monkey business" but is tight-lipped about what she may know regarding Eich's CIA experience. Unlike my mom, who was not interested in what my father was doing, she and Teddy would talk about operations. But just as a good spy never talks, neither does a good spy's wife. "It could incriminate someone who is still alive," Elaine explains. It's not unusual for family members to not know much or anything about what their spy husband or father does, especially when they are in counterintelligence, cultivating contacts, and assuming a cover. It's not advisable to let your family into this secret world.

As far as my dad's behavior, Elaine reiterates what she had

told me before: my father was funny around money. "Shortly after the divorce," she says, "for which Teddy and I gave Eich $10,000, your father came to visit us at our summer home in Nantucket." I realize this encounter must have been around the beginning of Eich's stint with INTERSER, the consulting group's short-lived offices at 1 Rockefeller Plaza. In Elaine's telling, when Eich saw their home, a modern design set off the dunes next to the ocean, he exclaimed, "I didn't know you were rich!" Certainly, my father knew it was gauche to comment on a friend's wealth. But perhaps for a moment, Eich let down his guard to reveal how different his background was from theirs.

My father grew up the only child of his widowed mother during the Depression. He would have been thirteen when the stock market crashed in 1929, a formative experience for anyone aware of the value of a dollar. Yet, I also assumed Eich grew up with some luxury after reading through the newspaper clippings that Delores, the daughter of my dad's girlfriend, sent me and saw the photo of my grandmother, Mary Eich. My grandmother was sitting around the McCann & Company's polished boardroom table accompanied by a ring of men who were executives like her. My brain just automatically associated executives with wealth and the trappings of affluence, a big home in an exclusive neighborhood.

In addition to the newspaper clippings, I found a letter with the address of my father's home when his father was still alive, and then another address where I assumed my grandmother moved after Eich was on his own. As part of this quest to know my roots, Richard and I went to where my dad grew up in Pittsburgh. To my surprise the grand house I imagined Mary Eich living in was instead the second floor of a modest brick apartment building.

It would be easy to suppose that my dad was accustomed to wealth given some of his associates, such as the Roosevelt cousins Kim and Archie. Many of the founding members of the CIA and the OSS came from the country's elite and attended Ivy League schools. Not my father. He needed to earn his status. This may be even more reason Eich set his sights on the security that came with getting rich. It explains why he was surprised by Teddy and Elaine's second home and attracted to friends who had already achieved his aim.

My mother's friend is interested in hearing that I've been corresponding with Lorraine Copeland and had recently spoken to Lucky Roosevelt. Before we leave, she offers to lend me a couple of books for my research. On a bookshelf, next to a Kuwaiti chest that looks much like ours but for the brilliant polish, Elaine pulls out Archie Roosevelt's memoir. She points out the author's 1988 tender inscription to her and Teddy on the first page of *For the Lust of Knowing*.[139] Touched that she entrusts me with this memory of her past, I promise to care for it.

Elaine draws another book from the shelf, *Legacy of Ashes: The History of the CIA*.[140] I'm surprised she has a book whose title admits failure at an endeavor in which her husband spent his life— but do not say as much. She has read the two-inch-thick tome and thinks I should have it, maybe because it will support my point of view: no good comes from a price paid with deceit. My Aunt Elaine remembers my rebellious roots, buried with little trust for what passes as success in the great game. When I was a teenager, my mother called Teddy when I needed a fatherly talking to. It didn't do any good. Although he tried, he couldn't be a father to me.

I found another way to build a life, quite the opposite of my father's. It is located on the end of the road we now travel. Key West, the small rock in the middle of the sea, was the birthplace of my new beginning. We lived there fifteen years, and now fifteen years later, we are returning. There is nothing more precious for Richard and me than to spend time with our family. It's been a year since we have all been together, a year too long for me.

124 Mohamed Heikal, *Cutting The Lion's Tail: Suez Through Egyptian Eyes* (London: Cirgi Books, 1986), 118.

125 Kermit Roosevelt Jr., *Countercoup: The Struggle for Control Over Iran* (McGraw Hill, 1979).

126 Mohamed Heikal, *The Cairo Documents: The Inside Story of Nasser and His Relationship with World Leaders, Rebels, and Statesmen* (Garden City: NJ. Double Day & Company, 1973), 58.

127 History, July 19, 1956 "United States withdraws offer of air for Aswan Dam," accessed June 9, 2021, https://www.history.com/this-day-in-history/united-states-withdraws-offer-of-aid-foraswan-dam.

128 Aburish, *Nasser, The Last Arab*, 90.

129 BBC broadcast of Nasser's speech, accessed June 26, 2021, https://www.youtube.com/watch?v=Qt1Xah1qR14.

130 Ibid.

131 Heikal, *Cutting The Lion's Tail*, 138.

132 Daniel Yergin, *The Prize: The Epic Quest for Oil, Money & Power* (New York: Simon & Schuster, 1991), 462.

133 Miles Copeland, *The Game Player* (London: Aurum Press, 1989); Nina J. Noring (ed.), 207, Foreign Relations of the US 1955-57, Suez Crisis Jul 26-December 31, 1956 Volume XVI (Washington: US State Dept Office of the Historian, 1990); Statement Issued by the Second Suez Canal Conference at London, September 21, 1956 Source: Conference doc. SUEZ II/56/D/10; Department of State, Conference Files: Lot 62 D 181, CF 782; Also printed in *The Suez Canal Problem*, July 26–September 22, 1956, pp. 366–367.

134 James M Eichelberger, letter to author, December 14, 1982.

135 Ibid; "The Suez Crisis An affair to remember," *The Economist*, July 27, 2006, http://www.economist.com/node/7218678.

136 Wilfred P. Deac, "Suez Crisis: Operation Musketeer" Military History, June 12, 2006. http://www.historynet.com/suez-crisis-operation-musketeer.htm.

137 Mark Thompson, "The $5 Trillion War on Terror" TIME, June 2011. http://nation.time.com/2011/06/29/the-5-trillion-war-on-terror/.

138 James M Eichelberger, letter to author, 1982.

139 Archie Roosevelt, *For the Lust of Knowing: Memoirs of an Intelligence Officer* (Boston: Little, Brown & Company, 1988).

140 Tim Weiner, *The Legacy of Ashes: The History of the CIA* (New York: Doubleday 2007).

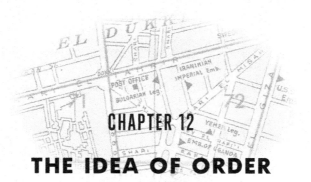

CHAPTER 12

THE IDEA OF ORDER

Our trip to Florida, that I had looked so forward to, is not going as anticipated. Our first evening in Sarasota, friends invite us to dinner at their home on nearby Siesta Key. As soon as we line up for a buffet of couscous and grilled vegetables, I realize I have a stomach bug and spend the rest of the evening between the bathroom next to their kitchen and the couch, conveniently close to the dining area where the eleven others gather. I recover the next day, but when we drive to the Ft. Lauderdale airport to pick up Jamila and Jai Gopal, we find that they are battling fever and a cold.

It is not the best circumstances for Jai Gopal's first visit to the island and the first time in seven years the five of us have been together in Key West. What was I thinking coming during the busiest week of the year? Tourists have overrun the city, and the duplex we rented on Truman Annex is not big enough to comfortably spread out. Everywhere is approaching its carrying capacity.

Richard and I sleep on the pull-out couch in the living room. Christmas morning I wake at dawn, as always, the first up. Feeling better after the initial virus, I slip out of bed and into my shorts and sandals for a bike ride. The island is peaceful at this early hour. I ride past the old weather-beaten church on Whitehead Street, now someone's home, with pink flamingos in Santa hats out front. Past the Southernmost Point, hugging the island until I get to White Street Pier where I turn left to get to Laird Street. I park my rented bike in front of what had been our home for twenty years.

We sold it in 2005 after Hurricane Wilma left two and a half feet of water inside, just six weeks after Hurricane Rita left six inches. The new owners tore it down before the financial crash two years later, and it has been an empty lot since. Only the mahogany tree from which we strung our hammock and rocked the babies is still standing. As disappointing as it is to not see our house, it's better this way, I rationalize. With climate change, this side of the island will succumb to the sea faster than Old Town. Our neighborhood started as a mangrove swamp, then was filled with marl in the 1940s for new housing. Let it return to nature.

The new owner hung a Private Property: Do Not Trespass sign on the half of the front fence that is remaining. I walk in the opening and search the grassy lot for any trace of our past. There is none. Instead there is an odd feeling that reflects my mood this morning. Christmas 2012 brings with it the blues, a soulful longing. I have a husband who loves me, three grown children successfully engaged in their own lives, and a career to which I devote much of my passion now that they have moved away. But aches still plague me. "Sodade," the haunting melody of Cesária Évora, floods my memory. Richard learned this favorite song of ours on this spot of land and has sung it hundreds of times since. Its meaning, a longing for what was but could never be, captures my mood. Is this the human condition, to always want something more, something out of reach, something invisible, something that was but could never be? I am thinking of my father and this quixotic quest to know him. I'm thinking of my younger years.

What had been our home has disappeared, like my father and so many relations, but my memories of what took place on this homesite linger. The most protracted drama was the hard-fought recovery of my marriage. When Jamila was two years old, my brief bout of infidelity had Richard wandering the streets of our island home with a knife and thoughts of killing my paramour. My deceit tortured me and hurt him. We separated for nine months when my mom was struggling with cancer and Jamila and I moved to DC to care for her.

The subsequent decision to not abandon our relationship after my treachery is what prompted me to write Eich and ask why he had left his own marriage. It was also what prompted Richard and me to buy our first home. Seven years after moving to Key West, we conceived Rio in the carport-turned-bedroom, now lost to the wrecking ball. Then Taylor arrived two and a half years later, nine months after Eich's death.

There had been happy days of birthday parties in our back-yard—blindfolded kids lined up for pin the tail on the donkey, musical chairs, and watermelon seed-spitting contests. And music, always lots of music. For these gifts I am lucky to have married a musician. I am also lucky that Richard did not leave after my unfaithfulness. I had pushed him away for many reasons, but he refused to give up on our marriage. The gradual healing of our relationship has allowed me to face my father's deceit and his abandonment, the hole in my heart.

I only have one book of my father's, a book of poems by Wallace Stevens, his favorite poet. Stevens wintered in Key West at the Casa Marina, five blocks from our house on Laird Street. This grand hotel stands at the terminus of the railroad Standard Oil's cofounder, Henry Flagler, had built from mainland Miami, which like our home was also wrecked by a hurricane. When we arrived in Key West five months pregnant with Jamila, Flagler's hotel was the site of Richard's first piano gig. For years he continued to play for the tourists and corporate clients relaxing in the Casa Marina's backyard overlooking the blue expanse of sea.

In "The Idea of Order at Key West," Wallace writes of a woman singing by the sea and how the sea shapes her song, yet she is the maker. In a letter to poetry publisher Ronald Lane Latimar, Stevens writes of the poem, "It may be that every man introduces his own order into the life about him." I have tried to read the renowned poet, but to my linear mind he rarely makes much sense. The words are like pretty-colored balls of yarn sitting in a basket. I want someone far more skillful than me to knit them into something with shape and meaning. But in "The Idea of Order at Key West," I understand it is for me to make sense of "ourselves and our origins."

Since our return home, the flu that I had been nursing in Key West has now turned into bronchitis. All I want to do is lie on the couch. It is New Year's Eve and Richard has a gig. I am home alone and have made a fire for cheer, pushing the couch up against our brick hearth for its comfort. It's an apropos time to reflect on the past year. The connections I have made searching for my dad are the highlights. West Virginia television aired Jerry Davis's documentary on Frank Kearns and a friend who lives there recorded it on her VCR, mailing us a copy. I was thrilled to see that Jerry used the photo I provided of Eich's military ID and the scan of Mom's address book with Kearns's Cairo address. It was Jerry who reconnected me to Lorraine Copeland.

Lorraine has been so kind toward my parents in her emails. In her last one she wrote, "I adored your father for his sympathetic explaining of complex intellectual concepts and clear thinking, and general 'niceness'." Whether true or not, reading her high regard for him helps increase empathy for the man who did a lot of double-crossing. Lorraine has opened my eyes to my father as a spy, my father as a two-timer, but also my father as a friend, my father as a thinker: "Eich's perspectives on politics were very worldly—not idealistic. He took a very philosophical view of human endeavors. I thought the world of him. He was hugely respected by everyone as a thinker. He occasionally coached us in intellectual ideas—for example, he made us question a 'given' that majority rule is fair and sensible."[141]

I knew Eich had attended graduate school at the University of Chicago (presumably on the GI Bill) after the war. I figured he'd continued his studies in Political Science, as this was the subject of his undergraduate degree from the University of Pittsburgh. After writing the University of Chicago Registrar in October, I was sent his transcripts. To my surprise, my father studied philosophy. From the spring quarter 1949 through spring 1951 he took courses in Ethics, Aristotle, Kant's Critique of Pure Reason, Advanced Symbolic Logic, The Pragmatic Movement, and other ideas borne from Western Philosophy.

From an early age, and without knowing my father's philosophic interests, I have trod a different path, my worldview shaped by Native American and Eastern spirituality. When Taylor was eighteen and left home for a year-trip around the world, I took a two-hundred-hour yoga teacher training course. After thirty years of mothering, I wanted to mark the transition from active parenting to letting my children go. Having all three of our offspring out of the house was a monumental transition. I felt like I was losing my mooring and needed a new anchor now that they all had cast off and set sail into their own lives. For nine months, as with gestation, for one long weekend per month, I attended trainings led by devotees of Yoga Bhajan, an Indian spiritual master who brought Kundalini Yoga to the West in the 1960s.

In Kundalini yoga, human beings have ten bodies, which are not actual physical bodies but powerful capacities of the psyche. The mind itself has three bodies: negative, positive, and neutral. The Negative Mind, the second body, is our protective mind. It instills a longing to belong. Unbalanced, the Negative Mind is overly influenced by others and does not feel contained within our own center.

With the kids independent and out in the world on their own journeys, my Negative Mind is getting the best of me. I feel their leaving as a compounding force to the loss of not having my father as I grew up. I have a longing to belong to something bigger than myself. When I am not doing yoga, enjoying nature, or tending to my marriage, I throw myself into work to outrun this need to belong. I can't imagine where I would be without it.

I am grateful for the sense of belonging I get from helping to protect the air. The air I breathe is what gives me life and connects me in the most intimate way to the natural world. We have just one Earth and the trees are her lungs, absorbing carbon dioxide and releasing oxygen in exchange. The Earth's lungs are my lungs. As I deeply breathe the oxygen she provides, I am thankful for the breath-focused yoga practices that connect my small self to this greater whole.

When Patanjali compiled the Yoga Sutras over seventeen hundred years ago, he named eight interrelated aspects of yoga to develop the full spectrum of the body and mind. At the base of this eight-limbed path are the Yamas and Niyamas. Yamas are moral practices such as non-judgment and compassion. Niyamas are daily practices such as gratitude and acceptance. Yamas and Niyamas master the Negative Mind, keep it in balance. It is one thing to know something intellectually and quite another to put it into practice.

I would like to be less judgmental of my father. I want to cultivate more compassion for his role in my life, more gratitude for all he is teaching me. Holding onto the loss and pain of what he did is not serving anyone, least of all me. I need to accept who he was and what he did to fully accept myself, flaws and all. He is a part of me, for better or worse.

---

141 Lorraine Copeland, email to author, September 19, 2011.

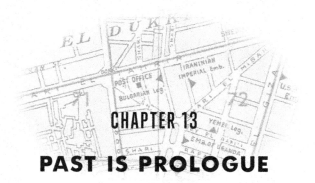

CHAPTER 13

PAST IS PROLOGUE

Hugh Wilford emailed while we were in Key West requesting Jerry Davis's contact information. He wanted to know if the Frank Kearns documentary is more generally available. Jerry had told me the West Virginia station is not offering it to the public because they're using it as part of their membership drive fundraising campaign. I am certain he will give Hugh a private link and am grateful to connect these two men, both helpful guides to my father's past. I hope there will be others. I still want to uncover more of my dad, especially the missing manuscript he'd been working on over his last years.

In April, Jerry Davis emails: "It's with a heavy heart I tell you about the sad news I received this afternoon from Stewart Copeland that Lorraine Copeland died." Another loss. I knew it was coming, but death is a stranger, easy to ignore. My parents' friend in Cairo and Beirut—an archeologist, mother of four, grandmother of fourteen—was ninety-two. In the chase of my father's ghost, she was one of precious few links still alive who knew him. It is a hard reminder that as old people die, living history goes with them; their recollection of direct experience, the vivid images captured by their own eyes, gone. What remains is interpretation, never again enhanced by the deceased's unique memories or countered by their reasoned objections.

By my account Lorraine had a remarkable life and a peaceful death. As a Scottish lass she worked in WWII London for Britain's clandestine secret service that carried out reconnaissance and sabotage in occupied Europe. There she met and married Miles Copeland, Jr. and before the war's end they had their first child, Miles III. Lorraine died at Château Marouatte, the castle that her eldest bought in the 1990s and her granddaughter Barbara now runs as an inn. "She is about to make me a great-grandmother," Lorraine wrote me in 2011. Oh, the blessings of meeting four generations of kin before dying at home.

Miles III had purchased the 270-acre fourteenth-century estate in the 1990s with proceeds from a lucrative music production career. He had managed Sting and his brother Stewart's band, the Police, through their rise to stardom, along with many other groups. The Police had a string of hits in the late seventies and early eighties. Another band Miles produced, the Bangles, recorded the number one hit in 1987: *Walk Like an Egyptian*. But I did not much follow the British punk rock to hit maker pulse that Miles Copeland had his finger on. In 1987 Key West I rocked more to reggae. Bob Marley's *Is This Love* coursed through my veins on Duval Street dance floors when I was lucky enough to have a babysitter. You could say we've traveled in different stratospheres. Now my castle is a one-room cabin with a million-dollar view.

Hugh Wilford provided me with Miles III's email last fall, and his mom's death is good reason for me to reach out to him now. I write a note of introduction with my condolences, explaining how Jerry Davis reconnected me with his most remarkable mother. Assuming he does not remember me, I explain that our fathers had been partners in Beirut and worked closely in Cairo and in the OSS during the war. Our mothers had been close friends. "I would greatly appreciate the opportunity to speak/meet with you sometime about the early years in the Middle East," I write before hitting the *send* key from our home computer. I don't know what to expect. I had tried to reach his brother, Stewart, a few years ago through his fan club to no avail.

Miles writes back the next day. Los Angeles is home, he explains, but he will be in France for six weeks this summer. "You can call me on the phone number below or email any questions, and I will do my best to get you answers." I call right away and leave a message with my numbers—cell and work.

Work is busier than usual. In February, the US Department of Energy awarded us half a million dollars to develop a project bringing together partners in five states to collaborate on petroleum reduction initiatives. The North Carolina Department of Transportation has also awarded us new Congestion Mitigation Air Quality money, and we have recently hired two new team members. All four of us are going to DC at the end of the month for the Alternative Clean Transportation (ACT) Expo. The California consulting group organizing ACT is bringing their annual conference to the East Coast for the first time to attract the attention of national policy makers and build on the growing interest in alternatives to oil. Gasoline prices are still high—hovering at $3.50 for a nationwide average—making it easier to raise awareness about the problem of our oil dependency.

Gathering facts from the Energy Information Administration and other government sources is part of our effort to make the case for change. The alarming reality is that the US, with under 5 percent of the world's population, consumes about 22 percent of global oil production. Transportation uses about two-thirds of the total US share—about thirteen billion gallons a day. I have memorized these facts from years of giving presentations. What surprises me is that we are the world's greatest single user of oil according to *The CIA World Factbook*,[142] and only two other countries charge lower gas taxes than the US. Of note also is that in late 2012, for the first time in fifteen years, the World Factbook added a new major category to each country it covers: energy. Interestingly, the two other countries—Kuwait and Saudi Arabia—with lower gas taxes than the US, are where my father invested a sizable portion of his career and intellectual capital.

Federal taxes on gasoline and diesel have not been raised in the US since 1993. They are not even adjusted for inflation, which has grown over 60 percent in the ensuing twenty years. The increased revenue could help expand alternatives, such as buses and trains, to reduce the use of single occupancy vehicles clogging our highways. A raise in the gas tax could also help support the use of lower carbon, less polluting fuels while encouraging fuel conservation. I am deep into thinking how the state agency I work for, which is not an advocacy group, can promote policy change when my cell phone rings.

It is Miles Copeland III. My heart skips a beat catching up with the unexpected caller. Without written questions in front of me I feel unprepared. At the same time, I'm elated he has called. Miles is ten years my senior, so I ask if he remembers Eich in Beirut. Yes, he remembers all of us. My father was tall with brown hair and a close friend to his father, although he was not much paying attention to these types of things as a teenager. Our conversation pings around as he hits on his own memories of those years.

"We used to make a game of how many capitals we could visit in one day—Cairo, Damascus, Beirut—with no passports, no customs, no security it was so easy to travel."

I wish I had been old enough to do such things.

He continues, "In Cairo, I could ride my bicycle to nearby ruins and explore any neighborhood I wanted. Arab, Jews, Christian, it didn't matter."

"It sure is different now, from what I have heard," I remark.

"Yeah, it's not the same. I was there not long ago. What a tragedy," Miles tells me.

"Especially Syria," I say. "Five thousand people on average are dying there each month—ninety-three thousand since the beginning of the uprising."

Thankfully, he steers away from politics. I don't know why I brought it up. I certainly do not want to get into a conversation about how I think our fathers' work contributed to the mess the Middle East is in now. It is not the kind of subject to bring up on a first phone conversation. I do mention my work promoting alternative fuels as an antidote to imported oil and his offhanded comment on the outsized role oil plays gives me the sense he gets the irony.

"I have been managing belly dancers recently—the Belly Dancer Superstars—it's a lot of fun. We have been touring the world, twenty-two countries including the Middle East. Belly dancers are easier than musicians to deal with. I'm through with managing musicians. They are too much trouble." Miles's tone of finality does not invite further discussion on the matter. I already know something about the troubles of managing Sting and the Police to fill in the blanks.

I tell him about my quest, that I am looking for letters Eich might have written his dad and a draft of my father's autobiography. Perhaps Eich had sent it to his dad to review. "It could be at my home in France," Miles replies. "My father saved everything. I'll look when I go next week."

Thanking him, I share my appreciation of his dad for including so much about my dad in his memoir. "He even titled a chapter 'Copeland and Eichelberger,'" I say."

Miles responds that his dad was really upset with the publisher over *The Game Player* because they had only included half of what he had written. "I'm going to put the entire manuscript on the internet," he retorts.

"Of course, I'd love to read it," I tell him. "Maybe, there's more reference to Eich in the cut pages."

"Could well be," he says as I hang on to every word of this possibility.

"Have you ever considered making a movie about the Middle East spy world in the 1950s and '60s?" I pitch to the music mogul.

"Yes, I am talking to some producers about it now."

"I think it could be a big hit," I reply. "The times and places are ripe with exotica and intrigue."

We touch on a few more topics. He wonders if I have the other half of a tapestry that our mothers found together at the Muski souk in Old Cairo. It is wool and cotton with painted designs and scenes. I remember Lorraine asking me the same thing. Both our moms wanted the Persian wall hanging, so they had the souk salesman cut it in half. "I wish I did," I reply, flattered he knows this story about our moms but disappointed I can't offer to reunite the missing piece with the section he has in France. At least he will be on the lookout for letters from Eich, I hope, as we hang up.

I have the morning of June 24, 2013 free. The ACT Expo starts at the DC Convention Center this afternoon, so I'll use the window of time to visit the National Archives in College Park, the place where Hugh Wilford had found Eich's memo. Two statues catch my attention as I look for the free staff and researcher shuttle to the Maryland branch facility in front of the National Archives downtown. An old man in draped dress, his granite brow furrowed, is sitting with a book in his lap. STUDY THE PAST is carved underneath. Nearby another statue, this one a woman, has

WHAT IS PAST IS PROLOGUE chiseled in the gray-speckled granite. The stone woman is speaking to me.

So is something at the bus kiosk. It is a large color poster of a guy in his twenties with longish hair and a beard, holding a black lab puppy. "Hitchhiker with his dog" is barefoot wearing a macramé necklace, tank top, and colorful flower patches up both legs of his old jeans. His image is part of the Searching for the Seventies photography exhibit currently at the National Archives. His pants look like the patches I sewed on the sleeping bag my boyfriend and I used while hitchhiking through South America in the early '70s. The poster jolts this thought: my generation has become living history. I am fifty-nine years old and still feel like the blonde-haired hippie chick who once picked magic mushrooms in a cow pasture along Ecuador's coast, only now I am a government bureaucrat dressed in business attire, my long hair wound in a bun, who is searching for her dad instead of psychedelic revelations.

Inside the rounded glass entrance to the College Park facility, a self-service kiosk issues me a photo ID, after which a woman at the front desk directs me to the second floor. There I submit my request form for the record groups Hugh Wilford recommended just in time for the 10:30 pull. The archivists have pull times listed on a sign in front of the desk. There are four more today: 11:30, 1:00 p.m., 2:00, and 3:00. I should have plenty of time to look through the four record groups Hugh gave me before catching the shuttle back to DC.

While waiting, I check in with a military archivist in the room adjacent to the request desk. He locates my father's military file, but when I open it the information has nothing more than what I already had through a written inquiry: he was an army captain who received a French Reconnaissance Medal in 1946. What act the medal honored I have no idea, and neither does the thin-faced older gentleman helping me. "My father served in the OSS and then went to work for the CIA after the war," I tell him. "That explains it," he says. "Military records are often stripped for service men who worked for the CIA."

I go back to the front of the desk in line with the several others awaiting their files. The room beyond has light streaming in from its expanse of window-lined walls. It is quiet with the intent of researchers trying to solve their own private mysteries. Some files arrive for those waiting and new people arrive with their requests for the 11:30 pull time. I assume nothing will come during lunch, so I ask for directions to the CREST computers, which Hugh told me about, where recently declassified CIA records are available.

When I type in "James M Eichelberger," a few references come up, nothing directly related to my father. I scan the only one that catches my eye, published the year I was born, and print it on the complimentary machine attached to the computer. A November 1954 *Newsweek* article titled, "Middle East: Fabulous Onassis and Oil" prints on blue paper. Since I grew up in DC in the shadow of John F. Kennedy's assassination in 1963, anything to do with the Kennedys holds my interest. Jackie Kennedy married Aristotle Onassis fourteen years after *Newsweek* published this article about an apparent "explosive situation" the Greek shipping magnate had created. Reading it now, I am learning Onassis made a deal with the Saudis to ship Saudi Arabian oil to Europe. This move cut the US-led ARAMCO from the global delivery line to a region that depended on the Middle East for 75 percent of its oil. The article states, "The possibility of Saudi Arabia developing into another Iran represented a terrible threat to American policy in the Middle East." It would be twenty-two more years before the Arabian American Oil Company fully controlled the oil under its own sands in the desert kingdom. No wonder this was explosive news in the US. We did not want anyone taking over the play in our sandbox. Did this article come up in the search using my father's name because he was working on countering Onassis's moves? As interesting as it is, this is not exactly what I came looking for. I want to find direct evidence of my father—a letter or a signed memo like the one Hugh Wilford discovered.

Back at the front desk, the pull team delivers more boxes on wheeled carts. The 1:00 p.m. pull approaches. I am feeling very impatient. Why is my request taking so long? They have already served everyone who was waiting with me. I ask what the delay is at the desk. The receptionist looks at my request and replies, "Sometimes when a researcher requests a lot of files, it can take some time."

"Oh, I didn't realize I ordered so many," I reply like the novice researcher I am.

Finally, after two more hours, my files arrive. A gray-haired librarian wheels out a tan cart with eighteen file boxes. All three of its shelves are full. I had underestimated the time I'd need. Everyone else I chatted with while waiting is spending several days here. Why did I order all the files Hugh listed for me? He also spent several days here. I only have forty-five minutes before I need to catch the shuttle back to DC and the conference my work paid for me to attend.

I steer my cart to a vacant table next to an older woman with platinum hair in a blue sweater and sneakers, bent over and examining her files. I open one of the boxes Hugh told me was most productive for CIA and Nasser-related State Department files: Record Group 59. Boxes 33 and 34 have documents on Project Alpha, Mask, and OMEGA. I lift the lid from the gray file box #33, pull the first folder out, open the manila sheath, and start to read the onion skin document on the top.

Already the age of this document, its history, feels precious in my hand. Dated November 10, 1955, it has TOP SECRET and THE MIDDLE EAST centered at the top. The body of the memo begins with, "The Premise 1) Our policy in the Middle East has been directed toward retaining the area within the free world, developing the oil resources." Further on, I read about how the "Russians have elected to open a new cold war front" and how a "consistent long-term policy must be devised" for the Middle East. "There is no short cut," it says.

My pulse quickens reading point four. "This Western policy must be based upon the need to have most of the inhabitants of this large area with the West and upon their willingness to let the West have easy access to their oil fields." Who wrote this document? It could have been my father. Whose hands have touched it in the sixty years since? Not much has changed except the price we have paid—are still paying—in blood for "easy access to their oil fields." We still have no long-term policy to wean ourselves from these precedents. However, back then there was no widespread movement to promote the alternatives.

I look up at the clock. It is already time to stop reading and gather the couple of files I want to copy at the pay copier across the room. The memo in my hand is evidence of the dominance oil has played in our political landscape for over half a century. I feel like I am at the right place at the right time. Finding this document buoys the importance of the work of the thousands of participants at the ACT conference I am here to attend. It is no accident that my passion and that of my colleagues for promoting alternative fuels is undoing the work of my father and his colleagues. Examining the past is the only way we can understand how it may inform the present. And now I understand it is critical to acknowledge the underbelly of our political desires to rectify the hidden agendas. This is the way we can grow and change as a people, as a nation.

142 The CIA Fact Book, https://www.cia.gov/the-world-factbook/.

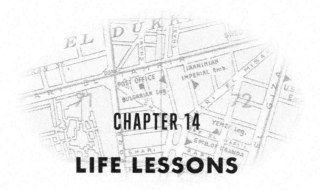

CHAPTER 14

LIFE LESSONS

Another year had flown by. Over the holidays Rio made the decision to move to Washington, DC from Boone, NC, the mountain town where he went to college. The past two years since the fire have been a challenge. After eight months on narcotic pain meds for his injuries he quit them cold turkey. But after quitting alcohol for a year and a half before his rooftop jump, Rio has gotten a DUI since. Our twenty-six-year-old needs a change. On New Year's Eve he took the bus to DC from our house and is crashing with friends till he finds his own place. Richard and I are excited and nervous for him. I distract myself with work and thoughts of my dad. The two seem to go hand in hand these days.

One day, I call a long-time colleague, a man named Earle Spruill, and what was meant to be a forty-five-minute conversation about his extensive career in the ethanol business is lasting close to two hours. He is getting passionate about the challenges. "The oil companies don't want to give up any ground to renewables!" he explains. Earle has been a mentor to me for over a decade now. We do not talk as much as we used to, but in the early days of my alternative fuels work he would patiently explain the ins and outs of the liquid fuel business. Earle started in petroleum and owns his own ethanol distribution company. After the first gasoline crisis in the early seventies, he discovered the benefits of home-grown fuels. We end up with him asking me about my current passion. I explain my wanting to dig deeper into the connection between my work promoting alternative fuels and my father's work for the CIA.

Earle tells me about a high school friend in Christiansburg, VA, whose father was in the CIA. "They [the CIA] were giving him experimental drugs to see when he would break, when he would start revealing things he was not supposed to reveal," he says. "He actually died in CIA custody." The man did not know the people he worked with were giving him LSD. My colleague must be talking about MKUltra, the mind control project the CIA started in the 1950s, but I do not want to go there. I cannot imagine what this kind of duplicity must do to a family. I do not tell my colleague that Eich must have known about this unfortunate program, that my father thought mind games were "better and more effective than LSD."[143]

According to Miles Copeland, Eich was a proponent and practitioner of gas-lighting—manipulating someone by psychological means to make them doubt their own sanity—until Kim Roosevelt reprimanded him for employing these tactics on a contact friendly to the US. The way Copeland portrays it, Eich enjoyed seeing how he could mess with someone's stability. I've had my fill of shame and anger for the dark arts my father allowed his brilliant mind to play in. All to gain the upper hand in the Middle East for the US government, for business, for easy access to oil. I want to discover what drove his younger years. This is my focus now. The years before the CIA.

I suspect WWII had an oversized effect on the young man that became my father. If the "make love not war" landscape of my teen years shaped my generation (and it did), the duty of war is what molded my father's generation. Over the course of World War II, the United States inducted more than ten million men into the military. The bare bone facts of my father's early military service are revealed through a search on Ancestry.com, keeping in mind one of the few tidbits my mother had told me about my father's early years: when Eich was in high school he had convinced his mother to pay for private French lessons.

I imagine my father took to traveling, as I did, to satisfy a yen for adventure and to put his fate in the hands of the universe. He would have also wanted to practice speaking French. Unlike my early avoidance of college, my father's path was more focused. After high school he went to the University of Pittsburgh for a degree in Political Science, then Europe to be a writer.

In 1938, Paris was a mecca for writers and artists. Eich followed the footsteps of twentieth-century literary greats like Lawrence Durrell, F. Scott Fitzgerald, Ernest Hemingway, James Joyce, Henry Miller, and Anaïs Nin. When the Germans bombed Paris and the Vichy Government broke relations with Britain in 1940, there was a mass exodus of expat writers. Some like J.D. Salinger and my father returned to serve the war effort as intelligence officers. From this I deduce that it was his going to Europe as a writer that put Eich in position to become a spy.

I wonder if Eich wrote about Kristallnacht as a freelance reporter when he first arrived in Europe? In November 1938, the "Night of Broken Glass" was a coordinated attack on Jews throughout the German Reich. The firestorm of violence started in Paris with the murder of a diplomat and spread to other cities. Mobs roamed the streets of Berlin and Vienna, breaking windows in synagogues and destroying more than seven thousand Jewish-owned businesses. Although fewer than one hundred died, authorities imprisoned thirty thousand Jewish residents of Germany and Austria. This was the beginning of what would become genocide, the killing of six million Jews.

While ramping up aggression toward the Jews, Germany was

touting new opportunities for tourism. The German autobahn had opened a few years earlier, and tourism posters of the day featured motor tours and car travel. Was Eich penning vacation-themed articles rather than reporting on the growing aggression of Nazi Germany? *In The Game Player*, Miles Copeland writes that after the war my father "remained behind in Paris, moved into an apartment on the Left Bank and [had] begun writing whimsical articles for the New Yorker." From this I speculate my father's reporting before his military service was on the less serious side. Or it could be that after the war my father needed to find his lighter side.

No doubt Eich was more aware than most Americans of Hitler's menace. Many in the US wanted to look the other way when Germany took over France. I need to remind myself that the US did not enter the war for a year and a half after France's occupation. As a young man traveling in Europe, did Eich see what was coming? Could he have imagined that he would soon be using his fluency in French (and possibly German) as a spy serving the Resistance? My father's war time is a puzzle to piece together, to gather intelligence, as it's called in the spy trade.

My father enlisted as a private in the US Army on August 11, 1941 in New Cumberland, PA. At twenty-four years, he was 5'11, weighed 149 pounds, and listed his occupation as an author, editor, and reporter. He had returned from Europe to New York nine months earlier aboard the Vulcania, an Italian passenger ship later taken over by the US to serve the war effort.

In Copeland's memoir my father's war story begins in 1942 London where Miles, Frank Kearns, and Eich shared a furnished flat. The Ovington Square apartment near Harrods Department Store came with a gardener, maid, and housekeeper. As members of the Counter Intelligence Corp (CIC), they talked their way into the posh accommodations by explaining their extended special duty need to be near the African and Asian diplomatic establishments and the US Embassy on Grosvenor Square. World War II training videos for the Office of Strategic Services (OSS) to which Eich, Kearns, and Miles also belonged, show officers gathering intelligence in London's crowded pubs by listening to conversations of their enemies. The phrase "Loose lips sink ships" came from this wartime espionage tactic.

I imagine my father spending hours in popular watering holes, sometimes using an assumed identity to make it easier to gather or pass valuable information. But Miles recounts their time in London as spent plotting the murder of a wealthy English industrialist rather than German or French spies. The intended victim was the manager of a talented and beautiful pianist who was a love interest of Miles. "So," Miles says, "during the next few months, Frank, Eich, and I—in all seriousness—spent most of our time planning to murder a reputable British citizen, and we did so with all the care and professionalism that I later brought to bear on problems of national import when I was working for the CIA."[144]

While I have heard that Miles was an exaggerator—some, like Aburish, say Miles was an outright liar—this story disturbs me. Although the planned execution never took place, to read that Eich focused his attention on the murder of someone standing in the way of his friend's love interest is upsetting. Was this planning exercise to hone their skills or just for amusement? To understand my father, it helps me to put into perspective how different my experience has been from his.

My father was twenty-five when he was in a world war plotting to kill someone from a luxury apartment in London. I was at the same age giving birth to Jamila in a small two-bedroom house that Richard and I shared with a housemate in Key West. Our dear friend and midwife, Gazelle, helped me usher Jamila into the world, one of the most blessed experiences of my life. Could our mindsets have been further apart? I was celebrating new life and my father was plotting death.

In his book, Miles admits to killing six people over the course of his life. Although the retired military man and CIA operative acknowledges what he calls a "glandular deficiency in the morality department,"[145] there is no specific reflection in his writing on the morality of taking another's life, nor the loss of seeing comrades die at the hand of an enemy. Under wartime circumstances and a later career with the CIA, this adaptive remolding of his inner compass was an effective form of protection. The sorry state of my father's life in later years—poverty, alcoholism, and an unfulfilled dream to publish his manuscript evidenced he was not so fortunate.

The thread I see connecting war experience with spy craft is what makes a person a good spy—the ability to deceive an enemy. But what if the enemy is yourself? To possess the skill to pretend, to trick someone else into believing a lie, is also the very thing that cultivates the ability to betray oneself. But that is exactly what you need to do in war time, especially if you are a spy. You most certainly need to deceive. You may need to kill. You may need to pretend to make friends with or even feign love for an enemy in order to survive.

Having lost his father at an early age and betrayed by failed ambition at the end of his life, I believe my father may have been too injured to examine his own pain. He could have been too adroit at deceit for his own good. No matter how proud he acted, the idealism of his youth became a hostage to the disillusionment of experience and misled dreams. Eich was afflicted with scars he nursed with the bottle. It eased the suffering, then created more. His enemy became the despicable inner voice that says we should not trust anybody or anything. And World War II became its proving grounds. Out of necessity the war was a place to hide his sensitivities and test his mettle.

With the German takeover of Paris in June 1940, millions fled south. General Philippe Petain, a World War I hero, set up a government in exile in Vichy, a small spa town in central France. The US initially supported Petain. The aging hero's followers were the nation's industrialists, bankers, and the Catholic hierarchy. This group of elites blamed the leftists, Communists, trade unions, civil libertarians, Freemasons, and Jews for France's defeat by the Germans. However, when the Vichy government became a proxy for the Nazis, the Americans switched allegiance, and the French underground coalesced out of the chaos.[146]

Is this when Eich first met the French poetess with whom he reconnected after he left my mother in Beirut? Copeland mentions the French poetess he had met during the last days of the war.[147] Had they first met in a Paris café and in the clutches of danger done something daring to help defeat the enemy Hitler? Eich must have done something heroic to have been awarded a medal from the French government after the war. It pains me now to be left in the dark surrounding this honor.

Leading up to D-Day in 1944, ninety-three small teams of three agents (one American, one British, and one French) went into France to coordinate actions immediately before the invasion. Having Charles de Gaulle, the new head of the French government, in exile in London made it possible for the Allied command led by General Eisenhower to pass orders to the French Resistance fighters. Their mission was to attack key targets ahead of Operation Overlord, the surprise landing of Allied troops on the beaches of Normandy. D-Day was the largest, most complicated amphibious maneuver in history. While the operation led to the end of German-occupied Western Europe, victory came at great cost. Three-quarters of a million soldiers and citizens across France, Belgium, Holland, and Germany died in the process.

Agents like my father assumed identities and entered occupied territories undercover. They supported actions to divert attention away from the planned landings by blowing up bridges, railway lines, and petroleum depots. They also supported the Resistance with "black" propaganda. By spreading rumors, developing printed materials, and even conducting whole radio shows identified as Nazi programming, the Allies led their enemies astray.[148] Miles Copeland described my father as a propaganda expert when he arrived as a CIA agent in Cairo. I imagine World War II provided his start in this dark art of lies. Perhaps this is how Eich met the French poetess he took up with at the end of the war. Maybe they worked together on an underground paper. Maybe they were involved in broadcasting coded messages signaling the Resistance to begin wreaking havoc on its German occupiers.

World War II research is rooting into my consciousness, fed by stories of people who were there. The investigation is fertilizer for my understanding of pivotal years in my father's life. I check out books from the library with firsthand accounts, follow the OSS listserv, and search the Internet, but the most meaningful stories come from a personal connection. On the Web, I find an account posted by a childhood friend, Duncan Caldwell. I remember playing with the Caldwell kids in their suburban Virginia home outside DC after my parents' divorce. Robert Caldwell's name is on the OSS[149] along with my father's. Duncan's parents and my parents had been good friends. Duncan's father—I called him Uncle Bob—worked with Eich in the CIA, and his mother Ru was an artist like my mom; they painted together. Duncan published Bob's biography *The Spy Catcher* online, crediting his nephew for recording the interviews before Bob's death from a stroke in 2007.[150] It is not my father's story, but it is the closest I have.

According to the book, after one battle, Bob's commanding officer declared, "This is the time, you know, to get medals." He then explained not everyone could get one. Bob's superior wanted his favorite soldier decorated—a fellow Yale graduate—although several men had participated in the same rescue. "So, what I'd like to know," the major continued, "is would the rest of you write up an affidavit telling how he risked his life to save the ensign?" The favoritism made Bob bristle and grow cynical about war medals. Especially after his commanding officer asked them to write an additional recommendation so that he, "the superior," could receive a Silver Star.

Reading about the underhandedness over medals in the US Military makes me further appreciate the recognition my father earned. After the war, the French government awarded the "Medal of Gratitude of a Liberated France" to allies for their notable contribution to freeing France from German occupation. The way I see it, there is no personal stake behind a medal bestowed by a foreign government. Although he wrote about the war, Eich never mentioned the honor to me in his letters. Discovering the US government letter tracing its award to my father after the war is the only bit of information I gleaned through my research into his military files.

"What did he do to be honored by a country that he wasn't even from?" I ask my husband. "It's gnawing at me, another important event in his life and I don't know what he did, whose lives he may have saved and at what personal risks."

"Make it up," Richard encourages over dinner to soothe my frustration with this mystery.

"You know I can't do that," I reply. "I have no imagination for war." That's why I am so captivated with Bob Caldwell's story. It's real. It's close to home. I can imagine his experience as a proxy to my father's war experience.

Toward the end of World War II, Bob was in Germany. He oversaw distributing rations to thousands of concentration camp captives who were left near death by the retreating Nazis in the Landsberg Concentration Camp Complex—feeder camps for Auschwitz. On their way to the last stretch of war, the liberating troops who rolled past this sea of starving humanity brought with them their moral fatigue. How could he and his fellow soldiers have become so unsympathetic, Bob wondered? This insensitivity haunted him. I answer him with my thoughts. We become inured by the devastation. It's a form of protection.

When the Army supply train supporting Bob's efforts moved on, he pled with the mayor of a nearby town for help. The man— who met Bob in full Nazi uniform—adamantly denied that such a horror was taking place nearby until my father's friend forcibly took the mayor to see firsthand the piled bodies of the dead and the barely living emaciates left behind by the retreating Nazis. Denial is also a form of protection, I muse.

After D-Day, the Allied troops were on the offensive beating back the Nazis. They were moving quickly. General George S. Patton's army was racing across France and Germany, but by September 1944 the "Lucky Forward" had to slow down due to a lack of gasoline. Access to oil was a key strategic asset. All the major weapons systems of World War II were oil-powered: surface warships, submarines, airplanes, tanks, and a substantial portion of sea and land transport. Oil was the lifeblood of the war, and supply of the tactical resource affected decisions on the ground.[151]

My father must have known this. He must have seen firsthand what a crucial resource oil was to the future. This must have played into his support of our actions in the Middle East to control more of such assets. While the United States entered World War II with a surplus production capacity of over one million barrels of oil per day,[152] Germany had no such good fortune. One of the reasons Germany turned against its ally, Russia, was that Hitler wanted control of its ample supply.

While Russia was a US ally in World War II, the relationship was more a marriage of convenience than anything else. General Patton was troubled, some say prescient, by the potential threat that Russian communism would play in the West after the war. Thus, Patton was furious he was not allocated petroleum supplies, while other US commanders were. He thought his troops should be sent to the front to finish the war rather than allowing the Russians to take the lead. I wonder if my father agreed.[153]

Immediately after the war, Patton became the Governor of Bavaria, where he headed up "denazification" efforts. At a conference in Potsdam, the three Allied leaders—England, US, and Russia—decided to put on trial all Nazi war criminals and dismantle German industrial assets. Patton was at odds with the US Administration; he believed that rebuilding Germany was critical to holding back the Communist threat of Russia after the war. It made no sense to the General to dismantle Germany's industrial prowess.[154]

Patton's loose lips led the Truman Administration to remove him from his post, not long after the assignment began, for being too soft on the Germans. In reading the press coverage, it is unclear on why with one hand the US government took a course of action and with the other wrote quite a different playbook. Our government relieved Patton of his duties in Germany for being overly concerned about Russian aggression and not concerned enough about the Nazis. At the same time, US counter-intelligence agents were helping Nazis. Miles Copeland describes how the US recruited the best and brightest of these war criminals to help the US government. During the "Paperclip Operation," my father's close friend discloses that, "in every command which housed extensive card files on POWs an especially 'trusted sergeant' sworn to secrecy was to go through the files and affix a paper clip to POWs that could shed some light on German technological superiority."[155] The Counter Intelligence Corp then pulled scientists and spies that could be of use to the US from the POW camps and gave them new identities. The seeds of the US space program sprouted from Nazi brain power cultivated in the ruins of post-war Germany. Miles loved the idea of harnessing German technical knowledge and at first wanted to oversee the "Paperclip Operation." He goes on to write that my father and "others in our Paris CIC unit who were still university liberals at heart would have nothing to do with it, and the Jews among us were practically in tears when they heard about it."[156] As a university liberal at heart, I hang on to these words about my father.

In May 2014 I am in California for the ACT conference in Long Beach. I've arranged to meet with Hugh Wilford who teaches at the nearby California State University. He suggested King's Fish House as convenient to both of us. It's a twenty-minute walk down Pine Street away from the boat docks next to the convention center.

I'm relieved to be in the fresh air under a blue sky, away from the air conditioning. In my briefcase I have Hugh's book, *America's Great Game: The CIA's Secret Arabists and the Shaping of the Modern Middle East*, for him to autograph.[157] When the publisher sent a complimentary copy late last year, I was gratified to see that he recognized me in the foreword and credited me under the photo of Eich. The photo caption reads, "James Eichelberger, the former ad man who coached the leadership of Egypt's revolutionary government while running the CIA station in Cairo." Below the black-and-white photo of Eich is one of Gamal Abdel Nasser, cigarette in hand leaning on his head, bent over a chess board. The caption reads: "Gamal Nasser 'He is very good at chess,' said a friend. 'It's never easy to know his intentions.'" Not so long ago, it would have been easy to say the same about Eich. Thankfully, a clearer picture of my father is starting to emerge.

Hugh is of average height, a trim-framed man with short, graying hair and beard. We greet each other warmly before settling into a wooden booth in the busy restaurant. He tells me about his four-year-old son, and I remark that it is my daughter Jamila's thirty-fifth birthday. "It goes quickly," I say. "Before you know it, they'll be leaving you." We get the waitress's attention to order a couple drinks—he a beer, I a margarita—and begin to discuss the book. The angle Hugh takes in America's Great Game is that early CIA operatives like my dad had the best of intentions to serve the Arabs and Iranians of whom they were fond. They treated Muslims and Arabs with respect and empathy but were engaged in what Hugh refers to as "a modern rematch of the Great Game." It was a 1950s and '60s US redux of the nineteenth-century struggle between Britain and Russia for control over central Asia. Their plans went awry—propping up authoritarian regimes and staging coups—contributing to the sorry state of the Middle East now.

Unintended consequences, rather than maleficence, is easier to stomach than the narrative that so often arises when I think of my father and his colleagues. I am grateful Hugh is showing me that they had good intentions—they supported the Arab cause, loved the culture, and were adventurers at heart—rather than focusing on the way they "played the game" and what the game was all about. In my estimation, the game's goal—resource control and wealth accumulation—has spawned tremendous animosity in the Middle East toward Americans. I would mention the 9/11 attacks, but instead choose to savor the moment.

The drink, the delicious crab cake, the side of sautéed spinach, the honor of Hugh's company, and conversation fill me with a sense of satisfaction. As we split the check, I pull out his book for him to autograph. "To Anne Eichelberger Tazewell with many thanks for all your assistance. Hugh Wilford," he writes with a flourish of blue ink.

I thank him and give him a hug. It means a great deal to me to have made a connection with someone interested in my father, and to have contributed in some small way to this historian's project. More than he could imagine. Finally, I am beginning to understand that cultivating disdain or continuing to judge my father's misguided actions will not bring me peace.

143 Miles Copeland, *The Game Player*, 130.

144 Ibid, 27.

145 Ibid, 64.

146 Lorraine Boissoneault, "Was Vichy France a Puppet Government or a Willing Nazi Collaborator?", SmithsonianMag.com, Nov 9, 2017, https://www.smithsonianmag.com/history/vichy-government-france-world-war-ii-willingly-collaborated-nazis-180967160/.

147 Copeland, *The Game Player*, 218.

148 "The Office of Strategic Services: Morale Operations Branch," News & Information. Historical Document, The Central Intelligence Agency, July 29, 2010.

149 "OSS PERSONNEL FILES—RG 226 ENTRY 224," The US National Archive and Records Administration, accessed July 14, 2021, https://www.archives.gov/files/iwg/declassified-records/rg-226-oss/personnel-database.pdf .

150 Duncan Caldwell, *A Biography of Robert Granville Caldwell, Jr. Part 1: Spy Catcher*, 2009, http://www.duncancaldwell.com/Site/Spy_Catcher,_My_fathers_biography.html.

151 David S. Painter, "Oil - Oil and World Power," accessed June 26, 2021, https://www.americanforeignrelations.com/O-W/Oil-Oil-and-world-power.html.

152 Ibid.

153 Lovelace, A., "George Patton," Encyclopedia Britannica, February 9, 2021, accessed June 16, 2021, https://www.britannica.com/biography/George-Smith-Patton.

154 History.com Editors, "General Patton questions necessity of Germany's "denazification," accessed July 25, 2021, https://www.history.com/this-day-in-history/patton-questions-necessity-of-germanys-denazification.

155 Copeland, *The Game Player*, 64.

156 Ibid.

157 Hugh Wilford, *America's Great Game: The CIA's Secret Arabists and the Shaping of the Modern Middle East* (New York: Basic Books, 2013).

The only picture I have of my father with his parents, Homer &
Mary Eichelberger, Pittsburgh, PA. (Circa 1926)

My father, James M Eichelberger (Eich) learned spy craft
as a Captain of Military Intelligence in WWII.

My mom Alice Hirshman Eichelberger, an artist,
in her sassy days at the Art Institute of Chicago.

Alice (pregnant with me) , Eich and our poddle Robert AKA Go-Go,
on the beach, perhaps in Alexandria, Eqypt 1954.

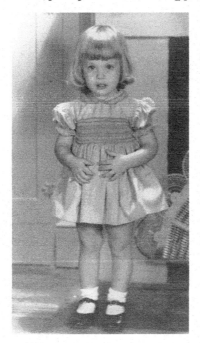

Ann Mary Eichelberger 1956.

Left to Right : On the fence Stewart Copeland, Ann Mary Eichelberger &
Ian Copeland, in our Beirut Lebanon back yard circa 1958.

My dad, James M Eichelberger, the idea man. I wonder what he was thinking.

The look of love: my baby brother James (Jay) Kurz Eichelberger
with Mom and me in Beirut, Lebanon 1959.

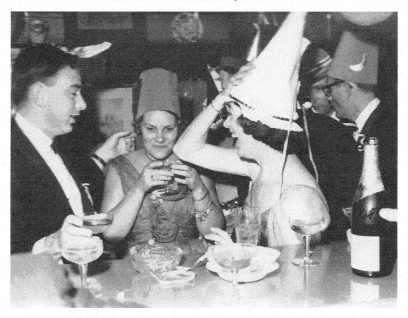

Party on: My mom Alice (on right) celebrating New Years Eve in the
Middle East with Lorraine Copeland (center) and unidentified man.

Left to Right: In our Beirut back yard on Rue Maamari, Stewart Copeland, my nanny, me (Ann Mary) and, my neighbor hood friend Renda.

Key West Sunset at Mallory Pier 1979. Left to Right, Richard Tazewell,
Din Allen, Jamila Tazewell, Anne Tazewell and Quint Lange.

Jamila and Richard in the Cameron Highlands of Malaysia 1981.

Anne & Jamila, in our yard at 1211 Laird Street, Key West Florida.
Photo courtesy of Karen Gladstone.

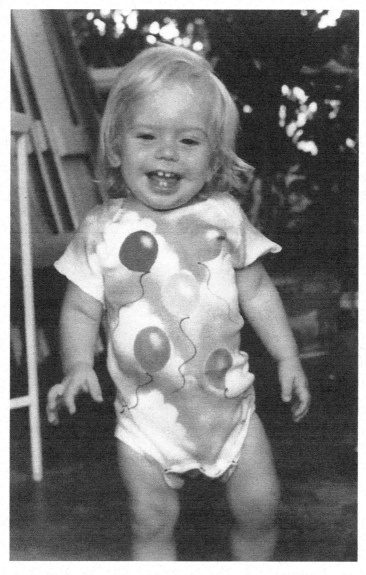

Rio Walke Tazewell modeling his Mom's airbrushed children's
clothing on our Key West porch 1988.

Taylor Kurz Tazewell enjoying the airplane his Dad made from scrap
wood and a bicycle tire at Laird Street Key West, 1992.

CHAPTER 15

A LOOK AT LIFE BACKWARDS

After California in May I have another work trip that takes me to DC in June. The US Department of Energy's Annual Merit Review of all the grant projects they support is at the old Wardman Park Hotel near Calvert Street and Connecticut Avenue. I have never actually been in the historic hotel but certainly knew about it growing up. This part of the city was my stomping grounds. My home from second through twelfth grade is only a couple of miles from the Wardman. With my morning session over and a free afternoon ahead, I decide to try a Capitol Bikeshare rental to visit my old neighborhood. Rio had already shown me how easy it is to use the ubiquitous banks of big red bikes that invite short-term use.

Climbing on the hefty machine, I head north on Connecticut Avenue and turn left at Van Ness Street. I peddle slowly up the hill, formerly the leafy grounds of the National Bureau of Standards when I was growing up, but now the campus of the University of the District of Columbia. At Reno Road I turn right, approaching our old two-story brick home in anticipation. What first catches my eye is how much the Japanese maple has grown. Its crimson leaves in the fall are still burned in my memory. This is the first home I remember. To my surprise the front door is open, allowing a glimpse of a workman sanding the stairway to our second floor. After parking the bicycle, I gently rap on the door and explain to the young man that I grew up in this house. "Do you think I could come in for a moment and look around?" I ask.

"Wait a minute," he instructs. "The owner is here, let me get her." A stylish woman with short dark hair and lovely eyes appears, introducing herself as Sonia. She is delighted to hear I grew up here. "Yes, please come in and look around, but pardon the mess; we are in the last stretch of a total remodel and racing to get it on the market." The owner introduces me to the woman next to her, her real estate agent. I inquire about the asking price for the three-bedroom house and she states that it is $1,090,000.

"Wow! My mother bought it for $20,000 back in 1961 and sold it for $300,000 in the late 80s," I tell her, as part of my family history with the house. "After recovering from cancer that left her legs partially paralyzed, my mother was unable to go up and down the stairs."

"Take your time to look around," Sonia says. "I'm really sorry it's such a mess. I'm moving back to Spain next week, but I'll miss this house. My two children started their lives here, so it will always hold a special place in my heart."

The rooms are a jumbled mess, yet the guts of my old home are the same. It is obvious Sonia's two young children had the bedrooms that were Jay's and mine. I pause to scan my second-floor room and peer out the side window. In eighth grade I jumped out of this window to get away from Mom during one of our fights. I landed on all fours and ran to my girlfriend's house about a mile away where I spent the night, hidden in her basement. The next day I returned home for a Christmas Eve reconciliation.

Walking into what was once my mother's bedroom, I notice the bed in the same place hers was three decades ago. The last eight months I lived here, Mom was lying in a hospital bed which was in the exact position that this queen size bed is now. I was caring for her with hospice help. She was an angel during this period. All malice drained from her bone-thin face, replaced with gratitude to be alive. Appreciation like I had never seen before sparkled from the windows of her eyes. A well of sadness surfaces in my seeing this empty bed and realizing just how much she must have suffered. My mother was younger than I am now when she lay here dying. Tears trickle down my face with this understanding. I am glad the others are downstairs.

After an unexpected recovery (whoever gets out of hospice alive?), Mom was wheelchair-bound for ten years until she died at sixty-seven. Here I stand, fit and fine, having just ridden a bicycle a couple of miles while anticipating a lovely dinner with my son this evening. Why did she have to become handicapped at fifty-six, then die so young? Before I had the courage to ask what happened between her and Eich, to the star-crossed union that created me?

Fear had trounced my courage. Fear of facing what had crippled my mother. Fear of facing my mother's pathos coupled with my father's abandonment. Fear of how their fractured dreams affected me.

I walk back downstairs and turn right into the living room. In the jumble of upended furniture, I notice our old fireplace on the south wall. It hasn't changed. That's where the brass peacock screen stood. I look to the wall behind me and imagine the Kuwait chest with the Paul Klee print hung above it. The signed Matisse print was on the opposite wall. It's odd that I can recall the exact placement of furniture and art but not my father's face. The only time I remember my father in this house was when he was in this room and Mom called me from my bedroom to ask with whom I would rather live. This was the moment I realized there was no right answer, that there would always be something missing.

"Did you go up to the attic?" Sonia asks as she walks in, interrupting my thoughts.

"Yes, it's stunning now, especially the deep red walls."

"I renovated it to be my architect studio. What about the bedrooms?"

"I loved seeing your son's things in the bedroom my brother had," I reply, walking around the corner past the basement stairs. The ground floor still has the circular layout I remember. Jay and I would run the round track between the living room, kitchen, and dining room, sliding across the tile of the dining room floor to catch each other as if we were on ice skates.

After a brief look at the basement—my teen hangout spot and where I slept while caring for Mom—I am ready to leave. It is a peculiar feeling to be here after so many years and see it in such disarray. Every room is torn apart, just as my life was torn apart by my parents' divorce when we moved here.

"Thanks so much for having me," I say to Sonia.

"Thank you for coming by. I knew this house had good karma—and that there had been other children who grew up here—so it's been a pleasure to meet you. Really, you've made my day."

"The pleasure is mine," I say, thanking her again and noting the humor of her assumption of a happy childhood, as I walk out the back door onto what was our screened-in porch. It is now an air-conditioned sunroom, the locust tree still shading it. Under the furrowed arms of this tree I had cajoled a young squirrel to come to my outstretched palm with a peanut. Through this daily ritual we became acquainted. I looked forward to seeing him after school. He was my introduction to nature—a world of trees, sky, acorns, rain—what would become my saving grace. Once I was able to pet his soft fur. Recalling this relationship with such a different creature is a reminder that I crave connection.

Back on my red bicycle, I ride up our old alley and out onto the side street, briefly stopping to pay homage to the oak trees on Warren Street. Crouched next to these trees collecting acorns, I first mused on my own mortality. As an eight-year-old I wondered: if forced to choose one of us to die, would I pick myself or my mother? Would I choose to live if it meant my mother had to die? Collecting the leathery green nuts, I could not answer this question.

I had already banished thoughts of my father in order to protect my mother. Thus, imagining life without him felt normal, but the idea of life without her stymied me. What good was whining about my concerns when she was already the walking wounded? My subconscious was a quick learner: my mother had a burden to bear bigger than me. She had lost her mate, someone to care for her. Before our move to Washington my mother did not even know how to drive. Other than organizing watercolor classes for her girlfriends in Beirut, she had not worked. But as I started second grade, walking distance from our home on the tree-lined streets of upper northwest, my mother was driving across the city to low-income neighborhoods as a traveling art teacher for the DC public schools.

Continuing up Warren Street, I spot an elderly couple sitting on the front porch of the house of Jay's best childhood friend. I have not seen Ruth and Fred Perna in thirty years, and they are just as surprised as I am. Jay keeps in touch with their son, so they have heard what I am up to, and I had heard their eldest daughter died of cancer last year. We remark on the coincidence of seeing each other after so long in a city that has seen such tremendous change. "Yes, they will be taking me out of here feet first," Mr. Perna says.

How quickly life passes. With each pump of the bicycle pedal my thoughts turn from moving to this neighborhood as a second grader to when I moved out after high school, only briefly returning when Mom was so ill. I think of my father's life at the same time and how separate we became. When I moved here, he was starting with Wanda Jablonski's *Petroleum Intelligence Weekly* in New York. When I graduated from high school in 1972 and left with my boyfriend for Jamaica, Eich had already moved to

Laurel, Maryland with Patsy Cooper—although I did not visit him there until 1981 when I took Richard and Jamila to meet him. And then again when I lived with Mom while she was in hospice. By then Patsy had died, and he had moved to DC to live on Sixteenth Street at the Roosevelt.

After so many decades, I am making up for lost time but with so many dead ends and jumbled thoughts, I am doubting that it will lead to what I am looking for. Passion is powerful fuel yet offers no guarantee of destination, nor does it explain what I am after. How to forgive a dead man? How do our small stories fit in a wider political whole? These questions drive me.

While I continue to pedal, looking for answers, I realize it is better to look at what is in front of me. Rio and I are spending the weekend together just over the Potomac River in Pentagon City. We have accommodations that my brother and sister-in-law are not using. It's a seventeenth floor two-bedroom suite with a view of the river, the Washington Monument, and other landmarks. I can even see the National Cathedral from our balcony since the church was erected on the highest point of land in the District. This landmark is where Mom would take Jay and me to church on Easter.

After crashing with friends for a couple of months, Rio is renting a room in Petworth. Our weekend apartment is a change of pace from his day job at the moving company and evenings spent writing cover letters for work applications to DC policy groups. On Monday he has a second interview with People for the American Way, a nonprofit started in the early '80s by Norman Lear—the creator of the long-running TV show *All in the Family*. They want Rio to prepare a sample press release as part of the interview process.

"Instead of writing a boring press release about some senator who has just announced a new bill to curb the influence of money in politics," I suggest that evening while we are soaking in the outdoor hot tub next to the pool, "why don't you write about something that will catch their attention?"

"Like what?" he asks.

"Like make the press release be an announcement about an anonymous donor who has just given PFAW $1M for a video contest. The contest can be about getting the money out of politics."

I love that my son is open to suggestions. We go back and forth on the idea. By Sunday morning, he has rewritten the press release and I am keeping my fingers crossed that he gets the job. He has had six or seven interviews in the six months he has been here and made it to the final round with a couple of them. The good news is, he has quit drinking again. In April he had a blackout experience that scared him. I do not ask for details and he does not offer any, but I always feel better leaving my son when he is not imbibing.

The summer passes in a rush of activity. In October, my team and I host six hundred attendees at the Raleigh Convention Center for the first Southeast Alternative Fuels Conference and Expo. Afterwards Richard and I drive to DC to visit Rio. Our son got the job with People for the American Way and is working with groups across the country to overturn Citizens United—the controversial Supreme Court ruling that cleared the way for corporations and other special interest groups to spend unlimited amounts of money on election campaigns. He gives us a weekend tour of his sixth-floor office on Fifteenth Street, all glass-walled with light streaming in from the October sky. It is much nicer than my office at NC State University where I only see a sliver of blue.

From there we go to his favorite Sunday afternoon DC happening, a drum circle at Meridian Hill Park. What began as a small group of African American drummers and dancers has grown into a multicultural mix of individuals and families celebrating the creative arts. As Richard, Rio, and I sit along the stone wall next to the line of conga players, I take in the view. There are picnickers and tightrope walkers on the lawn behind us, with hula-hoopers and jugglers spread around the cluster of drums. The sound is tribal, deep thumps from the skins like heartbeats from some long-ago time.

I remember Meridian Hill Park from when my dad lived on the next block over, Sixteenth Street. While Mom was in hospice and I was caring for her, I visited him at his apartment. Eich met me in the tiled lobby of the Roosevelt and escorted me to the fifth floor. At sixty-five his hair was still thick and mostly brown, but he moved slowly and complained about his gouty leg. Settling into his small living room, Eich had explained how Patsy's daughter Delores had helped him move after Patsy's death the previous year.

We sat close to each other, he in a worn leather easy chair and I on a straight-back. My father pointed to a Kodachrome of the two of us in our Beirut garden, tacked to the cork bulletin board propped on the radiator beside us. In the photo I am wearing a white smocked dress sitting in front of Eich, who is in a red plaid shirt and holding a drink. Go-Go is next to me, and the sun is shining on the three of us while the rest of the photo is in shadow. I know he pointed out the snapshot to say that he never forgot me.

Eich did not discuss the circumstances of Patsy's death, nor did he ask about Mom's health. Rather, he talked about his writing and inquired about Jamila and Richard. I did not tell him that Richard and I were having marital problems after the affair I had the year before in Key West. As I was departing, he leant me a chapter about World War II he was working on, and in the hallway introduced me to a friend, his next-door neighbor. Genie was a sprightly, gray-haired woman. I admired the silver pendant hung on a leather cord around her neck featuring a cross with a circle on top—Agape, the ancient Greek symbol for love.

Back at the house, when Mom and Jamila were asleep, I tried to read the typed document Eich lent me, but it made no sense. To my twenty-seven-year-old brain, the writing sounded like the scattered ramblings of an old man. The words provided no foundation from which to build meaning. I am not even sure I read through the whole thing; it was that confusing. Perhaps I took for granted that there would be other times to get to know him, after Mom died, so there was no urgency. My dying mother, my three-year-old, and my crumbling marriage were consuming me. There was little room for my father. When I returned the manuscript, I didn't have the foresight to ask about his war experience and the chapter I'd just tried to read. All I recall is Eich informing me his friend Genie no longer lived across the hall at the Roosevelt.

"After answering a knock on her door last week, she was beaten almost to death by thugs and has gone to live with her daughter on the Eastern Shore," my father explained.

Nearby Meridian Hill Park was a dangerous drug haven, Eich told me then, a place full of junkies and glue sniffers. Now the city block-sized park is known for its family-friendly drum circle, and I am visiting the neighborhood for the first time since I was twenty-seven with my twenty-seven-year-old son. While Rio and Richard find a grassy spot on the field to jam on guitar and melodica, I take a walk to look at the building where Eich lived. It is now much more upscale. As I peer into the window of the brass-rimmed front door and consider ringing the doorbell, a young man walks out. I take advantage of the opportunity to walk in. There is a grand piano to the right of the entrance and an African American woman behind a desk across the chandeliered lobby. I tell her my father lived here in the 1980s. She grew up in the neighborhood and remembers the place when it was an old folks' home. "It was almost torn down," she tells me. "There was a drawn-out battle with the city, and when the last elderly person died it sat vacant for almost ten years."

"It sure is beautiful now. Do you mind if I look around?"

"Certainly, please," she replies. There is a billiards room, a wood-paneled library, a stone wine cellar, and the more modern addition of a gym and climbing wall. I walk over to the elevator and remember Eich slowly pulling the metal-caged door closed, then pressing the round black button for the fifth floor. If the ghost of my father is living here, I expect he is happy. The dingy and run-down lobby is nothing short of grand now. It's troublesome that I can remember the lobby and his apartment thirty-five years later but cannot recollect anything Eich had written in the manuscript he lent me. The Agape necklace Genie was wearing is in the safety deposit of my mind, whereas my father's World War II story is missing from my memory.

Why hadn't I asked my father about his writing when he was alive? It didn't even occur to me to make a copy of the document he lent me. Although we rarely saw each other, I daydreamed that if my mother died before my father, he would come to live with us—that there would be time to get to know each other in his twilight years. Despite my mother's enrollment with hospice and her dire prognosis, she outlived Eich by four years.

"One understands life backward but lives it forward," a friend once commented. I have wedged this adaptation of Danish philosopher Soren Kierkegaard's quote in my consciousness for decades, shelved next to my thoughts on "Reading Life Signs and Making Meaning." I make sense of my avoidance of my father when he was alive by taking to heart Kierkegaard's saying. With age, my vantage point has shifted. I can look backwards. I can try to make connections. Because they are painful, I prefer skirting the edges.

"You won't believe how nice the Roosevelt is now," I say, returning to my music makers. I love that both our sons play music with their dad, that they share a language of rhythm and melody beyond words.

"Rio, I picked up a brochure from the apartment where your grandfather lived." The cover has a framed image of the building with the caption: "The picture of fine living." Inside is a photo of what feels like the two hundred steps I just walked up to the grassy field of the park. With all its steps, Meridian Hill Park reminds me of a Mayan Ruin.

"I'd love to live there," he responds. "I want to move closer to my office, someplace I can walk to. I'll definitely check it out. Thanks."

"Wouldn't it be something if Rio moved into the apartment where Eich lived?" I say to Richard on our drive home to North Carolina.

"Yes, it would."

"Then you two could jam on the grand piano in the lobby."

CHAPTER 16

MAGICAL THINKING

I t is February 2015 and Richard and I are in Key West, renting a friend's houseboat for a week. Our friend Kendal has driven down from North Carolina to join us. It is difficult to imagine the rest of the East Coast pounded with snow, ice, and freezing temperatures when we are sitting on the Garrison Bight pier in short sleeves, watching a manatee. The lumbering sea cow is drinking fresh water from a neighbor's hose. For Richard it is a work trip. He has a gig up the Keys at Little Palm Island—an exclusive resort previously used by Harry Truman as a fishing camp. The three-acre island is accessible only by boat or sea plane. A wooden launch used in *PT 109*, the 1964 movie about JFK's South Pacific WWII experiences, shuttles staff and guests back and forth. Picture Gilligan's Island meets the Ritz.

I am along for the much-welcomed sun and seeing old friends. Being here immerses me in the nostalgia for a part of the world where I spent fifteen years, yet my more current pursuit—understanding my father's world—surrounds me. Magically, everything feels connected.

"You know how it is when you first discover something, you start to notice it everywhere?" I ask Kendal as we are riding bikes to see my friend Mira in a play at the Red Barn Theater. "How when you become immersed in a subject you begin to make connections between it and everything else?"

"Yes, it's like what John Muir said: 'When we try to pick out anything by itself, we find it hitched to everything else in the Universe.'"

"Exactly, that's what I am finding in Key West."

I am thinking about my dad, and I've just realized that my affinity for tropical places was born in the Middle East. In Key West, the sultry breeze, the scent of jasmine, the rustle of the palms evoke my earliest sensual experiences. "This feels like home because it connects me to my beginning," I tell my friend as we near our destination, turning our bicycles off Duval Street toward the Key West Women's Club. We park down the narrow alley next to the Red Barn Theater, which some of our friends began in 1980, the year after Richard and I moved here pregnant with Jamila.

After the Red Barn show, we meet Bob over drinks at the Hard Rock Café's outdoor bar. Bob is Mira's neighbor on Sugarloaf Key. We are talking about the current price of oil, and I mention how Saudi Arabia's eighty-two-year-old Prince Talal is advocating for the creation of a fund independent of the government to help prepare for the post–oil era. "Oil could dry up, but there are alternatives in the market," Talal had said in a Valentine's Day 2013 interview.

"Don't get your hopes up that the rest of the Royal Family is listening," Bob says. "All they care about is the money. That's why they have not cut back on oil production, although the price dropped to $32 a barrel—about a third of what it cost at the start of 2014. If oil is above $20 a barrel, they make money."

I explain how the price drop is making my job more difficult, that alternative fuels are a much harder sell now that gasoline is $2.20 per gallon versus close to the four dollars it was a couple of years ago. "I am impressed that the elderly prince is speaking up for fuel diversity," I say to connect my father's world to mine and this friendly stranger's. Bob is an ex-military man and a United

Airlines pilot. He has businesses in Kenya and Tanzania, spends time in Saudi Arabia, and is friends with some of the Royal Family.

"The Saudis are good people. They make friends for life— unlike Americans who often let friendships fall by the wayside," Bob tells me over the course of our conversation. I lap up his wide-ranging insights along with my margarita. Through his charter airline business, Bob flies the Royals he is friendly with from Saudi Arabia to their private game reserves in Kenya. The princes are there to party. While their wives go to the cities to shop, the men enjoy high-end hookers imported from Russia.

I could have listened to him much longer than the evening allowed. Bob's firsthand stories corroborate my opinions on the excess and hypocrisy that has been undermining the Kingdom since its inception. Dating back to my father's days in the Middle East, there's been a struggle in Saudi Arabia between forces wanting progressive change, like women's rights, and those wanting to maintain the King's autocratic rule, guided by a religious council with a backward-facing interpretation of Islam. Women are stoned to death if found to have had sexual relations outside of marriage. In the 1950s, Prince Talal led the Free Princes, a movement through which a group of Royals advocated for establishing a form of representative government in Saudi Arabia. King Saud exiled Talal for a time because of this effort. Now the octogenarian is calling for the kingdom to consider alternatives to the oil that's made these men some of the wealthiest in the world. I wonder what Eich would think of Talal's efforts? Today, predicting the Saudis' next move in the oil game is lucrative business for investors. If my father was alive now, he could easily make a good living as an oil industry consultant.

At the houseboat the next day, I am scrolling through work emails while drinking my morning tea with Richard when I notice a message from Dan Egan. I remind my husband that Dan is the

Middle East researcher who thought he met my brother in a DC bar after the bartender mentioned my dad's name. We both reminisce for a moment on what a bizarre story that was. Now Dan tells me that on behalf of my quest to learn more about my dad's career he has emailed Raymond Close, whom he calls, "a CIA legend and great American patriot." Ray was in Beirut when Eich and Miles were working there as oil industry consultants. He didn't really know my dad but knew Miles well, having worked under him in DC from 1951 to 1953 when Miles was the Near East Division Chief. Taking a sip of his Cuban coffee, Richard asks what Raymond Close had to say about Miles Copeland in the email Ray had written that Dan had forwarded to me. After pausing to notice how the light is dancing on the water from the deck chairs squeezed onto the houseboat's narrow stern and realizing how my father would have loved Key West, I read Ray's email out loud.

"Anne might appreciate this personal observation from me: Anyone who knew Miles Copeland was aware of his lively imagination and charming personality. It was hard not to admire him for the first attribute and love him for the second. However, it must be said, I believe, that his creativity was not always balanced by sound judgment, and, frankly, many of his colleagues (certainly of my generation), were often apprehensive that Miles, at any moment, might do or say something that would embarrass his colleagues or cause problems that would make our jobs much more difficult or even dangerous."

I can just imagine Miles with his larger-than-life persona and seemingly come-what-may attitude causing consternation with his colleagues.

"You've been saying all along Miles was known as a liar at worst and an exaggerator at best," Richard says.

As I take my last sip of tea, I notice a pair of seagulls flying in front of our bow before replying.

"My mom did not like him, and Miles blamed her for my parents' marital problems. Ray also says Miles was making things up and inflating his position in his autobiographical writing. But in his defense, I don't think Miles could have gotten his memoir published had he not mixed made-up stories with the truth. The CIA is definitely tight-lipped about what it lets out."

"Yeah, but I get Ray's point and really don't like folks who make themselves bigger and more important than they are," my husband responds.

"I know. I tend to be more accepting of different personalities, but if Miles was really putting his CIA colleagues at risk, that's a different story."

In the email, Ray goes on to comment: "For many years we were all very thankful that Jim Eichelberger was there as sort of an *alter ego*, to give Miles sober advice when it was called for and to temper his sometimes-dangerous flights of fancy. (Some would even say that Jim was greatly appreciated for providing Miles Copeland with much-needed 'adult supervision,' but that might sound disrespectful of one of the Agency's legendary characters.)"[158]

Richard and I agree that it was nice that Ray took the time to shed some light on my dad. Even if Ray didn't know him personally, it says something about his reputation among his peers. On our bike ride to Fort Zachary Taylor to meet our friend Claudia, I ponder the past and how it makes its way into the present.

In addition to the happenstance conversation with a Middle East expert through Mira, and the unexpected email connection to my dad through Dan, a third link presents itself through Claudia. Her father was a German diplomat. Like my father, his job with the Embassy was his cover. Claudia's father worked for the BND, the German equivalent of the CIA. This was the first time I had thought to ask her about her childhood. While I have known both

Mira and Claudia since moving to Key West over thirty-five years ago, back in those days no one would have thought to ask about someone's past. We were who we were by *where* we were. Key West was the end of the road; a one-by-four-mile island where we could be who we wanted to be. It still is, just much more expensive and crowded in tourist season.

To make our livings, Claudia and I painted T-shirts to sell at the daily Mallory Square Sunset Celebration. We brought folding tables to the pier at the western tip of the island to display our wares. Mine were airbrushed children's outfits, hers hand-painted adult tees. In the mid-1980s, I was a board member of the Cultural Preservation Society, the non-profit still managing the nightly dockside ritual. We were a group of street performers and vendors managing a carnival of commerce to celebrate one of nature's great performances. Everyone gathers to clap hands as the sun goes down. Sometimes there are majestic colors crowning the sky with red, orange, and purple. Other times the red ball slips unadorned behind the Gulf waters.

The circus atmosphere continues at Mallory Square. Over time the pier has seen tightrope walkers, jugglers, fire eaters, even performing cats and a man who balanced a bicycle on his head. My favorite part of the evening is after sunset when the last finger of light is giving way to dark. Everything quiets down. That is when I found Claudia this visit. She was packing up to pedal her bicycle rig back home across the island. We made plans to get together at Ft. Zachary State Park at the tip of the island where the Atlantic Ocean meets the Gulf of Mexico.

The following day, Claudia finds us at one of the picnic tables just off the beach. We get to chatting and I discover that, like me, her parents divorced when she was young. Claudia grew up in London, Paris, and Berlin not knowing what her father did with the embassies in these European capitals. It was not until much later in life she learned her father was a spy. Because he was quite strict and opinionated, Claudia became estranged from her father and rarely spoke with him after leaving home. He had prohibited her from studying art in college, so she pursued a master's degree in literature instead. Shortly after graduating from the University of Munich, she moved to the US.

"I called him on his fifty-eighth birthday but cut the conversation short because I was in a hurry to do something else," she explains with a touch of regret. "Shortly after that, he died suddenly."

Regret is something I am continually aware of as I search for a relationship with my father now in his grave. The feeling is a constant companion, although I try to pay it no mind. For Claudia, regret is more nuanced. It is not so palpable. She does not wear it on her sleeve. But both of us agree that there is struggle entwined with our misgivings. We tussle with hidden identities. Who were our fathers? Neither of us could say.

We corroborate on how the horror of World War II must have fed our fathers' demons. Like my father, a mandatory draft in World War II forced her father into service. After the war her father, like mine, worked undercover for his country on secret missions. We surmise, for a time, that they were both driven by what they believed.

"Toward the end of the war, in desperation, Hitler drafted young teens," Claudia explains. "My father was one of them. He became disillusioned though, by the end of his time with the BND. Alcohol had gotten the best of him."

"Same as my father," I say with a freeze-framed image from my last visit with my dad at the Roosevelt. Richard and Jamila were with me. It was brief, and I do not recall a conversation of any substance. Only the jumbled scene haunts me: overflowing ashtrays, plates of half-eaten food, stacks of books, and empty liquor bottles in the crowded living room, his tiny kitchen full of dirty dishes.

———————————

A week after our Key West sojourn, I am back in DC for two work-related meetings. Before moving over to Richard's cousin's house, where I often stay, I am overnighting with Rio in his ninth-floor apartment. In December he moved into the building *next door* to the Roosevelt. His living room looks out on the sidewalk treetops and the grandeur of Meridian Hill Park.

"I tried to get an apartment at the Camden Roosevelt, but they are too expensive. This place is cheaper, and the view is amazing."

"Yes, it certainly is!" I reply. From this bird's-eye view, the park looks even more like a Mayan temple with all its stone steps. "Cheers!" I say, holding up the cup of herbal tea, our shared beverage now that he has quit drinking. "Your ancestors are smiling down on you." Out of all the places in the City, what does it mean that Rio has moved next door to where his grandfather lived?

In addition to celebrating Rio's recent move, we are also catching up on his good fortune at People for the American Way. I tell him how proud I am of him.

"I can't believe you got a random call at work from a guy who found you on the Internet a couple months ago and now he wants to donate $100,000 to PFAW to run a video contest. That's exactly the idea I suggested for your press release when you were interviewing for your job."

"Yeah, amazing, right?" my son says. "Jeff started a direct marketing company in the '90s, made hundreds of millions, and had an epiphany on a hike that he wanted to get into social activism. This is his first foray, and he decided money in politics is the issue to tackle because it's related to solving every other issue."

"I can't believe your luck. I don't know anyone who has had

this kind of money drop in their lap to support an issue they are so passionate about."

There are a lot of details to work out, of course. Jeff started his own nonprofit last year focused on passing a Constitutional Amendment to overturn Citizens United. The forty-something-year-old has never worked with a national nonprofit before and PFAW has never worked with someone with ambitious ideas but no political experience. Jeff's initial offer of $100,000 and the potential for more is helping the process along. Plus, it's useful experience for my son to learn how to negotiate the needs of the many parties involved to make something happen.

Serving the needs of multiple stakeholders is also the aim of the meeting I am attending in DC. Many different business interests are pushing forward an agenda of fuel diversity and reduced dependence on oil. The US Department of Energy invited about one hundred industry experts to help chart the course of the Clean Cities program over the next five years. The strategic planning meeting is taking place at the US DOE headquarters on Independence Avenue SW, just down the street from the Smithsonian Museum of African Art, one of my mother's favorites. Much of DC is still etched in my mind, but the DOE building is new to me. Known as the Forrestal Building, it is a low-slung construction of glass and bare concrete, an aptly named example of Brutalist architecture. It's not exactly welcoming. Nevertheless, I am happy to be here. I really believe in the Clean Cities mission—building government coalitions—local, state, and national—with fuel providers, vehicle manufacturers, transit operators, and fleet managers. I don't always agree with the DOE's administration of the Clean Cities program, but it's satisfying to be part of an event that is bringing together multiple interests to forward an agenda of reduced petroleum dependence.

It is no secret that I have been trying to start a fourth coalition in North Carolina to cover areas not included in the three current coalitions in the Triangle, Charlotte, and Asheville areas. But the DOE cannot provide for new coalitions—there are just not enough federal dollars to support them. It's a struggle for resources, and they are not going to sacrifice relations with the existing coalitions. In some states, regional coalitions have expanded to represent the whole state, but that will never happen in North Carolina because of local politics and DOE's reluctance to get involved. Because NC State University, where I work, serves the whole state, the local coalitions see our bid for a fourth coalition as a potential takeover threat. This is not our intention, nor is it politically feasible.

I must adapt to the situation or continue to be frustrated. Or it could be said, "adapt to reality or watch my bitterness grow." How can I best serve? Considering the stakes in overcoming our fossil fuel addiction, it will take all of us pulling together. Though I will not be a coalition coordinator again, I am grateful that DOE now recognizes I can bring value and expertise to the big picture.

Inside the public entrance, I join the line to get my visitor ID, then get in a longer line to get my laptop bag security checked—catching up with professional contacts I have made over the years who are also waiting in line. Our meeting is in the basement, down a nondescript hallway, past DOE's travel center, inside a dark auditorium. First, we write down what we consider to be the best markets for each alternative fuel. Open discussion and breakout groups on natural gas, biofuels, fuel economy, propane, electric and hybrid electric vehicles, and idle reduction follow. Back in the auditorium, DOE staff summarize the points brought up in the breakout groups. For example, should they encourage propane or biodiesel-powered school buses as the best market for these fuels? Underlying this exercise is a competition for resources. It is a daunting task to synthesize and serve so many interests within the confines of government programs with limited funding, subject to political forces outside the administrators' control. The next administration may not like what DOE's Office of Energy Efficiency and Renewable Energy is doing and could eliminate or drastically reduce Clean Cities funding. I do not envy their jobs. By the end of the day, I am ready to leave.

I am meeting Delores and Robert for dinner at Zaytinya, a twenty-minute walk from DOE headquarters, across the National Mall, down Ninth Street. Zaytinya is a new Mediterranean restaurant by chef José Andrés getting rave reviews. Delores is waiting for me, but I didn't notice that it was her at first. It has been over three years since Richard and I met her at Mama Ayesha's. Her hair has grayed, but she still has the same pleasant countenance. We order drinks while we wait for Robert—Delores red wine, me a Kerasia. It has rum, elderberry liquor, cherry juice, and cava.

The drink matches the atmosphere—exotic, hip. Delores is an engaging conversationalist, yet like last time, she does not want to share more than the surface with me. I ask about Eich's manuscript. Has she read any of it? Yes, she has, but it was just the ramblings of a sex-starved old man. She dismisses it as nothing of value. This is disturbing. Maybe the parts she read were smut, but why does she have to cast off his life's writing as nothing of value? Mostly though, I am bothered by feeling that I can't have a deep conversation with her about my dad (and her mom).

Again, I ask if she looked for his manuscript in the attic of their Connecticut home. "No, not yet. Next time we're there, I'll try to get to it," she says. "The attic is so full, and there are just so many boxes from other family members to go through I don't want to get your hopes up. I really don't remember putting anything of Eich's up there."

I ask if any of her siblings might be willing to speak with me about Eich. Yes, maybe her sister, Maggie, would. She was a teenager when they lived in Beirut. She might have more memories. Delores will ask her.

I put the subject of my father to rest. When we order, I take to heart Chef Andrés's words on the front of the menu. "Food is about making an interaction with ingredients. If you talk to them, they will always tell you a story." Instead of my prying more stories from a childhood Delores is reluctant to reveal, we talk over our hummus and grape leaf dolmades about her and Robert's upcoming trip to Eastern Europe to explore his family roots. What I share with Delores is not just a story with words, I muse to myself. Maybe I am better off without my father's manuscript, as the loss is pushing me to try to tell his story in my own words. For the moment, the food we are eating is more about the feelings. Pleasure we can share, but not pain.

Delores had previously told me about her mother's unanticipated passing. Eich had found his paramour the afternoon she had died in their apartment. All I can recall from our brief conversation is that her death had something to do with alcohol. She and Eich were both binge drinkers. Patsy was only fifty-eight. I recall Delores telling me when he called her with the news, Eich was so drunk he was practically incoherent. After this disclosure, I did not have the courage to ask her any more questions.

---

158 Dan Egan, email to author, February 13, 2015.

CHAPTER 17

DENIAL IS NOT JUST A RIVER IN EGYPT

The first touches of spring are appearing. Crocus and daffodils color the view from my work laptop. It is set up in what had been Jamila's bedroom the year she lived with us before moving to LA. I email my thanks to Delores for our dinner in DC and ask if she has talked with her sister Maggie about my interest in speaking with her about Eich. She gives me Maggie's phone number, although her sister has told her she is not sure how helpful she could be. When I call the Boston area code, a British-sounding man's voice on the voicemail recording says I have reached Neville, Marjorie, and Ned. I leave a message, then write Delores again to make sure I have the correct number since there is no mention of Maggie. She assures me I do and encourages me to try again. I leave a second voicemail for Maggie but feel I have reached another dead end when I do not hear back after a few weeks. Again, disappointment and doubt begin to hound me.

I have better luck with my third try at reaching legendary drummer Stewart Copeland. I knew the first email via his Italian fan club was a long shot. Then a couple of years ago, Jerry Davis, the producer of the Frank Kearns video, gave me contact information for Stewart's assistant, Adrienne. This was shortly after Stewart's mom, Lorraine, had passed, and I wanted to send him my condolences and let him know how grateful I was to have reconnected to the family through her.

I imagine Stewart still gets fan mail. Even though the Police disbanded thirty years ago, in 2011 Rolling Stone readers ranked him as the seventh most influential drummer of all time. To prove that I wasn't just your average fan, I attached a photo of Stewart and me when we were kids and wrote in the email subject line: "FAMILY friend of Miles and Lorraine Copeland would like to get in touch with Stewart." I heard nothing back.

After a two-year hiatus I decided to try a third time to reach the aging superstar. I shortened the message I had sent his assistant previously. Instead of attaching the photo of Stewart and me as kids, I directly embed it in the body of the email so when she opened it, it would be obvious that Stewart and I had a connection.

The black-and-white snapshot is one of my favorites for the grin spread across my face. Even at five years old, I must have had a crush on Stewart. We are in our Beirut backyard, each of us holding one of my nanny's hands. The blond-haired future founder of the band the Police is a foot taller, although we are only two years apart in age. He is wearing a striped shirt and jeans with suspenders. I am in a dress with a cinched waist and full petticoat. A few steps away, my best friend Renda is holding a rag doll. I want Stewart's assistant to understand there is also a mission to my message. At the end of the email I wrote, "Stewart is coming to Durham, North Carolina at the end of March and I would like to say Hi to him."

Stewart's response, less than twenty-four hours later, has me giddy with excitement. It begins with, "Hello Anne, it's great to hear from you! I remember your garden and the Easter egg hunt that we had there—but not your little friend with the doll. Gene Trone?"

He must mean Genie. Gene Trone was her father, a CIA colleague of both our fathers. The names are a flash of childhood memory, like a bit of ember from a long-ago fire. The last time

I saw Genie Trone must have been in the mid 1960s after the Trones left the Middle East and moved into an old mansion in Leesburg, Virginia. I remember attending a party there with my mom. We drove from the city through what was then countryside in my mom's lime-green Dodge Dart. Genie and I would have been around nine or ten years old when we were sneaking around like invisible guests at the grownups' soirée.

About a decade ago, well before my current obsession with learning about my father's world, Genie contacted me. She was putting together a book for her father's ninetieth birthday and asked for photos of our parents from Cairo and Beirut. She and I have since lost touch, and I can't seem to trace her now. She has disappeared, like a ghost. Though Stewart misidentified my neighborhood friend in the photo as Genie, I am impressed he remembers our backyard escapades. Even better, he has "made this little movie" he thinks I will find interesting. The blue YouTube link on my screen takes me to another place and time. Stewart's narration begins by recognizing his good fortune of playing with "giant bands, giant orchestras, lions, and colorful musicians around the world," then moves on to where it all started, "out there on the other side of the back of beyond"— Beirut, Lebanon. The heart of the three-minute slide show is what his father and, by extension, my father did in the Middle East.

Stewart's deep voice is buoyed by lightheartedness. "He and his CIA cronies imposed the dictators, monarchs, and potentates upon the emerging nations that kept the peace for half a century, up until 9/11 shall we say. For half a century the cut-throats, colonels, and cult figures kept the peace. As my daddy used to say, 'They may be sons of bitches, but they are our sons of bitches.'" Unlike me, he does not seem the least bit disturbed by his father's work overthrowing governments.

Then Stewart gives voice to what our fathers' work was all

about. "The American agents had one overriding mission, and it wasn't social engineering. Their brief was to keep the oil flowing west to our factories rather than north to the evil empire of the Soviet Union."[159] It is the same perspective as I have, although he tells it with more flair. I especially like how he puts their mission in mythic terms, using "evil empire."

Midway through, Stewart says, "our guys had to prop the systems up, while the Russkies contrived to knock it all down." Here, a color photo of his father and my mother with another man appears on my screen. I hit the pause button for a closer examination. The three are on a patio with Beirut's arid hills, blue sky, and white bulbous clouds behind them. My mother is wearing a maroon sweater, the unidentified man in a bow tie is sitting on a rock wall, while Miles Copeland is standing.

"That's your parents in one shot, isn't it?" Stewart asks in the email. I let him know the man in the bow tie is not my dad. "Do you have any more shots of the time and place? Of your parents? Of the Philbys?" he asks.

The name Philby gives me pause. Kim Philby's defection from Beirut to Russia in 1963 no doubt would have made an impression on Stewart. At the time, the second youngest of the four Copeland children would have been eleven and still living in Beirut, while I was younger and living back in DC. Even so, I remember my mother saving the multi-page spread in *LIFE* magazine about Philby's double-crossing. The British Intelligence officer and Russian spy made espionage history when he slipped out of the Mediterranean seaport under cover of night on a Russian freighter. The wake of his treachery rocked our parents' world.

Unfortunately, I have not found any shots of the charming spy-turned-traitor among the photos I inherited from Mom. I email Stewart what I do have: our moms at a New Year's Eve party in animated conversation with an unidentified man and a shot of my dad flanked by two men whom I hope Stewart can identify. They are standing in a kitchen with tourist posters of France and Greece behind them. I also add photos I had sent to his mom Lorraine.

He responds: "Hmmm . . . can't ID any of the partygoers but now I can recognize both of your parents. Your Mom (Alice?) seemed to be enjoying the sleazy guy's banter! . . . The shot at the bottom is my Dad, brother Ian, Mom, and brother Miles. Got any more? It's kind of fun sleuthing out our parents' exotic history."[160] "I wish I did," I reply, then ask, "Are all of what remains of your parents' belongings—photos, letters, and such in France?"

He doesn't answer this question, replying instead with, "Here's a nice one of our two dads." It certainly is. In the black-and-white photo, our fathers are sitting on rocks that could be part of a ruin, next to the shade of a cedar tree. I am certain from the landscape that it was taken in Lebanon. There is a leather satchel on the ground to their right about which I ask, "Do you think that's a bag of $$?"

This is where my imagination goes. Among other things, our dads moved money around. I do not receive an answer on this question either. Fortunately, there will be time to talk about our mutual interests when we see each other in a few months before his concert in Durham.

The remaining ground of my father's CIA career yet to be explored is in the Congo. I know he was in the African hot spot because he mailed me a card from there postmarked June 1966, and with it an ivory necklace. I never wore the gift as a youngster. The choker has tiny carved elephants and round white beads strung on either side of a filigreed teardrop pendant of the now-endangered giant. As a twelve-year-old it looked too ethnic to me, something strangely out of place when I wanted to feel like I belonged someplace. I was in seventh grade at Washington DC's Alice Deal Jr. High School and had no inkling of the Congo except that it was part of Africa. The place was a mystery, like the phantom father who sent me the unexpected gift.

Now I know there are many ghosts haunting this land. Long before the Congo's release from French and Belgium yokes, the US cultivated relations with the mineral-rich colonies. Uranium from the Democratic Republic of the Congo (Belgium's colony) was in the atomic bombs exploded on Nagasaki and Hiroshima. The equatorial region also holds abundant stores of gold, diamonds, tin, and zinc. The land straddling the world's second largest river include rare earth minerals used in cell phones and electric vehicles. The "resource curse" is what experts call the troubles conferred on countries with a bounty of natural resources. It appears that the Democratic Republic of the Congo could be one of its poster children.

The central African country gained independence from Belgium in 1960. Just seven months after its first free elections, the Prime Minister Patrice Lumumba was murdered. To my surprise and good fortune, someone at the nearby University of North Carolina in Chapel Hill authored *The Guardian* article I'm reading about this. I call the number on UNC's website for Dr. Georges Nzongola-Ntalaja to request an appointment, in hopes he can shed light on what my father may have been doing there.

Dr. Georges Nzongola-Ntalaja's office is a twenty-minute ride from our home in Carrboro. I love being able to ride my bicycle to meetings. To be outside and feel the breeze as I peddle is a joy, especially on summer days like today. I am also happy that my bicycle provides me a carbon-free ride. No gas required, just pedal power. In comparison, getting in my car would feel miserably hot, claustrophobic, and a hulk of nuisance when it comes to finding a place to park in Chapel Hill.

I find Battle Hall, one of UNC's historic buildings on Franklin Street, lock my bike, and climb the creaky wooden stairs. The African Studies professor greets me at the door to his office foyer. The round-faced man is very polite, shaking my hand, opening the door to allow me into his office first, then inviting me to sit in the wooden chair in front of his massive desk.

Dr. Nzongola-Ntalaja listens intently as I tell him how I am trying to learn about my father by researching his life and work. Unfortunately, I do not feel prepared for the interview. I rushed to allow time for the bike ride and, due to a printer malfunction, my questions are only in my head. This will have to be a free-flowing conversation. I hope he is game.

"Do you think the US was involved with Lumumba's death?" I start off, knowing the expert will confirm what I had previously discovered.

"They were very involved with Lumumba's murder,"[161] Nzongola-Ntalaja replies.

I tell him my surprise in finding a National Security Council brief outlining plans for CIA support of the prime minister's assassination. "I would think that type of information would remain classified."

"The August 1960 brief ties President Eisenhower to the murder plot," says Nzongola-Ntalaja, expounding on the CIA's efforts and the president's involvement. "A few weeks after the president's directive, CIA scientists flew to Kinshasa with cobra venom that they handed to the CIA station chief, Lawrence Devlin, to put in Lumumba's food or toothpaste."

Georges paraphrases Devlin's reaction. "Are you guys crazy? How are we going to penetrate Lumumba's security to get at his food or toothpaste?" He then goes on to say, "The best way, Devlin concluded, was to support Lumumba's rivals, and that's exactly what they did. Project Wizard became a CIA system of bribing Congolese officials."

Georges Nzongola-Ntalaja was a young man at the time of Lumumba's murder, politically aware of what was happening in his country but not the authority on the subject he is now. In 2002 he wrote *The Congo from Leopold to Kabila: A People's History*[162] and, in 2014, published a short book titled *Patrice Lumumba*.[163] Regrettably, I have not read either book and admit as much to the professor. He seems a kindly man and does not appear to think less of me for being an amateur on the subject. I confess my awareness of the Congo in the 1960s has come mostly from Internet searches.

The US government considered Lumumba a "red threat." There was concern the young nationalist would turn into a "strong man" controlled by Communists. Lumumba unwittingly validated this assessment by turning to the Soviets for help in unifying the country. Internal rebellions had splintered the newly independent coalition government into rival central governments, with breakaway rebels vying for the mineral-rich areas.

I ask the professor what drove US involvement in the Congo—communism and cold war concerns, or access to resources? He answers, "I think it's more the latter; the Cold War was a justification. Everyone who followed Congo politics knew Lumumba could not have been a communist. He didn't know what communism was, except what he heard from the Catholic priests who denounced them. Belgium banned any communist literature from entering the Congo." The professor continues, "In 1956 Lumumba wrote a book, posthumously published as *Congo, My Country*.[164] As one of the Congolese civil servants, he liked the Belgian system (except for racism) and accepted the colonial propaganda of a Belgian *civilizing mission* in the Congo. So how could he have just changed within four years into another Fidel Castro like CIA chief Allen Dulles liked to describe him?"

Nzongola-Ntalaja speaks with a French accent softened by his decades in the US. In 1963 he was the second black person to attend Davidson College. He returned to North Carolina eight years ago after earning a Ph.D. in Wisconsin and teaching at DC's Howard University for nineteen years. He misses Washington, DC.

"I do too. It's a lot quieter here, but Chapel Hill has its pluses," I reply, sharing that my growing up years were spent in the Capital City after my parents' divorce.

It's only now, years into the process of investigating my father's life and the political landscape of my youth, that I can connect what I am hearing from Georges with my father's experience serving as an advisor to Egypt's Gamal Abdel Nasser. Politically speaking, Lumumba was like Nasser. Both turned to Russia for military support after the US was slow to act in their defense. The late 1950s and 60s saw the birth of the nonaligned nations movement and both leaders were passionately nationalistic. Newly liberated countries eschewed the tether of the USSR and the US alike.

Nzongola-Ntalaja summed up the reasoning behind US concern for the non-aligned movement. "The main thing is the US, a leader of the western world, did not want to see newly independent countries liberated from colonialism with leaders that would not want to follow Western business interests." Sad but true, I concur with the brown-eyed African expert.

Nzongola-Ntalaja corrects my misunderstanding about Lumumba's death. "For the record, as the Belgian sociologist Ludo De Witte has clearly shown in his 2001 book, *The Assassination of Lumumba*,[165] Lumumba and his two companions of misfortune were killed by a Belgian execution squad, the result of an assassination plot engineered by Belgium, the United States, and Lumumba's Congolese rivals."

For almost seven years, the US was funding covert operations supporting the rival faction of Army Chief of Staff Joseph Mobutu. In replacing Lumumba with a more moderate, pro-Western leader like Mobuto, the Congo's troubles did not stop. Mobutu became a "strong man" the US felt obliged to support. With crises erupting in neighboring countries and continued Congolese struggles, the US felt compelled to continue funneling funds into aircraft, boats, and military support to keep a central Congo government afloat. The alternative was chaos.

By 1966, when my father worked there, the CIA was looking to wind down their covert operations. Although I believe the US Government would have preferred some semblance of a democratic government in the Congo, a year before my dad arrived, Mobutu assumed total control of the government in a coup.

"Mobuto destroyed the country," Nzongola-Ntalaja says. "He didn't build a single hospital. He didn't build a single university. He didn't build a single major highway around the country. See Kinshasa on the map there," the UNC professor says, pointing to the capital on an old 1960s-style wall map of Africa. "On the bend in the Congo River, at Kisangani, Congo's third largest city, there is no single bridge connecting the two sides of the city."

Appalled by hearing the heartbreak of his country in the Congolese native's voice—heartbreak that the US contributed to—I ask, "Do you ever feel conflicted about living in the US?"

"No, it's not the American people's fault, they have no idea what their country is doing." It's true, most people are unaware of the workings of our shadow government. And why should they want to know of the covert dealings? Hypocrisy is no friend of honor.

It is only natural to want to believe we live in an honorable country, or at least look the other way and go about our business. If you don't, what are the alternatives? Alienation? Apathy? I spent a large chunk of my youth living on the fringes with little respect for a system hellbent on consumerism and material wealth as the measure of success. I saw my government as a tool of the "corporatocracy."

Once I had my children, that view began to change. I began to look more to the future and question what I was bringing to it. What other social structure is organized enough to stand up to the massive power of corporate interests if not the government? Just because monied interests have a disproportionate influence on our elected officials is no reason to give up. Rather, I have come to see it as a call for action. Elect more honest politicians. Hold them accountable. Join the collective action of nonprofits supporting what I believe. Get educated.

Going to college in my mid-forties changed my life. It gave me the tools I needed to do the work I am doing and the confidence to reach out to the professor I am meeting with now. As difficult as it is to look at the nefarious activities of my government and how my father was its tool, it is empowering to get educated. For me, in whatever way I can, it is important to be a force for the change I want to see in the world.

My mother's friend Bea Rames had told me that Eich was an economic advisor to Mobutu. I like to think my father was part of a CIA exit team. Allowing for the benefit of the doubt, I try to put him on the best side of history. Perhaps the intelligence community was winding down covert operations because they realized their mistake in cultivating Mobutu. Or perhaps they just focused on the upside: Mobutu was turning into a good, strong man in that he was keeping the rival groups from tearing the country apart. Perhaps it wasn't clear that corruption was rampant and conditions unfavorable for the economic development needed to foster a wide middle class. Mobutu had not yet amassed one of the largest personal fortunes of any African dictator—later estimated by Transparency International to be between $1B and $5B. He did not yet own his string of Mercedes or lavish palaces in Paris and Switzerland.

On the other hand, learning more about the international meddling my father and his colleagues were involved in puts another dark filter on the past. The wide-angle lens of history frames another picture of US intervention backfiring in the face of projecting democratic ideals. The Democratic Republic of the Congo was anything but democratic. Paradoxically, the communist threat which blew life into the Cold War became another opportunity to strengthen the military industrial complex that President Eisenhower warned about in his farewell address.[166]

What did my father think about his service to the Congo effort? I'd like to think he'd say hindsight is twenty-twenty and that we backed the wrong man in Mobutu. Perspective often sees the past more clearly. But perhaps my father would have denied his past mistakes or those of his country, as did Lawrence Devlin.

"You read CIA Chief Devlin's memoir, didn't you?" Nzongola-Ntalaja asks.

"Yes," I reply.

"Lawrence Devlin was basically Mobuto's top advisor. They were buddy-buddy. He makes no apologies there. He thinks everything was fine."

Thank goodness I'd read Larry Devlin's memoir, *Chief of Station, Congo,*[167] one of the books Dan Eagan sent me, as it gave me more background for the current conversation. Trying to rationalize Devlin's actions, I respond, "Denial is a strong human tendency. Most people do not want to look at a painful past."

Nzongola-Ntalaja continues, "I was at a conference with him

in 2004 at the Wilson Center in Washington. He was then eighty-two years old, and he had an incredible moment. When he liked something, he was very clear. Then when it came to something he didn't like, he said: 'Well, ladies and gentlemen, I am an old man. My memory fails me.' I said, 'Mr. Devlin, you are a damn liar. How can you just two minutes ago tell us things with such details and then all of a sudden you can't remember anything?' You know he's just a liar."

"A lot of people don't want to admit any wrongdoing. They take their pride to the grave," I say to the professor, thinking of my father.

With Eich, Lawrence Devlin and most of the people from my father's CIA days dead, what's left is to sift through the sands of time to draw my own conclusions. Like a flood that buries all that lies beneath its surface, denial is a mighty force. It can bury memory. It can carry away feelings. Later in life, it could simply have been too difficult to examine the years and admit the damage of unintended consequences. It would be far better to bury them. As a result, I believe my father, Devlin, and many other spy world heroes carried secrets to their graves.

After bidding adieu to the professor, I continue my rumination while riding home. Thinking of secrets carried to the grave makes me consider how little I know about Eich's burial and the blinders denial has put on my own feelings. I realize my memories of my father have been washed away by time partly because of our estrangement, particularly at his end. It was much easier to deny, then forget the memories, as the loss was just too painful. I don't recall hearing anything about the plans for my father's burial or even discussing this with my brother or Delores upon my return from Ecuador. All I know is that my father was cremated. But what did Delores do with his cremains? Maybe I can find some closure in knowing what happened to his last earthly remains.

I may have caught Delores off guard when I called to inquire about what she did with his ashes. The muddled notes I took of our brief conversation are evidence of how wrapped in a wad of nervousness I was in asking this question. Delores quickly ran through how her mother had died suddenly and that she and her siblings had little money for a proper burial. Patsy Cooper was buried in a Roman Catholic cemetery with no gravestone. Since Eich wanted to be cremated, and had not left any specific instructions after that, it occurred to Delores and her siblings that he would want his ashes spread on their mother's grave. This news shocked and surprised me, and a feeling of guilt that I was not more involved with my father at the end of his life resurfaced.

My only experience with cremains was with my mother. Through her will she instructed Jay and me that she wanted her ashes spread over flowers in Key West. Instead of sprinkling them over the flowers in our backyard, we picked an assortment of hibiscus, bougainvillea, blue daze, and butterfly bush and tossed them, bloom by bloom with her ashes, into the sea. I imagine Eich would have wanted his ashes spread amongst the sand of the Egyptian pyramids. This was not the least bit practical for Delores's family, but the symbolism of immortality might have suited his soul.

159 Stewart Copeland, email to author, September 1, 2015.

160 Ibid.

161 Georges Nzongala-Ntalaja, interview by author, Chapel Hill, NC, August 25, 2015.

162 Georges Nzongala-Ntalaja, *The Congo from Leopold to Kabila: A People's History* (London: Zed Books 2002).

163 Georges Nzongala-Ntalaja. *Patrice Lumumba* (Athens: Ohio University Press 2014).

164 Patrice Lumumba, *Congo, My Country*. (Connecticut: Praeger Publishing 1962).

165 Ludo Dewitte and Renee Fenby et al., *The Assassination of Lumumba*, (London: Verso Publishing, 2001).

166 Transcript of President Dwight D. Eishenhower's Farewell Address, accessed June 17, 2021, ourdocuments.gov/doc.php?flash=false&doc=90&page=transcript.

167 Lawrence Devlin, *Chief of Station, Congo: Fighting the Cold War in a Hot Zone*, (New York: Public Affairs, a Member of the Perseus Books Group 2007).

CHAPTER 18

HOW WE ARE HAUNTED

I t feels like divine providence. I hadn't expected to go grave hunting when I made plans to visit my brother Jay and sister-in-law Maryrose for the long weekend. Now I am following my brother's friend Dave as he leads me to the old Catholic seminary where I think Delores and her family spread Eich's ashes. Dave told me about the cemetery, not far from Laurel, Maryland where Eich and Patsy lived. On my way, I call Delores's cell phone and leave a voicemail apologizing for the short notice. I ask her to call back as soon as possible since I am on my way to St. Charles College in Catonsville, MD. "I hope you can give me some details as to what part of the cemetery your mom is buried in and how I can find her since there is no headstone," I blurt out. Most importantly, I want her to verify that I am headed to the correct place. At the same time, I had trepidations about leaving such a message on Delores's voicemail, given the painful memories the subject may conjure for her and the uncomfortable nature of our previous conversation.

I met Dave Stout and his wife Jackie at my brother's house last night. They are here from Arizona to visit Dave's mom, who lives in a nursing home on what had been the seminary grounds. In the early 1970s, Dave had planned to be a priest and went to college there. His priesthood ambitions changed when he met Jackie. When I asked if there happened to be a graveyard at the college, he replied, "Yes, the seminary closed in 1977, but you can still visit the church and the old Sulpician cemetery there." After discussing the possibilities of how Delores's brother-in-law might have arranged for Patsy's grave at such short notice, I jumped at Dave's offer to lead me on his way to visit his mom the next day.

It is a cold January morning with blue skies and white wisps of clouds. Fortunately, the light traffic makes it easy to follow Dave on the interstate. After the guard at the Charlestown Retirement Community waves us through, my guide motions me to a parking area before continuing to the adjacent nursing home complex. The lot is close to the cemetery. I park my Chevy Volt and walk around the grounds first to give Delores more time to call me back. The only person I see is a man sitting on a park bench next to a fountain behind a large, three-story brick and stone building, what must have been the seminary. I like that he is wearing a red Santa hat with a white pom-pom dangling down his back. It's quiet and peaceful; the air is full of contemplation.

The door of Our Lady of the Angels Chapel is slightly ajar. After noting a few people setting up the altar for an event, I stay in the back of the church. The vaulted ceiling and Italian marble walls are stunning. In an alcove to the side I pause in front of a white marble statue of Mary, the miracle worker, her hands cradling the shoulders of a child.

Guide me to some sense of resolution, I ask her.

Go to the graveyard, she responds.

There is no reason to continue waiting for Delores's return call. The black wrought iron gate of the cemetery is already open. I scan the brick wall confines of the yard and walk the center path alongside a grassy area. Black metal crosses mark the men buried here. The cemetery dates back to Colonial times. Many of the original priests were born in France, dying far from their place of origin to be buried here in the eighteenth and nineteenth centuries. I walk the perimeter and notice a few gravestones the size of large shoeboxes, most of them commemorating men long gone. There does not appear to be any place for an unmarked grave along the sides of the yard nor in the center.

Flummoxed, I am about to depart when an elderly woman walks into the graveyard, accompanied by a nun. We exchange hellos, and the gray-haired woman, hunched over her cane, tells me she has just heard that there is a woman here researching her father's life. "So am I!" I say, surprised at the serendipity of our meeting. The nun steadies the woman with the cane. They both have sparkling eyes. The two are friends, and the nun is visiting the old woman from the Eastern Shore. "The woman researcher didn't know her father and thinks he might be buried here," continues the elder.

"That's why I am here too," I reply before realizing the old woman must be talking about me. She is Dave's mother, and I am the gullible one who believed there could be someone else out here on a cold January day, looking for an unmarked grave where her father was put to rest over a quarter of a century ago.

So goes my quixotic search for my father. Two months have passed. It is March 31, 2016 and I am looking forward to meeting Stewart Copeland this evening at his show at the Carolina Theater. Built in 1926, the downtown Durham landmark is a source of civic pride for a thriving city in what I like to call the New South—one that embraces the creative arts and diversity. Richard and I invited our drummer friend, David Shore, to join us since Stewart is one of his heroes. David and Richard play together in Southern Routes, a band Richard formed over a decade ago for a new take on old melodies and rhythms from Africa, Europe, and the Caribbean. Their repertoire ranges from reggae to jazz, Ry Cooder to Motown.

Leading up to his tour date in Durham, I had invited Stewart to dinner. He's traveling by bus with a band, he replied, and their road tour does not lend itself to this kind of leisure. Instead he will leave my name at the box office and we can meet backstage an hour before the show. Walking up the theater's stone steps, I snap a picture of its black-and-white marquee advertising "Stewart Copeland and Jon Kimura Parker & Company Tonight 8:00 p.m." next to the names of several films playing at the adjacent cinema.

We present our tickets at the box office. I give the attendant my name and tell her we are here early to meet with Stewart. Another woman with a walkie-talkie asks us to wait in the lobby before coming back with three backstage passes that we peel and press onto our coats. We follow her downstairs, through a labyrinth that takes us by a green room with a banquet of food and drink, to the wooden floor and black velvet curtains of backstage.

Stewart appears, tall and lanky. His blond hair now white, he is still a head taller than me. Although it has been well over fifty years, we hug like old friends. "I remember your mom's backyard Easter egg parties in Beirut," he remarks after I present him with the print of the black-and-white photo of him and me in our pebble and palm fronded backyard. I introduce Richard and David, standing a few steps away. Quipping about the luxurious accommodations, Stewart invites us into his dressing room. We enter a small and narrow room. It has a hat rack by the door, a couch on one side, and a wall of mirrors with a built-in vanity Stewart sits on when he is not standing. Searching for a place to perch, I sit on the couch. David and Richard stand at opposite ends of the long room.

Our conversation flows like melting butter down the side of a hot pan. I want to take notes but quickly dismiss the idea. Our visit is not meant to feel like an interview. Stewart has plenty of those, and I would rather enjoy the insights he provides as an old family friend. The world-famous drummer clearly relishes researching and talking about our fathers' spy world as much as I do, which makes our time together even more precious. He asks if I have connected with Kim Philby's granddaughter. She is a journalist and has her own mothering blog now, he tells me. He found her while sleuthing online. "No, I don't know Charlotte Philby, but I will definitely look her up," I reply.

Stewart sent Charlotte a note about "what a time" his dad and her grandfather must have had. Then, wondering why he did not hear back from her, he showed his wife Fiona what he had sent. "No wonder she never wrote you back," she told him. Stewart enjoys looking at the past—is obviously entertained by it—and I imagine Fiona balances her mate, in this instance, by being sensitive to the dark side of the Philby family's past.

While I don't bring it up, I understand the confidence that comes with charm (of which Kim Philby apparently had plenty), coupled with his heavy drinking and deceit as a recipe for his unresolved pain. Kim Philby's children, including Charlotte's father John, the eldest, were left in England when he defected to Russia. John Philby was nineteen at the time, an art student who, like his father, had socialist sentiments. As a British elite, he was conflicted by the life to which he was born. By the time his father defected, his mother, who suffered from alcohol and mental problems, had already died and Kim Philby had begun a second marriage to a woman, whom he also deserted when he fled to Russia from Beirut.

Our conversation moves on to Stewart's own family. He and his second wife, Fiona, live in Los Angeles and together they have three daughters. He also has four sons, from two other women, and four grandchildren. "It's hard to believe I'm a soccer dad, with kids in high school, and a grandpa," Stewart remarks like the proud family man he clearly is. He is close with all his children, another admirable trait. I tell him we have a daughter in Los Angeles and two sons, one a musician in Austin, the other working in the world of DC politics.

The easy flow of our conversation suddenly changes course when I tell him how much I appreciated my email exchanges with his mom before she died, and that I continue to hope to get some letters my dad had written to his dad that his brother Miles may have in France. "Miles and I are not on speaking terms," Stewart says matter-of-factly. The last time they were together was at their mother's deathbed. Miles's wife had arranged a reconciliation but, as he puts it, "it was a show for our mom."

"What happened?" I ask.

"It's about money," he responds. When the Police were planning their 2007-08 reunion tour, Miles assumed that he would be managing it, like he had managed the band's rise to super-stardom in the 1980s. Stewart was okay with his older brother handling all the money and arrangements, but Sting absolutely refused to have Miles manage the reunion. "It was millions of dollars Miles lost out on by not running the world tour," he confides.

What is the appropriate response to this intimate disclosure?

"That's too bad," is all I can muster. It is almost axiomatic that families can feud and become estranged over money, but this doesn't make it any less tragic. "It's a blessing that you were all together with your mom when she passed," I say, which is the truth.

Someone knocks on the dressing room door. A man hands the star a bottle of Patron. "I love tequila, but only in moderation," I remark, wondering what will happen next. Will he take a sip? Offer us a shot?

"Yeah, I only allow myself one shot after the show," he replies. I ask Stewart if he thinks his father was an alcoholic, but he does not answer definitively. "He liked to drink a lot. Everyone did back then." Those were the days of three martini lunches.

"Especially in the spy world," I comment. "It got the best of my father in the end, though. That's likely why I am so moderate," I conclude before changing the subject.

Stewart is on a five-city tour, so it gives him a taste of the old lifestyle—the fancy tour bus and the rhythm of the road—but not the grind that comes with months of travel. The band will be playing in Tennessee next. I wonder if my musician husband feels a pang of jealousy. After making multiple millions, Stewart Copeland can do whatever he fancies with his music mistress. "You should come by the Grove, my home studio, the next time you are in LA," Stewart offers as we say our goodbyes.

"Would love to," Richard and I say practically in unison.

As we settle in our theater seats, I lean over to my husband and ask if he thinks Eich was jealous of the success Stewart's dad enjoyed as an author. Miles Copeland published several books, and they still fetch good money. A used copy of his autobiography, *The Game Player*, goes for over seventy bucks on Amazon; new ones are over one hundred. While my father was forced to live in subsidized housing, his old friend and partner likely did not have to worry about money later in life. In addition to his own resources, by the time Miles died, his sons had already made millions in the music industry. Adding to these accomplishments, before Miles became an author, before he joined the CIA, before he met my dad during WWII, Stewart's dad played trumpet in the Glenn Miller Orchestra. However, Richard is not interested in entertaining my musing on envy. "Be here now," my husband says as he takes my hand and the theater lights dim.

Spring continues to unfold in a whirlwind of activity. At work, between turnover in staff, starting new projects, and keeping the existing ones going, I alternate between feeling overwhelmed and incredibly lucky to have such a fulfilling job. My team of four and I are navigating phase two of a multimedia public education campaign, including radio, TV, and billboards, to raise awareness about clean air and alternative transportation options such as bikes, buses, and electric vehicles. We also have over a $1M in grant funding and are now in the process of awarding another $1.8M through our 2016 solicitation. Applicants as widespread as the City of Charlotte and UPS to small, obscure companies will be supported. Their clean air projects range from compressed natural gas trash trucks and propane street sweepers to electric docking stations for refrigerated trucks that otherwise would be idling their diesel engines.

My frustration now is that the Federal Highways Administration, which reviews the work we do for the NC Department of Transportation, notified us just days after our recent award announcement that we need to delay progress until further review. The eligibility of some of the applicant's technology is being questioned. How embarrassing to follow the award announcement with, "hold on, it's no longer a sure thing." Still, it is best to identify concerns now, before the distribution of any funds. Early in my career, I had a colleague in Georgia who awarded hundreds of thousands of dollars in transportation funds upon FHWA approval, but before official authorization. The legal challenges he faced for this misstep are not something I ever want to deal with.

A new project I am most excited about is developing sustainable fleet training for the premier organization for vehicle fleet managers. The opportunity came about when I met the outgoing chairman of their board last year at the Department of Energy meeting in DC. The North American Fleet Association (NAFA) likes the idea of being affiliated with a state university, and I see potential for co-branding our educational services. The project is not without its challenges. The NAFA person in charge of training is busy and difficult to contact. Then when we submit a training module, it's reviewed by a volunteer committee that provide minimal feedback. Moreover, we have competition. I was in Austin a couple of weeks ago at NAFA's annual Institute and Expo and saw they already have a California nonprofit—one much larger and more established than our program—delivering training on alternative fuels and more fuel-efficient driving practices.

Still I feel a point of pride, like a badge, that a national fleet management group values our potential enough to pay us to develop a product for them. After sixteen years of working in this field, I feel satisfaction in being a respected player, although sometimes I still feel like an imposter. The flower power maven who had never worked an office job or led a meeting until her mid-forties passes as a clean air and transportation technology expert. I have become what I imagined, and to some extent, what I pretended to be. I wonder if I am walking in my father's footsteps in this way.

He was many things in his life: a writer, a warrior, a diplomat, a spy, a consultant. And then he became something he likely never imagined: a destitute old man, a man who had his ashes spread on an unmarked grave. A man with stories to tell that were never told, despite his promises otherwise. He was a man who slipped away—a man who died without even an obituary, whose death barely registered with his offspring. I sloughed off his passing from this world, like someone late to a pressing engagement.

Did he succumb to some pressure or simply give up after a string of bad luck? The dichotomy of his life continues to influence mine. I marvel at the moments of history my father facilitated contrasted with the anonymity of his death. His sad demise pushes me ever more to not end up like him. I want my marriage to succeed, my close-knit family and my career to continue to flourish. I hope my good fortune holds.

After the NAFA conference, Richard and I had a reunion with all three of our kids in Austin, then a few days at Kindred Spirits, an aptly named Airbnb in the Texas Hill Country. What a pleasure it was to have Taylor, our "baby," play host on his home turf. He organized a potluck for us and his friends in the side yard of the tiny house he is renting. Next door is a small studio he has set up with a forge and anvil for his metalsmithing. To support all this, he is pedaling a pedicab, hauling around sightseers, such as ourselves, in a three-wheeled tricycle to downtown Austin attractions and on the greenway along the Colorado River.

Rio has a girlfriend now, whose parents emigrated from Liberia. Virginia is tall and beautiful and does not seem to be a binge drinker like my son. I hope she can keep him in check. Rio looked awful after an all-night party with Taylor's friends in Austin, friends he has known since Taylor began playing music with them in middle school. Rio's propensity to get blackout drunk worries me. Once, visiting a friend in Paris at age eighteen, he woke after an all-night party naked with paint and magic marker covering his body and his camera stolen. This is one of the more colorful stories. The scariest is when he woke up in a DC alley and had no recollection of how he got there. I have repeatedly told him that no one starts out thinking they will become an alcoholic, that it can just happen over time, that he should beware and consider giving it up altogether. To have to stand back now and realize there is nothing more I can do for my son is about as difficult as watching someone play frisbee on the edge of a cliff. He is an adult and the only one who can make decisions about his life.

I know Rio is genetically predisposed to alcoholism from my father and to a lesser extent my mom, who was what I would call a "controlled heavy drinker." But I believe that the joy and solace of drink need not take over one's life and health, as Eich's was overtaken. If the discipline of moderation is not effective or possible, total abstinence is key, as is the discovery of some other channel for one's life force.

Since Jamila has become so immersed in Kundalini yoga, she has not had a drink in years. This is a huge relief for me, as my daughter had been headed in the same direction as her brother with heavy alcohol consumption throughout high school and early adulthood. Taylor discovered the power of discipline in middle school, as he earned a black belt in Tae Kwon Do. Rio is on his own path of life lessons, and my role as mother now is to be supportive but not domineering. As they continue to individuate, I recognize that our three children could not be more different in temperament and lifestyles. Nonetheless, they seem to respect each other, and that is a blessing.

The next best thing to having my kids together in one place is hearing from all of them in one day. It is one of those times now. Richard and I are at our cabin for Mother's Day weekend. On Sunday we pay Annie Dillard and her husband, Bob Richardson, a visit at their place, a thirty-minute walk down our ridge and halfway up another. Her cozy shack, as Annie calls it, is next door to our friend Callie's cabin. She and Bob spend a couple of months here twice a year in the shoulder seasons between summering in Cape Cod and wintering in Key West. Bob lives in Callie's cabin and Annie lives a few steps away in her one-room perch. I feel honored to be sharing this beautiful forgotten place in rural southwest Virginia with such esteemed authors, although Annie does not have much regard for the writing world these days.

We are sitting on her small porch overlooking the view of Iron Mountain when I tell her I have started an MFA program in creative nonfiction. There is no note of encouragement in her response. Catching on that she is uninterested in my writing endeavors, I switch subjects to wish her a happy Mother's Day. Annie, the Pulitzer Prize-winning author, responds that she only started writing to pass the time while she hoped to become a mother.

Annie has one child, a daughter, and "no hope of becoming a grandmother," she laments between puffs of her cigarette. I am also dragging on one that I bummed from her. Smoking cigarettes is my guilty pleasure, one I try to keep in check by not purchasing my own very often. Annie knows this and does not seem the least bit annoyed by me asking for one or two every time we see each other.

Like me, she is hoping to get a call from her daughter today. Every year I also wait expectantly, wondering if one of my children will forget. Annie's daughter is a nature lover and writer like her mom but is gay with no interest in having a child. "I so much want to be a grandmother too," I say, stubbing out my smoke, "but there are no guarantees."

Inside Annie's cabin, the phone rings. I can tell by the cadence in her voice that her daughter has called. I gaze out at the vista before me and realize that so much of what I yearn for is out of my control. Where is my trust that the universe will provide what I need? After all this time, is it still held hostage by a need to make peace with my father?

The loss of my father, it seems, has affected my approach to all my expectations. This one loss seems to account for my innate desire for control. Now that the kids are grown, this control can no longer exert itself in the parenting realm. Increasingly, I must trust that my children are making their own way in life. My authority must be replaced with faith that they will make the right decisions for themselves. My work, on the other hand, is under my control. I think.

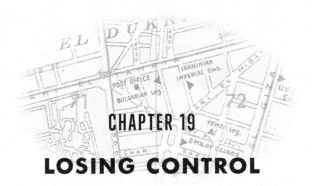

CHAPTER 19
LOSING CONTROL

I am blindsided. It is Monday, the day after Mother's Day, and my boss Steve calls me into his office. He asks me to resign from the Center, that effective immediately he does not want me managing the clean transportation program, that he will give me six months with pay to look for another job, that he will fire me if I do not resign. I am in shock. Steve recruited me to the Center at NC State University, and I built the program to five full-time staff and a couple of interns by bringing millions of dollars of grant money to the University. The clean transportation program is my baby. Now, after twelve years, I am being forced to let go of something I have conceived and nurtured like a child from birth into maturity.

It is no exaggeration to say that my entire sense of self is critically wounded. Now that my real children are grown and out on their own, my work has become my identity. With one blow, my ego is shattered into millions of painful pieces and my self-esteem is standing over the mess trying to figure out how to clean it up.

How did this happen? *You should have seen it coming*, my distrustful self is telling my ego as she lords over the rubble. Last Friday Steve had walked into a kerfuffle I was in with two of my younger team members. Although I have had trouble with people on my team before, I never thought that my boss would fire me as a result. Steve and I have always gotten along, and for the most part he has left me alone to do what I wanted. Regarding this incident, Steve planned to sit down with all of us together to work things out. This was an excellent idea from my perspective. Instead he called the human resources office who advised that he meet with each member of the team individually. I was the last person that he and our finance director were to meet with. I thought perhaps they would require me to take a management training class. We had talked about this before, but I always felt too busy with the mission at hand—reducing our dependence on oil, improving air quality, and saving the world—to take the time. Nonetheless, I knew all along that I had a problem.

I am a micromanager. When I sense others' frustration with my management style, I admit this tendency to my team members and justify it by explaining that I am so invested in what we are doing that I have trouble letting go of the reins until I have confidence with how they are handling a task. I don't want to be a micromanager, I explain to them individually when I begin to feel they are getting frustrated, but I need their help in overcoming this tendency. It takes time to build trusting relationships.

I ask them to come to me if they are having a work-related problem. "I have an open-door policy," I say. However, when they do come it is usually to complain about another team member, and I feel hamstrung in knowing how to respond and then delay in taking any action. Consequently, things fester. A recently hired team member was avoiding me rather than speaking to me about his problems. When I finally brought up the existence of a problem between us, he spit out that I was "creating a toxic environment."

My reluctance to confront challenging situations has likely aggravated things. I understand that if we are going to grow this program to its full potential that I can't do it by myself. I would like to work things out with my team, but in this case it's being worked out for me. There is a finality in Steve's decision (albeit impulsive, from my perspective) that no amount of pleading from me for another chance will change.

But I am not a quitter.

I do not want to walk away from twelve years of my life. I could already taste the bitterness of rejection in my mouth and feared the resentment it would feed. When Steve said he would give me six months' pay to look for another job, I pivoted the conversation. "Let me create a new position for myself," I said. "I can be the Special Projects Manager," a job title I thought of on the spot. "I can work with other staff to write grants and work on new projects as they come in." He agreed, "but give me your resignation letter dated six months from now in case it doesn't work out," he said.

We met with what had been my team the next day. I wanted to clarify that it was not my choice to step away from the program I had created and that, as the Special Projects Manager, I would be available to help them any way I could. For me this is the best path forward. I could not stomach feeling like a victim. I do not want my final act at the Center to be held hostage by their wish for my termination. At the same time, it is going to be a challenge for me to share the same office and not have a say in the goings on of the largest program at the Center.

To some colleagues, my new position looks like a step up. A couple even offered congratulations. At the minimum it appears to be a lateral move. I am saving face. When people ask what happened, I say that in Steve's *infinite* wisdom, he realized he needed my help. Being the Special Projects Manager means I get to work on all sorts of interesting subjects that need attention like increasing the use of solar, supporting energy efficiency, and enhancing the diversity of the clean tech sector.

Meanwhile, I have quietly begun searching for another job. There are none in North Carolina for a subject matter expert on transitioning to alternative transportation fuels. I have built a career in a very niche market. Furthermore, I am over sixty. I had never considered age bias before except when I was on the hiring end, passing over resumes of qualified applicants with advanced degrees from the mid-1970s who I thought might not be as tech savvy with today's communication, organization, and analysis tools. Forced to cast my net wider than the horizon of the Tarheel State, over the following few months, I have managed to have two in-person interviews. One job prospect flew me to Seattle and put me up in a downtown boutique hotel but ended up hiring someone younger than me, someone with experience in the region.

A young colleague at the Center who had never written a federal grant asked for my help with a proposal. Then I got engrossed in putting together another grant application to provide scholarships for solar design and installation training for underrepresented minorities. The clean tech sector needs more diversity, and solar panel installers get paid well, with opportunities for advancement. Despite the ego crush from losing the stature of running a program where I really had made a name for myself, my spirits have begun to lift as I am making myself useful. Moreover, having the weight of managing the transportation program removed has given me more time to think about my father.

By the time Eich was my age, his girlfriend Patsy had died, and he was living in the Roosevelt. It was so long ago now, and our visits were so infrequent, I am left with only the bare bones of his story from this time to consider how the sorry state of his later years have influenced me. The sudden turn in my career exposes a fear that in old age I could end in the same situation as my father. This is not rational. I'm in a more secure position than Eich upon his return to the US after almost two decades focused on Middle East affairs.

In 1967 Eich moved from Beirut to the US with Patsy and some of her children because of the Six Day War. Israel's victory over Egypt had inflamed anti-Western sentiments. Everywhere in the Middle East—including Beirut—people took to the streets calling for death to the West. How times had changed from when I was born in Egypt. Then Gamal Abdel Nasser and US leaders were courting each other with mutual affection and for a time my father was an undercover match maker. Re-establishing himself in the States could not have been easy after decades of living abroad under the auspices of the CIA. Especially since things did not go according to plan.

Eich and Patsy were not able to "bust her family trust," as Lorraine Copeland had described their mission. Although Eich told me he had pushed my mother into divorce because "he wanted to be free to marry again one day," Patsy and my father never married. Perhaps Eich and Patsy's relationship was bound more by the kinship of drink than any need to proclaim their commitment to each other through a piece of paper. Maybe the love he felt for her never met the romantic ideal of the perfect mate for matrimony. Or Patsy and Eich's informal union may have been due to her and her husband never divorcing. Patsy and Charles were Catholic, and divorce was more difficult in those days.

After he left our family, my father pieced together a living as a consultant for a while, but financial mishaps seemed to follow his every step. The oil deal in Kuwait with Former Treasury Secretary Robert Anderson went bust. Then there was the national tourist study of Lebanon for a group of Beirut banks that fell short of expectations. As part of the long biographical letter Eich wrote, he explained, "The guiding spirit behind the project—the owner of one of the banks—was put in jail (in another connection)." To get the needed expertise to do the job, my father gave more than half of the $50,000 he was paid to a US consultant he brought in to teach him how to do the work. The rest of the Beirut office lived on what was left, he told me, "since neither Miles nor Charles did an effing thing."[168]

It is difficult to take Eich's complaints seriously or give them much merit after learning that his Beirut partner Charles was Patsy's husband, and that my father began his affair with Patsy before he left my mother. During the period he was writing about, Eich was living with Patsy in the Cooper's Beirut villa. Eich expressed no guilt or remorse with what he was doing because, as he explained it, Charles was having problems of his own creation in Saudi Arabia with Prince Talal. It appears that my father felt justified in living with his partner's wife given he was doing all the work in Beirut and his partner was tied up in Saudi Arabia by a disagreement with a prince.

By my father's account, Charles had sued the Saudi Prince after Talal "justly fired him for drawing his pay while doing no work." Through my research, Prince Talal is a member of the royal family whom I have come to admire, but someone the CIA might not have seen favorably. As the leader of the "Free Princes," Talal advocated for representation for their people in a country rapidly accruing vast wealth from its oil—likely the opposite of what the CIA wanted for the kingdom. Did Talal terminate his relations with Charles because he caught on to what he was doing for the CIA, or was my dad's attitude about his former partner tied up with the fact that he was involved with the breakup of another family? I will never know.

Although my father blamed his personal troubles on everyone but himself, I have sympathy for the pressure he was under at the time he chose to leave us. The many layers of deceit and double-crossing must have been stressful—pressing, pressing, pressing on him like tectonic plates. Like at any moment he could crack under the pressure. Especially for a man with a poet's soul who spent his career under a cover of darkness, cultivating contacts and leading others astray.

With more free time to devote to research on Eich, I have

found another lens through which to see how he spent his life on something I am trying to undo with mine. The author of a Stanford University PhD dissertation analyzed the historical process that "culminated in the 1972 nationalization of the Iraq Petroleum Company (IPC)—a consortium that included four of the world's largest and most powerful corporations."[169] Right around the time Eich took leave of his family, he and Miles Copeland wrote a letter that was sent from Beirut to DC by Secret Air Pouch. The letter is titled "Views on Middle East Politics by Two Private American Experts" and "the ambassador's introduction to the letter stresses the credentials and reliability of the authors and states that he thought the letter was penned in early February 1960."[170] My brother Jay was just seven months old. I still hold an image of him in a tiny blue-striped bathing suit sitting with his ready smile in our Beirut wading pool.

The letter recommended interventionist activities in Iraq. My father was part of a euphemistically named "Iraqi Health Alteration Committee" plotting the assassination of the new leader of Iraq, Colonel Abd al-Karīm Qāsim, who himself came into power after executing the British-installed king and his royal family a couple of years earlier. This story dovetails with the UPI article I discovered early on in my research about the botched assassination of Qāsim that Saddam Hussein had attempted. It is good to have found this second source and to feel more confident of my understanding of Eich's dealings. Hussein's botched murder attempt of Qāsim, and my dad's subsequent interactions with him, took place just three months before the letter he and Miles wrote that this researcher discovered. In it, Eich and Miles advised that Iraq form an alliance with Egypt as the "best bet against the nationalist 'oil experts'" led by Saudi Arabia.[171]

While Qāsim implemented land reforms, expanded education opportunities, and championed women's rights, he also demanded that the Anglo-American-owned Iraq Petroleum Company (IPC) share 20 percent of the ownership and 55 percent of the profits with the Iraqi government. When the IPC rejected this proposal, Qāsim issued a law to take away 99.5 percent of the IPC's ownership and establish an Iraqi national oil company to oversee the export of its oil. British and US officials and multinationals demanded that the Kennedy administration place pressure on the Qāsim regime.[172]

Although protecting Western oil interests was the real driver, my father and Miles advocated for "external intervention" into Iraq's business because of the threat of communism. In the 1975 Congressional Church Committee hearing, it became known that the "Iraqi Health Alteration Committee" had approved a "special operation" to "incapacitate Qāsim." Plans were formulated to "mail a monogrammed letter with an incapacitating agent" to the Iraqi leader.[173] These CIA plans turned out to be unnecessary. Three years later, Qāsim was executed by a firing squad in a Ba'ath Party coup.

There is no telling if my father had a hand in this coup as well. A CIA official working with Eich's colleague, Archie Roosevelt Jr., on a separate plan to instigate a military coup against Qasim, "denied any involvement in the Ba'ath Party's actions." Instead the unnamed source stated that the CIA's efforts against Qāsim were still in the planning stages at the time.[174] I am still struck by the audacity of these men, that they can justify the struggle for power even if it meant murder. Nonetheless, my eyes always perk up when I see references to Archie and Kim Roosevelt.

Theodore Roosevelt's grandsons were more than just CIA colleagues to my father. They were his contemporaries and friends, men I imagine Eich resonated with intellectually, philosophically, and creatively. No doubt he also admired their social status. When Miles was recruiting Eich away from his job in

Chicago writing political speeches for J. Walter Thompson, "he and Kim took to each other as fellow literati."[175] Before my parents moved to Egypt where Kim became my father's boss, my parents moved to Washington, DC where he and Kim "had some fine times discussing highbrow literary topics in the evening, while devising propaganda themes during the day."[176] When Eich and Miles began the Beirut-based consulting group in 1958—after signing Gulf Oil as their first client—Kim Roosevelt effectively became their boss a second time when he became Vice President of Gulf. In a classic example of the revolving door between government and business, all three were capitalizing on their connections in one underhanded, dirty, double-crossing line of work—the CIA—to pimp for another—BIG OIL.

Of course, they would not have viewed it as such. They were just doing what men were expected to do in the 1950s and 60s—pursuits that are alive and well today. They wanted to get rich. But just as his marriage with my mom didn't last, neither did Copeland and Eichelberger's contract with Gulf Oil. The lucrative agreement ended when Roosevelt left the CIA—with his full roster of contacts still at his fingertips—to join Gulf Oil. With that development, Miles and my father's contacts and intelligence-gathering skills were not nearly as valuable. Miles blamed my father's "Dionysian temperament" for their losing the Gulf contract while Eich had a different viewpoint.[177] My father concluded that Gulf had decided they didn't need both him and Miles, since the oil conglomerate offered Eich "a very good job in their London office."[178] Instead, Eich turned down the London opportunity to join INTERSER, the ill-fated Kuwaiti oil deal with Robert Anderson.

I suppose we are all building on our family's legacies even if we are not aware of it. But what should I do with this new knowledge about my father's? Though in my daily lifestyle choices, I strive to reduce my planetary footprint, America's current level of consumption far exceeds the sustainable threshold which would forestall the looming climate catastrophe. It is discouraging to realize the US is ranked thirteenth for CO_2 emissions per capita as compared to the other 180 nations being tracked, emitting 16.02 metric tons in 2016. This is 99 percent greater emissions per person than the lowest ranking country, Burundi.[179]

It makes me want to fight even more for what I believe would be the single most effective solution: a carbon tax and dividend. We need to put a tax on carbon to support the investment in future generations who will pay dearly for our reckless consumption. Such a tax would help pay for the transition to a clean energy economy. The dividend could be weighted to better help the growing ranks of our nation's poor. For this to happen we need to help the organization Rio is working for, People for the American Way, and the many others trying to reduce the influence of money in politics.

My research reverie into Eich's sad story and my own role in trying to undo this legacy is interrupted by a phone call at my office from Rio's distraught girlfriend, Virginia. She is in tears. It is May 26, 2016 and my son is in a DC jail after a fight they had last night. They were in an Uber. Rio was drunk. He wanted Virginia to spend the night with him and she wanted to go home. To hold his girlfriend hostage and buy time for her to change her mind before the end of the ride, Rio grabbed her bag and cell phone, jumped out of the car at a downtown stoplight, and began running down the street. Virginia jumped out of the Uber to run after him. Passersby thought Rio had stolen her bag and apprehended him as the thief until the police came to take him away. She did not want to press charges, but they took him to jail anyway.

"I didn't want to call you, but I thought you should know," Virginia explains.

"I am so sorry this is happening to you," I reply. "Of course, I want to know."

I want to help, but there is nothing I can do, she assures me. The police have not charged Rio with anything, but it is unclear when he will be released. A friend of Rio's is at the jail now to see what he can find out. I call him. We speak briefly. It's midday and his friend Aaron is camped out on the jailhouse steps. He promises to have Rio call me upon his release. I want to manage this problem, but I can't. Now it's a waiting game.

When Rio calls, I am at home rehashing the news with Richard. "Maybe he will learn a lesson from spending the night in jail," my husband says to comfort me. All I can think about is Rio's impetuousness and the resulting trauma from his drunken actions, how a trigger-happy cop could have killed him while he was running down a dark DC city street clutching a woman's handbag, how this event will certainly end a relationship with a woman who really cares about him, how our son needs help— how our son could end up like his grandfather.

The night in jail was horrific. The cops first took Rio to the police station on U Street near his apartment, then he was transferred—shackled in the squad car—to the main jail in Southeast. He was put in a holding cell; a cage is how he described it. The police told him nothing. All night, Rio heard gut-wrenching screaming around him. My twenty-eight-year-old son got a real taste of the anguish and despair that less privileged men must endure daily. He was the only white person behind bars. The odds against them and the injustice was palpable. As dreadful as it was, he knows he is one of the lucky ones for the color of his skin.

As soon as Rio was released, he went straight to his office to speak with his boss, Marge. More than anything, he was concerned about not showing up for work that morning. It was three in the afternoon. He was exhausted from lack of sleep; his clothes were disheveled. Marge Baker is executive vice president at People for the American Way and has spent over thirty-five years in the trenches fighting social injustice. She must also have a big heart.

Rio was honest with her. He confessed that he missed work because he had been drunk and detained in the DC jail overnight. "It will never happen again," my son assured her, and she gave him another chance.

"You really need to get some help," I tell Rio while pacing the floor of our living room. "You should join AA."

"I tried that before in Boone. It doesn't work."

"Try again. You need a support group," I plead. For the umpteenth time, I launch into the talk I have given him for years now. "No one starts out to become an alcoholic. It just happens. Look at your grandfather. He had so much promise, so much going for him, and it ruined his life."

"I'll think about it," Rio says. I know he is passionate about his job and cognizant of the fact that his predilection for binge drinking is dangerous. He knows it has the power to derail his ambition and ruin his life. But for years he keeps going back to it, thinking he can control himself, thinking he can still enjoy the best of reckless abandon while avoiding the worst. This time he knows he went too far. For now, I can rest knowing he has quit drinking again. Miracles happen, every day, I tell myself.

168 James M Eichelberger, letter to author, December 14, 1982.

169 Brandon Wolfe-Hunnicutt, "The End of the Concessionary Regime: Oil and American power in Iraq, 1958-1972," March, 2011, iv. accessed June 17, 2021, https://stacks.stanford.edu/file/druid:tm772zz7352/Concessionary%20Regime%20%5Besubmit%5D-augmented.pdf.

170 Ibid, 49 "55 Beirut to State," no. 539, (Secret Air Pouch), "Views on Middle East Politics by Two Private American Experts" [Marked: 780.00/3.760], 7 March 1960, in RG59, Box 2030, Folder: 780.00/1, 460.

171 Ibid, 49- 51.

172 Douglas Little, *American Orientalism: The United States and the Middle East Since 1945*, The University of North Carolina Press, 62.

173 United States Senate Select Committee to Study Governmental Operations with Respect to Intelligence Activities (Church Committee), Interim Report: Alleged Assassination Plots Involving Foreign Leaders, (Washington DC: GPO, 1975): 181, note 1, paragraphs 4, 7, and 8 (see bibliography for web address), as cited by on pg. 52 of "The End of the Concessionary Regime Oil and American Power in Iraq 1958-1972," Brandon Wolfe-Hunnicutt, March 2011.

174 Bryan R. Gibson, *Sold Out? US Foreign Policy, Iraq, the Kurds, and the Cold War.* (Palgrave Macmillan, 2015). xxi, 45, 49, 57–58, 121, 200.

175 Miles Copeland, *The Game Player*, 129.

176 Ibid, 218.

177 Ibid.

178 James M Eichelberger, letter to author, 1982.

179 "CO_2 Emissions per Capita," World Atlas Data, Rankings, Environment, KNOEMA, accessed August 10, 2020, https://knoema.com/atlas/ranks/CO2-emissionspercapita.

CHAPTER 20

PERSPECTIVE

I n my search to more fully understand my father's work and motivations, and indeed my own, it may be best to consider Kim Roosevelt's grandfather, both a passionate conservationist and proponent of America's involvement on the world stage. At home President Roosevelt established the National Park system and fought mightily against the ascendency of corporate greed, two interests I passionately share. Yet, Teddy Roosevelt also thought it was our country's place to promulgate our "progressive ideals" around the world. He saw the importance of spreading these ideas whenever they helped US corporate interests (such as the Panama Canal). In doing so, he expanded our military and made popular the phrase, "Walk softly and carry a big stick."

Teddy Roosevelt considered his greatest achievement to be the construction of the Panama Canal. Making Panama a US Territory provided an access point between the Atlantic and Pacific oceans and was a tremendous boon to the US companies building the canal (such as US Steel), as well as companies selling their wares around the world.[180] Corporate welfare, it could be argued, was America's cloaked and veiled form of imperialism. The United States was not colonizing countries like the Europeans had across Africa and the Middle East; instead we were benefiting them with increased trade and commerce so they would want to become like us.

Roosevelt used the bold move of building the Panama Canal to establish what is called the Roosevelt Corollary to the Monroe

Doctrine.[181] Whereas the 1823 Monroe doctrine was a warning to the European powers to respect the Western Hemisphere as the United States' sphere of influence, the Roosevelt Corollary gave the US the right to intervene in other countries' affairs if they affected US economic and political interests.[182] This move focused on the Americas, but after the discovery of oil in lands that became Iran, Iraq, Kuwait and Saudi Arabia, I would argue that this ethos expanded to the Middle East and was enacted by my father and his colleagues.

The big stick is the US military, the largest in the world.[183] My father, Miles Copeland, and Kim Roosevelt were part of the "speak softly" side of the equation that has been our policy since Teddy Roosevelt's days. So softly that you will not hear this part of the story at most cocktail parties, nor on the radio. So softly that you wouldn't be sure of what you're hearing and what is true. My research into my father's life has confirmed what I've felt all along. Things are not what they seem and what passes as success may not be what is best for ourselves or the planet.

This is a valuable lesson, not only for our dealings in the material world but for matters of the heart. My escape to Key West as a young woman was a direct reflection of my not wanting to join the mixed up, hypocritical "do one thing and say another" world my father helped perpetrate. Now, with the perspective of age, I understand it was destiny that trouble would find me there. History repeats itself in families and on the world stage as it is wanting to do, coming from troubled beginnings. Yet perhaps I learned something.

I wanted to make my marriage work, not just for our daughter, which was of paramount importance, but because of our deep abiding love and that I am stubborn like my husband. We both refused to leave after my affair. I did not want Jamila's life to be upended by divorce the way mine had been. Besides, we were living our dreams in Key West. Life was a celebration of arts and the natural world on a small island in an ocean of turquoise. I did not want to ruin this life in hope of finding myself in another.

I wrote Eich in 1982 when Jamila was three to ask why his marriage with my mom came apart. He heaped all the blame on her. I could not do that. Although marriage troubles are never just one sided, I confessed immediately and accepted 100 percent of the blame for the damage my dalliance caused. Keeping the affair secret would have made the violation of our sacred trust worse. I must have known intuitively, from my father's behavior, that it was better to come clean. Thus began the five years—leading to my pregnancy with Rio—it took to build back the trust we had lost. Richard says that it was our trip to Bali, when Jamila was two, that saved our marriage. And maybe it was. Who knows, in the moment, what serendipitous events will shape the rest of our lives?

We had been planning a trip to Bali before we became pregnant with Jamila—an adventure we had all but given up on. Despite our efforts at saving, we were still $3,000 short when the window of time we had to go was approaching. Just then, I received a phone call from my mother. She had received a letter from the American Civil Liberties Union addressed to me at my childhood home in Washington, DC.

At a May Day protest I attended in 1971, President Nixon had ordered our arrest as we were being addressed on the granite steps of the capitol by Congresswoman Bella Abzug. She was wearing one of her trademark hats and I had skipped my eleventh-grade classes to hear her and Ron Dellums, the tall, black congressman from California, talk about legislation they had introduced in Congress to draw down our troops from Vietnam. While ten thousand people were detained during the week of demonstrations against the Vietnam War, the ACLU only sued on behalf of the 1,200 arrested on the capitol steps. What Nixon had done was illegal.

A decade later, my mother was holding a check in her hands for $3,245. The government compensated me $100 for each hour I was held in violation of my First and Fourth Amendment Rights—freedom of speech and false arrest and imprisonment—first in the DC Armory and then the DC Jail. This amount was just exactly what we needed to go to Bali.

I consider my three-day incarceration and arrest protesting the Vietnam War as a defining experience of my youth. In a nod to my protest of war, my father asked in one of his letters, "Does anybody in your generation ever think of the retreat from Dunkirk and what it meant?" I had never heard of the heroic efforts to save three hundred thousand British and French troops from German slaughter when I received this letter in 1988. The Battle of Dunkirk, the miracle evacuation from the beaches of northern France in May 1940, meant nothing to me. He wrote, "I was only a little fish of a captain, but I swam just under the waves made by the big names of the epoch." So wrapped in my own life, I had never considered the forces that shaped my father's as a young man.

On September 3, 1939, seven months before the retreat at Dunkirk, Britain and France had declared war on Germany while Eich was traveling around Europe after college as an author, editor, and reporter.[184] By June 22, 1940 France had surrendered. I am struck by how quickly everything must have changed for him. Within eight months of traveling around Europe, he was back there as a soldier spy. Again, I am hit with how much circumstance determines our lives. Not only that, but how my father's life is reflected in mine—in opposites, like the reverse images in a mirror. A pacifist was born from a soldier spy. Eich ends this letter with, "It is right for flower children to deplore war, but it's not so bad if you are lucky."

Considering the circumstances, my father was lucky. After seeing unspeakable horror, he made it out alive and with a sense of humor. Eich wrote, "I was in England, North Africa, France, and Germany and saw everything but the surrender. Where was I then? Probably in bed with the wife of the Archbishop of Canterbury." World War II made the boy a man, a man who had already shielded himself from the loss of his own father when he was eleven. My father was a man who loved the written word and poetry. He was also a man forced to disassociate from his heart. To survive, he had to rely on his wits.

It was during the war that my father found the people he most resonated with, other intellectuals who were soldier spies like him, much like I had found my tribe in Key West—new age seekers who had an appreciation for the community we were creating. As a young mother I, along with a cadre of women, started Key West's first recycling center. In 1988 the Women's Resource Center was an all-volunteer group of men and women who smashed glass, crushed aluminum cans, and bundled newspapers that were hauled by the tractor trailer load to mainland Miami. It was this experience that inspired me to go to college with hopes of making a career out of helping our planet, a planet facing a perilous future.

After graduate studies in philosophy, where Eich was on a PhD track at the University of Chicago, I am certain it was the abiding bonds of war experience that led him to join the Central Intelligence Agency. Miles Copeland came calling in Chicago and soon thereafter, my father met his boss and future friend Kermit (Kim) Roosevelt Jr. The deal was sealed. They were going to save the world from the growing threat of communism or, at the least, gather intelligence and protect US oil interests overseas. They may have been idealistic, but they were not naive. After WWII, I don't doubt that they realized our shadow government would do whatever it took to get a job done.

This type of treachery is still alive and thriving, especially in the digital age and an increasingly polarized political environment. Yet, I want to be a bridge builder. I want to have this disturbing reality bring me to a place of healing. I recognize my place of privilege and appreciate the fact that I live in a tolerant country where I can be who I want to be. I look back on my fifteen years living in Key West and starting our family, five years in Sarasota going to college and working as an energy efficiency consultant, then my life in North Carolina these past sixteen years. What surprises me the most is discovering my passion for reducing our oil dependence would be the magnet drawing my father and me together.

I find my views are not as black and white as I once thought, but a spectrum of color in between. There is no grand conspiracy by a few who want to control the world. Rather, we have a system that has been manipulated by a few to create advantages favoring one choice over another, say, fossil fuels over renewable options—a system of entrenched interests that rewards selfishness and exploitation over the good of the whole. And, as individuals, we have been lulled into believing that we can buy our way to happiness. This is a myth. I know this firsthand. After achieving a certain level of security and creature comfort, a bigger house or a fancier car will not buy me more peace. It's the service we can provide, the relationships we build and the moments we share that make for a successful life.

Through the current tenuousness of my work—the six-month trial to establish a new position for myself while looking for other employment—I am developing more compassion for the struggle my father faced in returning to the US. In 1982 he wrote, "I remain quite bitter about the world when I think of the hundreds of resumes I sent out without getting one single interview." A man who made his living in an undercover world, where no trace of your influence is the gold standard, would have a tough time adjusting to a system valuing resumes with noted accomplishments. On the other hand, wouldn't he have listed his many cover stories to document his worth? Perhaps Eich's struggles finding work were as simple as what I am now facing: age bias.

Before the CIA took my father to the Congo to write an economic development plan for the dictator, he wrote a documentary film script for Pan American Petroleum about their exploration successes in the Red Sea. He was grateful for the opportunity to see the pyramids a few more times. He also helped write the first Surgeon-General's report on smoking and ended up smoking more cigarettes than he ever had before. Because of this experience, the contrarian humorist I have discovered my father to be wanted to pen a book about how smoking is *good* for you. I will smoke to this, but only on occasion.

This is one of those occasions. Rio just called to let me know he has decided to join AA. His relationship with his girlfriend has ended, but he is committed to working the steps to recovery. The steadfastness in his voice does not waiver, and I give my son my vote of confidence that he will meet with success. We hang up and I head to our backyard. Lighting an American Spirit, I take a deep drag. It is a moment to pause, to say a prayer as the smoky rings dissipate into the evening sky. Like the Native Americans, I consider tobacco sacred. It brings me closer to the spirit world, especially my father. Especially now that Rio is facing his alcohol abuse, a nemesis he has not been able to conquer over the past fifteen years and that my father was never able to overcome. I, too, dance on the skirts of addiction—with tobacco—a waltz of love and loathing. I love the smooth taste as it fills my chest and calms my nerves. I loathe polluting my lungs and the planet's lungs with every breath. If I indulge too much, the yapping dogs in my stomach increasingly hound me to light up. This desire is my signal to stop. Then the yearning I feel from my withdrawal, in its own way, brings me closer to my father. It's the feeling of saudade, the desire for what was but could never be. It is my regret for not sharing more with him when he was alive.

180 "Roosevelt Corollary to the Monroe Doctrine, 1904", US Department of State Office of The Historian, accessed August 12, 2020, https://history.state.gov/milestones/1899-1913/roosevelt-and-monroe-doctrine.

181 Anya van Wagendonk, "How the Panama Canal helped make the US a world power," August 15, 2014, *PBS News Hour*, accessed August 12, 2020, https://www.pbs.org/newshour/world/panama-canal-helped-make-u-s-world-power.

182 "Monroe Doctrine" (1823), *OurDocuments.Gov*, accessed August 12, 2020, https://www.ourdocuments.gov/doc.php?flash=false&doc=23.

183 "Power Rankings," *US News & World Report*, accessed August 12, 2020, https://www.usnews.com/news/best-countries/power-rankings.

184 According to Ancestory.com, James M Eichelberger left Naples, Italy on the Vulcania and arrived in New York on Jan 17, 1940, then enlisted in the Army on Aug 11, 1941.

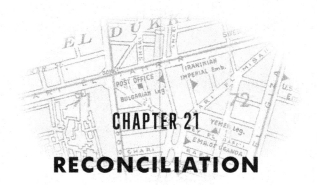

CHAPTER 21

RECONCILIATION

T he last letter Eich wrote me was in July 1989. The short missive was addressed to Richard's family's home in Norfolk, VA, referring to plans for him to visit; plans I have no recollection of now. Memory is no faithful recorder. It is a fickle friend. Without his letter in my hand, I would have no memory of this lost opportunity. Eich was letting me know that I would not be able to reach him at the Roosevelt. He was having another round of chemotherapy and would be in the hospital. The turn of events was unanticipated. Two months later he died.

I got the news while traveling with my family and friends in Ecuador. Nine months later, Taylor was born. I have rehashed this surprise sequence of events many times since. At the time there was no regret that I chose to continue with our planned trip. Now the horror house of mirrors that reflects Eich's life in mine is filled with remorse.

By not being with my father at the end of his life, I did the same to him on his death bed as he did to me as a child. I knew he loved me, and I abandoned him. "You did not," Richard exclaims. "It's totally different. You had your own family and other obligations to tend to." I agree. At the time, my father was not much a part of my life. Yet it is small comfort in this moment, and I have trouble walking away from the reflections of loss haunting me.

At work the daily climate change news arriving in my inbox is grim, matching my mood. NASA just determined that July 2016 was the hottest on record.[185] What makes matters worse is that habitat loss and our changing weather patterns are fueling a species die-off never witnessed by humankind.[186] I lament that the oil powering our cars and trucks are a primary culprit. Yet in North Carolina our leaders are in denial. There is no more planning, no more discussion on how the State can lead the way by reducing its carbon emissions. When I first started this line of work it was different. We are moving backwards.

As I consider the limited run left on my career and my life, I fixate on my father's final resting place. After I visited the cemetery in Maryland, where I thought his ashes were spread, I found my scribbled scrap of a note from when I called Delores to ask what had been done with his cremains. I distinctly recall the note indicating the cemetery is in Hyattsville, MD, not Catonsville where I had visited. Curiously, the online map I have just found shows no Catholic cemetery in Hyattsville. Now I am beginning to doubt my own memory. It's possible that I didn't write it down correctly given how nervous I was in asking the question in the first place. It's also possible my memory is failing. I am getting old. Yet I am not ready to let the subject go.

Instead I call the Catholic Cemeteries of Maryland for help, and a friendly woman answers the phone. I picture her older than me, with white hair and a rose-colored scarf around her neck. She sounds genuinely interested in helping me find my father. "Was your father Catholic?" she asks.

"No, but his girlfriend was," I say, explaining that she was buried in a Catholic cemetery and that my father is with her. "Her family didn't have money for a grave plot, though." Rosie, I want to call her, assures me some parishes provide pauper graves for the poor. "This grave doesn't have a headstone," I confess.

That doesn't matter. She says the parish priest would have a record and suggests that I call. But suddenly I am spooked, especially after confiding that Eich's ashes were spread on his girlfriend's grave. Catholics are not big fans of cremation, I learn, because they believe in the resurrection of the body after death. "But we are changing with the times," Rosie tells me. Her brother-in-law was cremated, and his cremains were buried in a Catholic cemetery. "We don't allow the spreading of ashes on graves, though," she says.

As helpful as this woman on the phone is trying to be, I cannot imagine calling cemetery offices to ask about Patsy Cooper's unmarked grave, like I am trying to pry secrets from the crypt. I thank the kindly woman for all her help and hang up. Sitting at my desk in Raleigh, I swivel in my office chair to look at the blue sky outside my window and take a deep breath.

A wave of acceptance washes over me. My father's final resting place is not somewhere on top of an unmarked grave in a Catholic cemetery. He is in me. A realization dawns: my father is my shadow side—the side that I must embrace to come into the light of my own true being.

The quest to square my journey of loss to one of forgiveness for my father is reflected in the despair and hope I feel for or our planet's future. It has all come to my understanding that there is no "us and them," that we reflect each other. I must accept my father, what happened when he left us, how he succumbed to the debilitating disease of drink, how he did not, despite his assurances to me otherwise, ensure that I would get his own story in his own words. I am partly at fault here too, just as I contribute to the travesty unfolding for our planet's future.

The last sentence of the letter my father wrote me, two weeks before his final brief note, says: "I have not talked to Art John recently but shall get the MS from him to you before venturing to the UK." He was going to London to author a book with Miles Copeland on covert political action. "Miles is imaginative and not much given to narrow-minded concerns about what is true or false," he wrote. My father's job was to keep his friend "to the straight and narrow path while infusing the work with literary merit." Eich then confides as an aside, "I was deputy to Kermit Roosevelt and, at an echelon just below, Miles was chief of the political action staff. Big job in the days when CIA people kept their identities really secret."[187] I like that he is bragging a bit. Of course, the trip to visit the Copelands did not happen, nor did I receive the manuscript from Eich's childhood friend Art John, who, as my father described him, was from "Pittsburgh, New York, Chicago, and Harvard." Nor did I make any effort to find Art John after my father's death—when there was a chance of finding him— now twenty-seven years past.

In this journey to discover what shaped my father's life, I have found the silhouette of what has shaped mine. All the loss and regret have contributed to who I am now. My father's hardships have fueled my strengths, not the least of which is dogged determination. I have hope for the future and am willing to fight for it. I see it in my children. I see it in the young activists around the world standing up to the injustices we have thrust upon the earth. I see it in all who dream to create the more beautiful world our hearts know is possible. No doubt, in some corner of his heart, my father did too.

My struggle into the future will be overcome by my willingness to accept the dark fears of my insecurities, my feelings of inadequacy in the face of so many problems, to embrace the long shadow of love. I am not alone, far from it. I am connected—to what has come before, my parents, grandparents and on back, and those who will come into the future—through love. In the end I must forgive myself as I forgive my father, just as I must acknowledge, then forgive, the injustices inflicted on the earth by my father, myself, and all our relations.

I am walking on the Virginia Highlands Horse Trail as I

formulate these thoughts. This sixty-eight-mile path along the ridge tops of southwest Virginia transects the common-area road leading to our cabin. Richard and I are here for a getaway weekend. The morning air is fresh, crisp, cleaned from last night's rain. It's now, with these realizations, that I step into the light of reconciliation.

185 "NASA analysis finds July 2016 is warmest on record," NASA's Goddard Institute for Space Studies, August 15, 2016, accessed August 12, 2020, https://climate.nasa.gov/news/2479/nasa-analysis-finds-july-2016-is-warmest-on-record/.

186 "Halting The Extinction Crisis," Center for Biological Diversity, accessed August, 12, 2020, https://www.biologicaldiversity.org/programs/biodiversity/elements_of_biodiversity/extinction_crisis/.

187 James M Eichelberger to the author, June 10, 1989.

EPILOGUE

Four years later, I am still working as the Special Projects Manager at the Clean Tech Center where my attention has increasingly shifted to solar energy. Renewable energy has seen dramatic growth since the years covered by my story. In 2019 solar energy accounted for nearly 40 percent of all new electricity generating capacity added in the US, the largest annual share in the industry's history.[188] People are often surprised to hear that North Carolina is ranked the number two state in the nation for installed solar capacity.[189] This is not because we have more sunshine in the Tar Heel state. Years ago, forward-thinking advocates and experts helped pass legislation—tax credits and a requirement for the state's utilities to utilize renewable energy—fostering the solar industry. Then a few years later, production and technology advances enabled a tremendous drop in solar panel costs.

With the resulting growth in this industry, and a change in the political landscape, doubts and worries about photovoltaics have arisen. I have heard all the unfounded concerns: that the glare from the panels might disturb air travel, that runoff from the panels might put toxic chemicals in the soil, and that too much of our farmland might be gobbled up by solar panels. Consequently, the clean energy industry is slowing here and moving to other nearby states. What is fueling this thinking? What is driving out an industry with zero emissions, an industry adding hundreds of thousands of dollars annually to the tax coffers of poor rural communities hosting these solar farms? It is fear and misinformation stoked by the fossil fuel industry. The old ways are changing, and legacy industries are doing their best to keep the status quo in place.

It is a common observation that our political system has become progressively more dysfunctional and polarized. At the same time, income inequality is increasing, our health is declining, and the effects of climate change from burning fossil fuels are becoming more pronounced. Since I am my father's daughter, and likely more sensitive to being manipulated, I have become increasingly aware of the efforts to divide and distract the nation as a whole from what is most important: our health and well-being, and that of the planet's.

My father, it could be argued, was a founder of what President Eisenhower presciently coined the "military industrial complex," a cluster of individuals and institutions who buy favors from the political leaders who are the face of government. This MIC is above truth-telling. It seeks autonomy, to ensure its own agenda is carried out. In World War II France, Eich was an author of "fake news" to lead the enemy astray. The propagandizing was widely accepted for stopping the devastation Hitler was inflicting on the Jews. But what about the misinformation campaigns polarizing our country now? We have not seen these kinds of bold-faced lies in public discourse, certainly not since my father was involved with this kind of subterfuge. For what purpose and whose gain is this disinformation campaign being waged?

In the essay he penned for Gamal Abdel Nasser's government in the early 1950s, *The Power Problems of a Revolutionary Government*, my father called for secret police and propaganda facilities as important components for maintaining the revolutionary government. Are these activities alive and thriving in our government now, over 225 years after the revolutionary war that established the United States? As the number of independent news outlets have dwindled and moneyed interests have increasingly bought the favors of our elected officials, I have to say yes. The efforts poured into *A Good Spy* were in part to expose this dark side of our democracy.

Eich's story continues to help me to read between the lines of everything I think and every news story I hear to ascertain what it is *really* trying to tell me. I do not doubt the existence and power plays of special interests. The revolving door between business and government is open 24/7 and gets lots of use. Our military and intelligence agencies, and all the private sector contractors hired by them, have benefited tremendously from the wars fought to promote the trappings of freedom while paving the way for fossil fuel companies to enslave us to the creature comforts they make possible.

I will not let my awareness of dark and nefarious efforts cripple me. I will not let my own feelings of self-doubt muzzle my hope for this passion play we call life. Rather, I am more committed than ever to choose a path of love and affirming action.

My father's absence and the lack of his love while he was alive were just the bitter medicine I needed. Investigating my father's life has given me the courage to examine my own and allowed me to tell his story through my own eyes. And through this almost two-decade experience, I have come to reconcile his life with mine. It is a humbling and empowering experience.

As I type these final words, I glance up from my writing desk for a moment. My eyes rest on a piece of embroidery I created more than forty-five years ago, with words that have guided my life since. "See God In Each Other," it reminds me in pink chain stitches across its center. "God Dwells Within You As You," it says in purple running stitches along the bottom. Two hands are rising from a sea of turquoise holding the Sanskrit OM symbol, the sound that acknowledges our connection to everything in the universe.

The dualities we see today, both personal and political, are part of a cosmic whole. An evolution of consciousness is afoot. Awareness that we are all in this together. Past, present, and future. All is one. In the fullness of time, we will find unity of purpose by facing our shadow sides with love, acceptance, and action to create the more harmonious world of our dreams.

I have my father to thank. He is my shadow side, the part of me that I have finally come to embrace. While I set out on this journey to get to know my long-dead father to reconcile a relationship with this man I didn't really know, I was also looking for a way to forgive myself. I wanted to still the voice inside my head that says I am not worthy, that there is something more I continually need to do; that whatever *it* is, is not enough. Yet in the face of all my inadequacy, my lack of trust, the deceit—especially when considering our collective future, I am reminded of Rumi. "Let the beauty of what we love be what we do. There are hundreds of ways to kneel and kiss the ground." It is through this—what I love—that I can bring light to the darkness, my father into my heart.

188 "SEIA/Wood Mackenzie Power & Renewables US Solar Market InsightTM", *2019 Year in Review*, Solar Energy Industries Association, accessed August 12, 2020, https://www.seia.org/research-resources/solar-market-insight-report-2019-year-review.

189 "SEIA, North Carolina Solar," Solar Energy Industries Association, accessed August 12, 2020, https://www.seia.org/state-solar-policy/north-carolina-solar.

HISTORICAL FIGURES
OF INTEREST

Hussein bin Ali (May 1, 1854 – June 4, 1931) a Hashemite Arab leader who was the Sharif of Mecca from 1908 and, after proclaiming the Great Arab Revolt against the Ottoman Empire, King of the Hejaz from 1916 to 1924.

Robert B Anderson (June 4, 1910 – August 14, 1989) a lawyer, businessman, and close confident of Dwight D. Eisenhower who served as Secretary of the Navy and Secretary of Treasury from 1957–1961.

Henry Byroade (July 24, 1913 – December 31, 1993) a career diplomat who served as the US ambassador to Egypt from 1955–56.

Camille Chamoun (April 3, 1900 – August 7, 1987) President of Lebanon from 1952–1958 and an important Christian leader during the Lebanese Civil War (1975–1990).

Miles Copeland, Jr. (July 16, 1916 – January 14, 1991) served WWII in the Counter Intelligence Corp (CIC), then worked for the CIA in the Middle East with posts in Syria, Egypt, and Lebanon. He was the author of several books including a memoir, *The Game Player.*

Allen Dulles (April 7, 1893 – January 29, 1969) a diplomat, author, and attorney, was the director of the CIA from 1953–1961 overseeing coup d'états in Iran and Guatemala, the Suez Crisis and the Bay of Pigs Invasion.

John Foster Dulles (February 25, 1888 – May 24, 1959) Allen's older brother, a diplomat and attorney specializing in international law, was Secretary of State from 1953–59 under Dwight D. Eisenhower.

William Eddy (March 9, 1896 – May 3, 1962) an academic, born in Lebanon to missionary parents, attended Princeton, joined the US Marine Corp in WWI, the Office of Strategic Services (OSS) in WWII, and continued intelligence work through the US State Department and CIA in Saudi Arabia.

James M Eichelberger (December 17, 1916 – September 28, 1989) a writer, philosopher, WWII Captain of Military Intelligence who served the CIA as a US State Department economic attaché to Gamal Abdel Nasser in Cairo, Egypt; an oil industry consultant in Beirut, Lebanon; and an advisor to Congo president Joseph Mobuto and other unknown leaders.

Dwight D. Eisenhower (October 14, 1890 – March 28, 1969) a US Army general who served as the WWII Supreme Commander of the Allies Expeditionary Force in Europe and the 34th US President from 1953–1961.

Wilbur Crane Eveland (July 1, 1918 – January 2, 1990) the author of *Ropes of Sand*, began his career during WWII in Army Intelligence and became a Middle East expert serving the CIA on a contract basis during the 1950s.

Crown Prince Faisal (April 14, 1906 – March 25, 1975) the third son of Saudi Arabia's founder, Ibn Saud, who assumed the title of king in 1964 after his brother King Saud was removed for mismanagement of the kingdom's finances.

King Faisal II (May 2, 1935 – July 14, 1958) ascended to the Iraqi throne at three years of age after his father King Ghazi died. His execution in 1958 marked the end of the thirty-seven-year-old Hashemite monarchy in Iraq. Faisal II was the great-grandson of Hussein bin Ali, the Grand Sharif of Mecca and grandson to King Faisal I.

Mohamed Heikal (September 23, 1923 – February 17, 2016) an Egyptian journalist, author, and confidant of Gamal Abdel Nasser who was the editor-in-chief of *Al-Ahram*, what was called *The New York Times* of the Arab World.

King Abdullah I bin Al-Hussein (February 2, 1882 – July 20, 1951) the Hashemite (a direct descendant of Mohammed) ruler of Jordan and its predecessor state, Transjordan, from 1921 until his assassination in 1951. He was the second of four sons of Hussein bin Ali, the Sharif of Mecca.

Ahmed Hussein (1902 – 1984) Egyptian Ambassador to the US from 1953–58 who promoted health, agricultural, and social welfare programs in Egypt, including Egypt's first social security pension system.

Saddam Hussein (April 28, 1937 – December 30, 2006) a Baathist's leader who in 1972 nationalized Iraq's oil industry, assumed the presidency in 1979, launched a 1980 attack to control Iran's oil and Kuwait's in 1990, was accused by US President George W. Bush as having weapons of mass destruction in 2003, tried by an Iraqi tribunal in 2005, and executed in 2006.

Wanda Jablonski (August 23, 1920 – January 28, 1992) the daughter of a Polish petroleum geologist who earned a graduate degree from Columbia University and established the renowned *Petroleum Intelligence Weekly* in 1961.

Frank Kearns (November 28, 1917 – August 1, 1986) served the WWII's Counter Intelligence Corp (CIC) and became a CBS foreign correspondent based in Cairo, London, Paris, and Rome who in later years taught journalism at West VA University.

Zakaria Mohieddin (July 5, 1918 – May 15, 2012) an Egyptian military officer, the first head of Egypt's intelligence organization, and Egypt's Vice President from 1961–68.

Mohammad Mosaddegh (June 16, 1882 – March 5, 1967) Iranian political leader who nationalized British oil holdings in Iran and, as the Premier in 1951–53, almost succeeded in deposing Mohammad Reza Shah Pahlavi. A coup orchestrated by the US and Great Britain removed Mosaddegh from power and sentenced him to a three-year prison term and house arrest for the rest of his life.

Gamal Abdel Nasser (January 15, 1918 – September 28, 1970) Egyptian army officer, prime minister, and then president of Egypt 1956–70 who also created the short-lived United Arab Republic with Syria from 1958–61.

St. John Philby (April 3, 1885 – September 30, 1960) a British political officer, explorer, author, and Arabist who became a special advisor to Ibn Saud and was the first to cross the "Empty Quarter" of Saudi Arabia.

Kim Philby (January 1, 1912 – May 11, 1988) a British intelligence officer and a committed Communist who became the most successful Soviet double agent during the Cold War period and defected to Russia from Lebanon in January 1963.

Abd al-Karīm Qāsim (November 14, 1914 – February 9, 1963) an Iraqi army officer who did not like the monarchy's socially conservative and pro-Western policies. Qāsim overthrew King Faisal II in 1958 to become prime minister of the newly formed Republic of Iraq and was then overthrown and executed in a 1963 coup.

Theodore Roosevelt (October 27, 1858 – January 6, 1919) a conservationist and statesman who at forty-two became the youngest US president after the assassination of President McKinley and served from 1901–1909.

Archibald (Archie) Bullock Roosevelt, Jr. (February 18, 1918 – May 31, 1990) Theodore Roosevelt's grandson was a soldier, scholar, Middle East authority, author, linguist, and a career CIA officer.

Kermit "Kim" Roosevelt, Jr. (February 16, 1916 – June 8, 2000) a WWII Office of Strategic Services Intelligence Officer, grandson to Theodore Roosevelt, credited with leading the CIA operation to overthrow Iran's Mohammad Mosaddegh, who became Vice President of Gulf Oil.

Selwa "Lucky" Roosevelt (January 13, 1929 –) the daughter of immigrant parents, Vassar graduate, married Archie Roosevelt, worked as journalist, served as President Ronald Reagan's Chief of Protocol from 1982–89, and received commendation from Barack Obama for her service.

King Abdulaziz – Ibn Saud (January 15, 1875 – November 9, 1953) the tribal leader who united the Bedouins to establish the state and monarchy of Saudi Arabia in 1932 and ruled to his death in 1953.

King Saud (January 15, 1902 – February 23, 1969) the eldest son of Ibn Saud who became king of Saudi Arabia upon his father's death in 1953. He proved to be an ineffective leader and was replaced by his half brother Crown Prince Faisal in 1964.

Hussein bin Ali, Sharif of Mecca (May 1, 1854 – June 4, 1931) an Arab Hashemite leader of the Great Arab Revolt against the Ottoman Empire whose sons were chosen by the British to lead newly formed countries of Transjordan, Syria, and Iraq after WWI.

Prince Talal bin Abdulaziz Al Saud (August 1931 – December 22, 2018) the twentieth son of Ibn Saud, and leader of the 1960s Free Princes Movement who proposed a constitutional monarchy for Saudi Arabia and championed other progressive causes.

Abdullah Tariki (March 19, 1919 – September 7, 1997) the first Saudi oil minister appointed by Ibn Saud, earned a graduate degree from Texas A&M in petroleum engineering and geology, and was a co-founder of the Organization of Petroleum Exporting Countries.

George Kennedy Young (April 8, 1911 – May 9, 1990) the deputy director of Britain's intelligence agency M16 with aggressive and activist views on spy craft.

SELECT CHRONOLOGY

1909:

- The Anglo-Persian Oil Company forms in London.

1914:

- **June 14:** an oil bill introduced by Winston Churchill calls for the investment of 2.2M pounds in the Anglo-Persian Oil Company, a 51 percent ownership of a private company by the British government.
- **August 1:** Germany declares war on Russia. Churchill orders the entire British fleet to "commence hostilities against Germany," starting World War I.

1916:

- **May 9 and 16:** Britain and France sign the secret Sykes-Picot agreement, setting up the division of Turkish held Syria, Iraq, Lebanon, and Palestine into various French and British administered areas after World War I.

1918:

- **June 28:** The Treaty of Versailles ends World War I.

1921:

- The British Empire administers Iraq until the establishment of the Kingdom of Iraq in 1933.

1927:

- **June 27:** Oil is discovered in Iraq.

1932:

- **September 23:** Ibn Saud establishes the Sunni kingdom of Saudi Arabia. King Faisal I rules the Hashemite Kingdom of Iraq.

1938:

- **February 11:** James Eichelberger, "Eich," graduates from the University of Pittsburgh with Advanced Standing in History.
- **March 3:** Saudi Arabia's first commercial well strikes oil.

1939:

- **September 3:** Britain and France declare war on Germany after the German invasion of Poland.

1940:

- US dominates world oil market with 70 percent of global output.
- **January 17:** Eich arrives in New York, NY aboard the Vulcania from Naples, Italy.
- **June 14:** Germany invades Paris.
- **June 22:** Armistice signed in Compiegne, France for the division of France into an occupied zone (northern France plus the western coast) and an unoccupied southern zone.
- **September 7:** Germany commences bombing of London and many other cities, military installations, and manufacturing plants.
- **October:** US draft begins.

1941:

- **May 10:** Germany ends London bombing.
- **August 11:** Eich enlists as a private in the US Army in New

Cumberland, PA. His profession is listed as author, editor, reporter.

• **December 8:** US formally joins WWII.

1942:

• **June 13:** Office of Strategic Services (OSS) forms.

1943:

• Lebanon becomes independent from the 1920 French mandate.

1944:

• **June 6:** D-Day, the Allied invasion of Normandy is the largest seaborne invasion in history.

1945:

• **May 8:** V-E Day (Victory in Europe), after Gen. Alfred Jodl of the German High Command signs the unconditional surrender of all German forces.
• **August 2:** US drops atomic bombs on Japan.
• **August 15: V-J Day** (Victory in Japan), when Japan accepts the terms of the Potsdam Declaration and unconditionally surrenders.
• **September 20:** OSS dissolves.
• **October 24:** Syria gains independence from France to establish a parliamentary republic.
• **December 20:** Eich is commissioned as a Captain in Military Intelligence.

1946:

• **February 25:** Captain James Eichelberger is awarded Decret No. 5 French Reconnaissance Medal.

1947:

- **June 14:** My mother Alice graduates from the Art Institute of Chicago with degree in Interior Design.
- **July 10:** National Security Act of 1947 passes, creating the National Security Council (NSC) and the Central Intelligence Agency (CIA).
- **July 15:** Eich's mother, Mary Eichelberger, dies.
- **October 18:** Alice Hirshman and James Eichelberger wed in Bedford, Ohio.

1948:

- **May 14:** The United Nations recognizes Israel as a state. Subsequent war and exodus of Arabs to other areas and neighboring countries is called the Nakba, literally "disaster" in Arabic.

1949–1950:

- Aramco's profits are nearly three times greater than royalty payments to Saudi Arabia when Ibn Saud negotiates a 50/50 split. Eich studies philosophy as a graduate student at the University of Chicago.

1953:

- Eich and Alice live in Washington DC.
- **November 9:** Ibn Saud dies; eldest son Saud succeeds him as King of Saudi Arabia.

1954:

- **July:** Israeli spies set bombs in cinemas, libraries, and other western targets in Egypt.
- **August 26:** Ann Mary Eichelberger is born in Cairo.

- **October 26:** Assassination attempt on Gamal Abdel Nasser in Alexandria; CIA supplies Nasser with a bulletproof vest.
- **November:** US announces $40M aid to Egypt.
- **December:** Israeli spies responsible for Lavon Affair go on trial in Egypt.

1955:
- Women are given permission to attend major speeches at the National Press Club, Washington, DC.
- **February:** Gamal Abdel Nasser's only meeting with Anthony Eden, Churchill's Deputy Prime Minister, at British Embassy. Brits push Egypt to join Baghdad Pact; Nasser argues that the best protection against communism is to support the people and the people won't support another super power pact. Eden makes clear the importance of Arab oil strategically and economically.
- **February 27:** Israeli Operation Susannah conducts raid on Gaza army post in retaliation of Egyptian execution of Lavon Affair spies. Israeli raid kills fifty-six Egyptian soldiers. Egypt does not retaliate. Nasser uses Gaza as the rationale for his 1955 arms deal with the Czechs/Russians. Raid is condemned by UN Security Council.
- **May 22:** Nasser meets with US Ambassador Byroade to let him know he has offer from Russia to purchase arms.
- **September 27:** Nasser announces "Czech" arms deal which had been finalized a week earlier.

1956:
- US President Eisenhower sends Robert Anderson to Cairo to forge peace with Israelis as part of Project Alpha. Alpha backfires because Nasser thought he was being blackmailed by linking Aswan Dam aid to settling Palestine problem.

- **March:** Wilbur Crane Eveland is sent to London where he meets Eich for "talks with the British government." British press lashing out at the "communist serving Nasser."
- **April:** Soviet premier Khrushchev visits London. British Prime Minister Eden urges no more weapon sales to Egypt. Khrushchev agrees if part of a general embargo overseen by UN.
- **May 2:** Eich writes Memo for Middle East Policy Planning Group "Cairo Station Views Pertinent to Omega Planning."
- **May 16:** Nasser recognizes Communist China.
- **July 18:** US withdraws offer to help finance Egypt's Aswan High Dam.
- **July 26:** Nasser's speech in Alexandria announces the nationalization of the Suez Canal.
- **August 18-23:** Eich attends first Suez conference in London with John Foster Dulles.
- **September:** Eich attends another London conference of eighteen "concerned nations" who form the Suez Canal Users' Assoc. to run the canal on Egypt's behalf. Instead, the Soviets and Egypt want the UN to discuss threat of French and English troops in Mediterranean.
- **October 29:** Israeli armed forces push into Egypt toward the Suez Canal, initiating the Suez Crisis. The Israelis are soon joined by French and British forces.
- **December 22:** The last British and French troops are withdrawn from Egyptian territory while Israel keeps its troops in Gaza under the pretext of protecting the Canal from the two belligerents.

1957:
- **January 5:** Eisenhower Doctrine is introduced, and Congress approves in March.

- **February 22:** *Petroleum Weekly's* Wanda Jablonski states that Abdullah Tariki, Saudi Arabia's first Director of Petroleum and Mineral Affairs, is "a force to be reckoned with." He is a spokesman for a "new generation" of educated Arabs who are putting the international oil companies and their governments on notice.
- **March 19:** US finally compels the Israeli Government to withdraw its troops from Egypt.
- **May 31:** Eich resigns from State Department Foreign Service Staff Officer Group 1-C FS 53.
- **July:** My parents and I move to Beirut.

1958:

- **February 1:** Gamal Abdel Nasser joins Syria's president, Shukri al-Quwatli, in announcing the formation of the United Arab Republic (UAR).
- **March:** Due to King Saud's excesses, Saudi Arabia is grappling with staggering debt.
- **April:** Prince Talal gives Saud an ultimatum demanding transfer of all executive powers to Crown Prince Faisal. Faisal restricts family purse to no more the 18 percent of government revenues.
- **May:** Unknown assailants assassinate editor of the Beirut newspaper Al Telegraf, which sets off riots that eventually lead to the burning of the United States Information Agency.
- **July 14:** Iraq's King Faisal II and four members of the royal family are executed in the Baghdad palace courtyard in a coup d'état led by Iraqi military men under the leadership of Abd al-Karīm Qāsim.
- **July 15:** President Eisenhower authorizes Operation Blue Bat, US troops land on Beirut beaches.

- **July 17:** My mother and I depart from Le Havre, France to Southampton, NY on the S.S. Liberté.

1959:
- **February:** Under mounting pressure from the oil glut's financial drain, the major oil companies, starting with British Petroleum, begin to cut the price of crude 10 percent to about $1.90 a barrel.
- **March 10:** Eisenhower reluctantly announces the US's first mandatory oil import quotas. The independent oil producers are pleased, the major oil companies disappointed.
- **July 28:** James Kurz Eichelberger (Jay) is born in Beirut.
- **August:** Oil prices have settled to what they were in 1950.
- **October 7:** Twenty-two-year-old Saddam Hussein botches assassination attempt of Iraqi Prime Minister General Abd al-Karīm Qāsim.
- **December:** Gulf Oil ends contract with Copeland and Eichelberger. According to Miles Copeland, Eich leaves "his wife and went off to Paris to resume a romantic relationship with a French poetess."

1960:
- **September 14:** Saudi Arabia, Venezuela, Iraq, Iran, and Kuwait announce formation of the Organization of Petroleum Exporting Countries and in the Congo, Army Chief of Staff Joseph Mobutu carries out a virtual coup by establishing a College of Commissioners to administer the country on an interim basis.
- **September 30:** St. John Philby dies in Beirut. My mother registers at American University of Beirut 1960–61 first semester.

• **October 17–23:** Eich attends second Arab Petroleum Congress in Beirut. Saudi Oil Minister Tariki gives a "riveting" speech on plan to limit oil output by dividing market by hemisphere and forcing oil companies to get rid of international subsidiaries.

1961:
• **January 17:** Congolese Prime Minister Patrice Lumumba's death by firing squad.
• **February 21:** Letter from American University of Beirut to my mother thanking her and Eich for book donation to the Education Library.
• **June:** With end of British protectorate, Kuwait, the Middle East's largest oil exporter, becomes independent and pressures BP and Gulf Oil to let go of half its acreage.
• **August:** Wanda Jablonski begins recruiting to start her own industry weekly; Eich works for her for four weeks.
• **September:** I start second grade at Phoebe Hearst Elementary School, Washington DC.

1963:
• **November 22:** President John F. Kennedy is assassinated in Dallas, Texas.

1966:
• I receive a postcard from Eich in Leopoldville, Congo.

1968:
• **April 4:** Martin Luther King is assassinated in Memphis, TN.
• **June 6:** Presidential candidate Robert Kennedy is assassinated in Los Angeles, CA.

1971:

- **April:** I am expelled from West Nottingham Academy, Rising Sun, MD.
- **May 5:** I am arrested on the US Capitol steps protesting the Vietnam War.

1972:

- **June:** I graduate from Kingsley Hall School, Westbrook CT.
- **September:** I fly to Montego Bay, Jamaica with my high school boyfriend.

1973:

- **March:** I take the mail boat from Jamaica to Dominica with new boyfriend, Bill.
- **April:** President Richard Nixon ends Mandatory Import Program, which limits oil imports.
- **October 20:** OPEC plus Egypt, Syria, and Tunisia begin US oil embargo in response to Yom Kippur War.
- **Late fall:** Bill and I fly to Columbia, spend Christmas with campesinos in a one-room hut after being framed by 'cops' who came to our hotel room and 'found' the pot they had stashed in the bedside table drawer.

1974:

- Bill and I hitchhike through Columbia and Venezuela and take open boat across "Boca del Dragon" to Trinidad. Spend February in Trinidad. Take mail boat to Dominica where we and another couple are attacked by four men with machetes while we are sleeping in an isolated spot along a river. After a couple of weeks in the hospital, the government pays for Bill to fly home to Norfolk, VA for further treatment and I take the mail boat back to Jamaica with friends.

- **March:** the Arab oil producers lift US oil embargo.

1975:
- Bill and I hitchhike to CA, attend month long retreat in Eureka with Swami Muktananda.

1976:
- With three partners I open the Amrit Restaurant, meet Richard Tazewell.

1978:
- **May 20:** Anne Eichelberger and Richard Tazewell marry.

1979:
- **May 7:** Jamila Starwater Tazewell is born at home in Key West, FL.

1981:
- **September 15:** Richard, Jamila, and I fly from Baltimore to Bali.

1982:
- **January:** Return from trip to Indonesia, my mother is terribly ill and had emergency cancer surgery while we were in SE Asia. I care for Mom at home.
- **September:** Richard, Jamila, and I reunite in Key West.

1983:
- **Summer:** Richard and I work at the OMEGA Institute in Rhinebeck, NY then drive to Mexico with Jamila.

1986:
- Richard, Jamila, and I visit Eich at the Roosevelt.

1987:
 • **October 1:** Rio Walke Tazewell is born in Key West, FL.

1988:
 • We visit Eich at VA hospital to introduce him to Rio.

1989:
 • **September 28:** My father, James Manning Eichelberger, dies.

1990:
 • **June 24:** Taylor Kurz Tazewell is born in Miami, FL.

1992:
 • **October 22:** My mother, Alice Eichelberger, dies in Jay and Maryrose's home in Columbia, MD.

1996:
 • **May:** I graduate from New College, Sarasota, FL with a BA in Environmental Studies.

1998:
 • Labor Day weekend: Richard, Rio, Taylor, and I set off for "year trip" in a twenty-foot motorhome to camp across the country, concentrating on national parks in the West and three months in Mexico. We cut the trip short to return to Key West to take over repairs on our house after Hurricane Georges.

1999:
 • **July 1:** I start work at Triangle J Council of Governments in Research Triangle Park, NC.

2001:

- **September 11:** A series of four coordinated terrorist attacks by the Islamic terrorist group al-Qaeda against the United States kill 2,996 people. I purchase my first hybrid electric vehicle, a 2001 Toyota Prius.

2003:

- **March 20:** US ground troops invade Iraq upon direction of George W. Bush.
- **July:** First biodiesel B20 station in NC opens at a Handee Hugo BP in Garner.
- **December 13:** Saddam Hussein is captured.

2004:

- **July 1:** I start work at the NC Solar Center/NC State University (later renamed the NC Clean Energy Technology Center.)

2006:

- **January 31:** State of the Union President George W Bush declares, "Here we have a serious problem: America is addicted to oil, which is often imported from unstable parts of the world."

2008:

- Average price of a barrel of oil in the US is $91.48.

2009:

- **March:** 38 Retail stations sell biodiesel blends (B20-B100) and 11 retail locations sell E85 (a blend of 85 percent ethanol, 15 percent gasoline) in NC.

2012:
- I buy my first electric vehicle, a 2012 Chevy Volt.

2016:
- **September 3:** President Barack Obama announces the US formal entry in the Paris Climate Agreement to limit global warming to 1.5 degree Celsius compared to pre-industrial levels. NOAA records the hottest year in 140-year climate record.

2019:
- Petroleum products account for 91 percent of the total US transportation sector energy use. NOAA records the second hottest year on record and the average temperature around the world is 1.71 degrees F (0.95 degree C) above the twentieth century average.

BIBLIOGRAPHY

Aburish, Said K. *A Brutal Friendship: The West and The Arab Elite,* New York: St. Martin's Press, 1998.

Aburish, Said K. *Children of Bethany: The Story of A Palestinian Family,* New York: Bloomsbury Publishing, 1988.

Aburish, Said K. *Nasser: The Last Arab: A Biography,* New York: Thomas Dunne Books, 2004.

Aburish, Said K. *The St. George Hotel Bar,* London: Bloomsbury Publishing Ltd., 1989.

Aburish, Said K. Website http://www.iiwds/said_aburish/a-lostvictories.com

Alsop, Stewart, and Thomas Braden. *Sub Rosa The OSS and American Espionage,* New York: Harcourt, Brace & World, 1963.

"Annual Energy Review 2011." US Energy Information Agency. September 2012.eia.gov/totalenergy/data/annualarchive/038411.pdf

Bellow, Saul. *To Jerusalem and Back A Personal Account,* New York: The Viking Press, 1976.

"Big Oil, Bigger Oil". *Financial Times.* February 4, 2010.

Bird, Kai. *Crossing Mandelbaum Gate: Coming of Age Between the Arabs and Israelis, 1956-1978,* New York: Scribner, 2010.

Brown, Anthony Cave. *Treason in the Blood H. St John Philby, Kim Philby, and the Spy Case of the Century,* New York: Houghton Mifflin Company, 1994.

Caldwell, Duncan, "A Biography of Robert Granville Caldwell, Jr. Part 1- Spy Catcher" 2009. http://www.duncancaldwell.com/Site/Spy_Catcher,_My_fathers_biography.html.

"CO_2 Emissions per Capita," *World Atlas Data, Rankings, Environment, KNOEMA,* accessed August 10, 2020, https://knoema.com/atlas/ranks/CO2-emissions-per-capita.

Copeland, Lorraine, email to author, September 8, 2011.

Copeland, Lorraine, email to author, September 19, 2011.

Copeland, Miles. *The Game of Nations: The Amorality of Power Politics,* New York: Simon and Schuster, 1969.

Copeland, Miles. *The Game Player Confession of the CIA's original political operatives,* London: Aurum Press, 1989.

Copeland, Stewart, email to author, September 1, 2015.

Davis, Gerald. *Algerian Diary Frank Kearns & "The Impossible Assignment" CBS News.* Morganton: West Virginia Press, 2016.

Deac, Wilfred P. "Suez Crisis: Operation Musketeer" *Military History*, June 12, 2006. http://www.historynet.com/suez-crisis-operation-musketeer.htm.

Devlin, Lawrence. *Chief of Station, Congo: Fighting the Cold War in a Hot Zone*, New York: Public Affairs, a Member of the Perseus Books Group 2007.

DeWitte, Ludo and Renee Fenby et al. *The Assassination of Lumumba*. London: Verso Publishing, 2001.

Dickinson, Elizabeth. "Anatomy of a Dictatorship: Hosni Mubarak." *Foreign Policy*, February 4, 2011.

Dillard, Annie. *Pilgrim at Tinker Creek,* New York: Harper & Row, 1985.

Egan, Dan, email to author, February 13, 2015.

Egan, Dan, phone call with author, May 31, 2011

Eichelberger, James M., letter to author, December 14, 1982.

Eichelberger, James M., letter to author, June 10, 1989.

Eveland, Wilbur Crane. *Ropes of Sand: America's Failure in the Middle East,* New York: W.W. Norton & Company, 1980.

Farmaian, Sattareh Farmen, Dona Munker. *Daughter of Persia: A Waman's Journey from Her Father's Harem Through the Islamic Revolution,* New York: Crown Publishers Inc, 1992.

Gibson, Bryan R. (2015). *Sold Out? US Foreign Policy, Iraq, the Kurds, and the Cold War,* Palgrave Macmillan. pp. xxi, 45, 49, 57–58, 121, 200.

"Halting The Extinction Crisis," Center for Biological Diversity, accessed August, 12, 2020, https://www.biologicaldiversity.org/programs/biodiversity/elements_of_biodiversity/extinction_crisis/.

Heikal, Mohamed H. *Cutting The Lion's Tail Suez Through Egyptian Eyes,* London: Cirgi Books, 1986.

Heikal, Mohamed H. *The Cairo Documents: The Inside Story of Nasser and His Relationship with World Leaders, Rebels and Statesmen,* New York: Double Day & Company, 1973.

Helman, Christopher. "The World's Biggest Oil Companies," *Forbes,* Dec. 14, 2014 http://en.wikipedia.org/wiki/Saudi_Aramco.

Kinzer, Stephen. *The Brothers John Foster Dulles, Allen Dulles And Their Secret World War,* New York: St Martin's Press, 2014.

"Kuwait Population." *PopulationOf.net,* accessed April 6, 2021, http://www.populationof.net/kuwait/.

Little, Douglas. *American Orientalism: The United States and the Middle East Since 1945.* The University of North Carolina Press, 2002.

Lumumba, Patrice. *Congo, My Country.* Connecticut: Praeger Publishing, 1962.

Maass, Peter. *The Violent Twilight of Oil,* New York: Alfred Knopp, 2009.

Macintyre, Ben. *A Spy Among Friends: Kim Philby And The Great Betrayal,* New York: Broadway Books, 2014.

Meyer, Karl E & Brysac, Shareen Blair. *Kingmakers: The Invention of the Modern Middle East,* New York: W.W. Norton & Company, 2008.

Mills, C. Wright. *The Sociological Imagination.* Oxford: Oxford University Press, 1959.

"Monroe Doctrine" (1823), *OurDocuments.Gov,* accessed April 6, 2021, https://www.ourdocuments.gov/doc.php?flash=false&doc =23.

"NASA analysis finds July 2016 is warmest on record," NASA's Goddard Institute for Space Studies, August 15, 2016, accessed April 6, 2021, https://climate.nasa.gov/news/2479/nasa-analysis-finds-july-2016-is-warmest-on-record/.

Neff, Donald. *Warriors At Suez: Eisenhower Takes America into the Middle East in 1956,* Brattleboro: Amana Books, 1988.

Noring, Nina J. (ed.) *Foreign Relations of the US 1955-57, Suez Crisis Jul 26-December 31, 1956 Volume XVI* (Washington: US State Dept Office of the Historian, 1990).

Nzongola-Ntalaja, Georges. *The Congo from Leopold to Kabila: A People's History.* London: Zed Books, 2002.

Nzongola-Ntalaja, Georges. *Patrice Lumumba*. Athens: Ohio University Press, 2014.

Nzongola-Ntalaja, Georges, interview by author, Chapel Hill, August 25, 2015.

O'Neill, Patrick. "Going for homegrown at the pump." *Indy Weekly*, July 9, 2003.

"OSS PERSONNEL FILES - RG 226 ENTRY 224" The US National Archive and Records Administration, December 23,2010. http://www.archives.gov/iwg/declassified-records/rg-226-oss/personnel-database.pdf.

Pace, Eric. *"ROBERT B. ANDERSON, EX-TREASURY CHIEF, DIES AT 79."* *The New York Times*. (August 16, 1989), accessed April 6 , 2021, http://www.nytimes.com/1989/08/16/obituaries/robert-b-anderson-ex-treasury-chief-dies-at-79.html.

Painter, David S. "Oil: Oil and world power" Encyclopedia of the New American Nation, accessed October 28, 2018, http://www.americanforeignrelations.com/O-W/Oil-Oil-and-world-power.html#ixzz33yqCXcDn.

"Population of Kuwait." *Muzaffar.com*, accessed April 6, 2021, http://muzaffar.com/Kuwait/population.htm.

"Power Rankings," *US News & World Report*, accessed August 12, 2020, https://www.usnews.com/news/best-countries/power-rankings.

Roberts, Paul. *The End of Oil: On the Edge of a Perilous New World*, New York: Houghton Mifflin, 2004.

"Robert B Anderson: Papers 1933-89." Dwight D. Eisenhower Library Abilene, Kansas. July 2004, 2.

Roosevelt, Archie. *For the Lust of Knowing Memoirs of an Intelligence Officer*, Boston: Little, Brown & Company, 1988.

"Roosevelt Corollary to the Monroe Doctrine, 1904", US Department of State Office of The Historian, accessed April, 4, 2021, https://history.state.gov/milestones/1899-1913/roosevelt-and-monroe-doctrine.

Roosevelt, Kermit Jr. *Countercoup: The Struggle for Control of Iran*, New York: McGraw Hill, 1979.

Rubino, Anna. *Queen of the Oil Club: The Intrepid Wanda Jablonski and the Power of Information*, Boston: Beacon Press, 2008.

Sale, Richard. "Exclusive: Saddam Was Key In Early CIA," *UPI*, (April 11, 2003): https://www.upi.com/Defense-News/2003/04/10/Exclusive-Saddam-key-in-early-CIA-plot/65571050017416/.

"SEIA, North Carolina Solar," Solar Energy Industries Association, accessed April. 4, 2021, https://www.seia.org/state-solar-policy/north-carolina-solar.

"SEIA/Wood Mackenzie Power & Renewables US Solar Market Insight™," *2019 Year in Review*, Solar Energy Industries Association, accessed April, 4, 2021, https://www.seia.org/research-resources/solar-market-insight-report-2019-year-review.

Sherrill, Robert. *The Accidental President*. New York: Grossman Publishers, 1967.

Statement Issued by the Second Suez Canal Conference at London, September 21, 1956 Source: Conference doc. SUEZ II/56/D/10; Department of State, Conference Files: Lot 62 D 181, CF 782.

Stenger, Wallace. *Discovery! The Search for Arabian Oil,* Vista CA: Selwa Press, 2007.

"Suez Crisis: Operation Musketeer," *Military History*, June 12, 2006.

"The Office of Strategic Services: Morale Operations Branch" News & Information. Historical Document, The Central Intelligence Agency, July 29, 2010.

"The Suez Crisis: An affair to remember" *The Economist*, July 27, 2006. http://www.economist.com/node/7218678.

Thomas, Gordon. *Her Majesty's Secret Service: The First 100 Years of British Intelligence inside M15 and MI6,* London: Thomas Dunne Books, 2009.

Thompson, Mark, "The $5 Trillion War on Terror" *TIME*, June 2011. http://nation.time.com/2011/06/29/the-5-trillion-war-on-terror/.

United States Department of State. *The Suez Canal Problem, July 26–September 22, 1956: A Documentary Publication*, Washington, 1956.

United States Senate Select Committee to Study Governmental Operations with Respect to Intelligence Activities (Church Committee), *Interim Report: Alleged Assassination Plots Involving Foreign Leaders*, (Washington DC: GPO, 1975).

US Department of State, *Omega*, James Eichelberger. Omega Folder Vol 4, Record Group 59, Lot 61D417, Box 55. College Park, MD: National Archives and Records Administration, Retrieved 2013.

US Energy Information Agency 2019, "Frequently Asked Questions," accessed April 4, 2021, https://www.eia.gov/tools/faqs/faq.php?id=709&t=6 .

Van Wagendonk, Anya. "How the Panama Canal helped make the US a world power," August 15, 2014, *PBS News Hour*, accessed August 12, 2020, https://www.pbs.org/newshour/world/panama-canal-helped-make-u-s-world-power.

Weekes, Richard. "Secrets of world's oldest boat are discovered in Kuwait sands." *The Telegraph*, April 2001, accessed January 19, 2015. http://www.telegraph.co.uk/news/worldnews/middleeast/kuwait/1314980/Secrets-of-worlds-oldest-boat-are-discovered-in-Kuwait-sands.html.

Weiner, Tim. *Legacy of Ashes: The History of the CIA*, New York: Doubleday, 2007.

Wilford, Hugh. *America's Great Game: The CIA's Secret Arabists and the Shaping of the Modern Middle East,* New York: Basic Books, 2013.

Wolfe-Hunnicutt Brandon, The End of the Concessionary Regime: Oil and American Power in Iraq, 1958-1972, Stanford University, March 2011 (iv).

Yergin, Daniel. *The Prize: The Epic Quest for Oil, Money & Power.* New York: Free Press, 2009.

Yergin, Daniel. *The Quest: Energy, Security, and the Remaking of the Modern World.* New York: Penguin Books, 2011.

ACKNOWLEDGEMENTS

First, gratitude goes to Richard Tazewell, my husband of forty-three years, without whom this book would not have been possible. Thank you for understanding its importance.

To my children: Jamila, for always being there for me with artistic eyes and a compassionate heart; Rio, for your commitment to the cause and allowing me to share a part of you through this book, and Taylor for your principled dreams and deep thoughts. You three are my inspiration for trying to capture in words the legacy of family.

This book has been calling me for close to two decades. I have been guided by many. To David Taylor who has been reading my attempts and advising me on storytelling from the beginning, and Joyce Allen, my first writing teacher. To my faculty mentors Wil Hylton, Jacob Levenson, Phillip Gerard, and Meline Toumani and fellow Gophers at Goucher College's Creative Non-Fiction MFA program. A special thanks to Madeline Blais and Meline for your encouragement to keep going and Leslie Rubinkowski whose grit has kept this most remarkable program thriving through thick and thin. I also want to recognize the fine work of editors Anne Dubuisson and Caleb Guard.

To my first and second draft readers and editors, some who gave tremendously of their time and talent: Cindy Calderwood, Roxanne Henderson, Kendal Brown, Lila Pague, and Jerry Davis.

And finally, to the guides chronicled in this book, Dan Egan, Jerry Davis, and Hugh Wilford who especially seemed to care about my quest.

To all those named and unnamed, please know in your heart I owe you a debt of gratitude.

ABOUT THE AUTHOR

Anne E Tazewell has been a vegetarian restaurant owner and chef, a textile artist in Key West, and an award-winning advocate for the environment for over three decades. For the past seventeen years she has served as a clean energy expert at NC State University where she has received grants totaling over $15M for her work. She holds an MFA in Creative Non-Fiction from Goucher College and lives in Carrboro, North Carolina.

For more information about Anne, visit her website www.annetazewell.com. To share your thoughts about the book or ask questions, email Anne directly at agoodspybook@gmail.com.